Praise for *Torah Tutor*

"Rabbi Bohm's important work opens up each weekly Torah portion in ways that will touch the soul of individual seekers and will serve as the basis for creating community through shared study and conversation. Her beautiful language is accessible and rich, allowing Torah to touch our hearts and minds. This book provides a compelling and persuasive argument for the contemporary relevance of Torah study, explicitly in its introduction, but implicitly on each and every page. This new book is a vital resource for adult learners, rabbis and educators."

Rabbi Leon A. Morris, President of Pardes Institute of Jewish Studies, based in Jerusalem and New York City

"What I really love about this book is its accessibility. A lay-leader could pick it up and use it to lead a Torah study group with great success. Yet at the same time, it offers a grounded, scholarly, feminist perspective on each Torah portion, offering a rich source of sermonic material. A genuinely useful book!"

Rabbi Kari Tuling, author of *Thinking about God*

"Rabbi Lenore Bohm has written a very accessible, appealing, and challenging book that is a gem for Christians as well as members of the Jewish community. She has done the work of Torah which, as its name implies, 'instructs' and 'guides' adults through key passages of the Hebrew Bible. Using an approach that explains stand-out phrases and verses, offers questions to illuminate the texts and invites readers to make practical connections to their own lives, this book ultimately leads to personal reflection and prayer. With the help of Rabbi Bohm's knowledge and creative insight, adults will discover or rediscover trustworthy wisdom for life in today's world. I heartily recommend this treasure for seekers and for those charged with bringing the scriptures alive for their communities."

Barbara Quinn, RSCJ, Associate Director of Spiritual Formation, Boston College School of Theology and Ministry

"This book is for those more spiritual than religious, for the seekers and the shape-shifters who want to be drawn to Torah but need a guide, a reason, a rabbi. Rabbi Lenore Bohm offers her heart and wisdom but also, importantly, her expertise in arranging, managing, and navigating the immensity of Torah study. In this short, brilliantly organized book, Rabbi Bohm provides scaffolding for accessing Torah—for learning to talk about, think, and focus on Torah. This is a gift of a book by a very gifted rabbi."

Jessica Pressman, Professor of English and Comparative Literature, San Diego State University

"Rabbi Bohm's book manifests excellent teaching skills and important Jewish feminist insight. Throughout *Torah Tutor*, Bohm renders complex religious issues, both ancient and contemporary, easily understandable. The book offers something for every reader, including Jewish and Christian religious leaders preparing to preach. The seeds of many sermons are here! The audience is diverse, including Jews interested in exploring Torah and its relevance to their lives, Christians interested in how Jews today interpret Torah, and those seeking enrichment or personal spirituality. I highly recommend it and plan to return to it often."

Bishop Jane Via, co-founder of Mary Magdalene Apostle Catholic Community in California

"As a Christian, I have always loved the stories and wisdom in the Bible. Rabbi Bohm expresses that same love in *Torah Tutor*. With each portion of the Torah, she lovingly crafts questions and insights that draw us in to the heart of God. Here you will find all the drama of creation and humanity made plain from ancient times. Here you will find parallels and deep connection to the issues and concerns of today. *Torah Tutor* can be used privately or in group study or by clergy preparing messages. Rabbi Bohm demands brave encounters with difficult and disturbing stories in the Torah. She offers a fresh spiritual approach, calling us to love and care more deeply for one another and the world around us."

The Rev. Sharon A. Buttry, retired American Baptist minister, co-author of *Daughters of Rizpah*

"Rabbi Bohm, a popular and beloved teacher of Torah, has crafted a very accessible and rich approach to Jewish sources. Well organized, the materials stimulate thought and conversation while featuring diverse voices and opinions."

Rabbi Deborah Prinz, author of *On the Chocolate Trail*

"Rabbi Lenore Bohm's *Torah Tutor* is for adults—thinking, questioning, skeptical adults. In it she puts aside children's Bible stories to reveal profound, often contradictory, and sometimes frustrating narrative investigations into what it means to be human. Torah is a tough book for tough adults looking for a challenge that is at the same time political, social, and spiritual. A skilled Torah teacher, Rabbi Bohm is the perfect guide to this indispensable book."

Rabbi Rami Shapiro, author of *The Tao of Solomon*

"We describe Torah as *Torat Hayyim*, a living tradition. This requires that our lives be deeply informed by ancient wisdom and practices, and that Jewish traditions learn and grow from our insights and lived experiences. We are living through a moment of transformation in which ancient Jewish texts are being interpreted by an ever-expanding circle of people. Judaism is being transformed by this generation of learners. And so are we, as people who now have access to Torah study in previously unimaginable ways. This book is a sturdy walking stick, a bridge, and a trail map that invites anyone and everyone to come and drink from the well of Jewish wisdom."

Rabbi Ari Lev Fornari, Senior Rabbi of Kol Tzedek, Philadelphia

"*Torah Tutor* is the perfect companion to jump into the sea of Torah. Rabbi Bohm has created a masterful and wide-ranging text to study the weekly Torah portions. She brings together the best of contemporary commentators and helps us focus our questions through carefully crafted and insightful teachings. I can't wait to bring this book to my regular Torah study group."

Rabbi Denise L. Eger, Senior Rabbi of Congregation Kol Ami, West Hollywood, California

You couldn't do better than picking up this book and reading her commentary, indispensable even among thousands of years of conversation on a text that begs for those like her to help us—even those like me who study and teach it for a living—encounter even more in it. The insights here you won't find anywhere else, and you'll use them every day of your life. Many have written commentaries on the Torah, and this rises up with the very best of them. It really is that good."

Rabbi Scott Fox, Senior Rabbi of Temple Israel of Long Beach, California

"Rabbi Bohm's book is a unique and useful offering to the rich world of Torah study. Part anthology, part manual and part spiritual guidebook, *Torah Tutor* is a fresh treasure trove of ideas, sources, questions and practices that are sure to deepen and enliven any Torah study group."

Rabbi Lisa Goldstein, former Executive Director of the Institute for Jewish Spirituality

"As a participant in Rabbi Bohm's Torah study sessions for over a decade, I heartily recommend *Torah Tutor*. This elegant and eloquent presentation of weekly *parshiyot*, accompanied by insightful commentary, fills the reader of Torah with renewed awe. Rabbi Bohm masterfully weaves contemporary themes and current issues with the wisdom and foresight of our rabbinic sages. *Torah Tutor* is a wonderful companion for those who wish to connect or reconnect to our greatest treasure."

Michael B. Maskin, ABPP, Clinical Professor of Psychology and Psychiatry (retired)

"I have attended numerous Torah study sessions with the brilliant Rabbi Bohm over many years. This book is modeled on these sessions—but for a much wider audience. Rabbi Bohm brings the same expertise to her book as her in-person Torah study sessions."

Glenda Sacks Jaffe, Hillel Director, University of San Diego and California State University at San Marcos

"Rabbi Bohm's book is indeed a treasure—both for those who think that they know the Torah already and for those who have never studied at an adult level before. Her book will open your mind to some of the questions that the Torah asks of us as well as to some of the questions that we should ask when we confront the Bible. I promise you that this is a book that you will find well worth reading—and that you will want to reread many times."

Rabbi Jack Riemer, author of *Finding God in Unexpected Places*

Torah Tutor

A Contemporary Torah Study Guide

Rabbi Lenore Bohm

For David, my husband:

I have found the one in whom my soul delights.

Song of Songs 3:4

Contents

Foreword

Albert Einstein said that "coincidence is God's way of being anonymous." That thought occurred to me when Rabbi Bohm invited me to write this foreword. She was not aware that for many years, I have wanted to write just such a book, a guide to Torah Study, that would remind readers how an ancient, revered document can be compelling even today. Unfortunately, I never found the time to fulfill this wish, but I am glad Rabbi Bohm did. She has created a work that makes the words of Torah easily accessible to all: rabbi or congregant, teacher or student, individual or group.

I encourage anyone who seeks greater spirituality to use *Torah Tutor* as a guide to enter the eternal conversation between God and the Jewish people.

Torah Study has always been at the very heart of Jewish life. Generations ago, our sages engaged in a discussion about which was more important: study or practice. Rabbi Akiba said study takes precedence. Rabbi Tarfon said doing deeds is greater. The lively discussion continued until the majority agreed with Akiba who said that study is more important because it leads to practice. *Talmud Torah k'neged kulam*, which means "the study of Torah is equal to everything."

Why? Because it leads to discovering and understanding our Jewish obligations (*mitzvot*) and our responsibilities as human beings.

Torah Study asks: What did Hillel see? What nuances came from Rashi's daughters? What did ibn Ezra contribute from his perspective?

How do female scholars such as Nechama Leibowitz and Aviva Gottlieb Zornberg deepen the conversation? All these commentators—and so many more—can help us find that kernel of wisdom to keep us connected to each other and guide us in meeting personal and societal challenges.

A well-researched volume relying on the wisdom of many scholars, *Torah Tutor* is organized according to the weekly portion, or *parasha*. After summarizing the *parasha's* basic events, Bohm draws our attention to verses that stand out, some of which we may not have realized originate in the Torah. This is followed by ideas to think or talk about, making the portion easy to approach for individual study or group discussion. Finally, Rabbi Bohm offers a focus phrase to strengthen our spiritual awareness during the week.

Rabbi Bohm encourages us to set aside time to reflect on what the Torah teaches, always remembering that a biblical story or character, a verse or even a word, can be understood differently through different perspectives of time and place. Where we are in our own lives at a particular moment enriches the search and the discovery.

For some, it may be best to begin Torah Study alone. Others may prefer to join a group—most synagogues have them. Another option is to sit down with a small group of family or friends and rediscover Torah wisdom in this setting. The most important thing is to start the habit of Torah Study, to set aside a fixed time to do it. I recommend an hour on Shabbat! Before long, you may find yourself looking forward to these weekly moments of challenge and connection. Reading this may become one of the most meaningful parts of your week, renewing, enriching and energizing you for the other tasks that fill your days.

Kol hakavod to Rabbi Bohm for sharing with us her gifts of heart, mind, and spirit, and making this unique and important contribution to the study of Torah. May we welcome her efforts with open minds, and may she go from strength to even greater strength in her learning and teaching.

Rabbi Sally J. Priesand, North America's first female rabbi, was ordained in June, 1972. She has served congregations in communities in New York and New Jersey and also has served on national Jewish boards. Through the years, she has become a sought-after speaker, teacher and contributor to many books about Judaism.

Introduction

Is this book for you?

Yes it is, if you want to learn about the Torah and the roots of Judaism from an adult perspective. You are not alone if you had little Jewish education or were bored by the Jewish education you received in your youth. Imagine if your exploration of love, food, travel, or music halted in middle school! How deprived you would feel not to have developed an adult appreciation of what you encountered as a child. I suspect this is why some Jews think of religion as "childish." Perhaps they participated as adults in child-oriented holiday celebrations, but their most comprehensive exposure to their religion was probably in Hebrew school. This book is designed to show that the Torah, Judaism's foundational narrative, can be meaningful and impactful for adults.

This book is for you if you identify as spiritual more than religious. The Torah records the journeys of seekers such as Abraham, Hagar, Rebecca, Jacob, Joseph, Moses, and Miriam. Following their stories and transformations, you might recognize the experience of hearing a call to grow and expand. Spiritual seekers who use this book alongside the Torah will likely find biblical parallels to their journeys. Prayer, fasting, and other types of spiritual practices found in the Torah are highlighted in this book. Together with the Torah, this book can accompany you on a spiritual path. There are many spiritually rich words and phrases in the Torah. These phrases will grab your attention when you study the weekly portion. In addition, the focus words at the end of each portion are there for you to include in your meditation or mindfulness practice.

You might also enjoy beginning or ending each Torah Study session with a few minutes of contemplative silence.

This book is for you if you are in a Torah Study group, a Christian Bible Study group, or if you want to assemble one. *Torah Tutor* can provide structured content to help inform your study sessions. For each Torah portion, I provide questions that illuminate the text and motivate personal and spiritual reflection.

And finally, this book is for you if you are a rabbi, Jewish educator, or Christian clergy. The book directs you to salient words and concepts in each Torah portion. Many rabbis, clergy, and educators are pressed for time. If this is true for you, you might find this book useful in developing study sheets, *divrei Torah* (lessons or homilies based on the Torah portion) or sermons.

Why Is it Valuable to Study Torah?

The Torah addresses central human concerns: family relationships, the pursuit of justice, the meaning of power and the power of desire, the purpose of celebration, the sanctity of human life, the importance of animal life, and the value of confronting one's finitude. When we return to the Torah's stories each year, we can identify changes in our own lives and in the world around us. For example, in one year, I might identify with Miriam, who prioritizes faith over fear. In another year, I might identify with Leah, who resists being overlooked and asserts her strengths to earn respect. In one year, my Promised Land is far away and I despair of reaching it. In another year, I see it from the mountaintop and feel confident that I am approaching my goals. In one year, I hear God's voice calling me to change. In another year, I am tempted to give up entirely; my energy has dissipated and I am stuck.

The Torah is a history, a family epic, an ethics primer, a creedal inventory, and a self-help manual. Because the Torah is all of these things, it can be helpful to consider it not as one unified book, but as a bookshelf containing different manuscripts.

Nonetheless, for all its diversity, themes that are eternally relevant permeate the Torah: human dignity, agency, responsibility, and concern for the vulnerable.

Here are some specific reasons why Torah Study might appeal to you:

When you grapple with the Torah, you become part of an ancient and continuing Jewish conversation. By joining this conversation, you are connecting with Jews who are spread over thousands of years and thousands of miles.

Torah Study provides a source of affirmation for Jews and those who are part of Jewish families. It is an identifiably Jewish way to understand our human natures and aim for transformation.

Do you like a good story? The Torah exposes us to time-honored stories that permeate not only Jewish and Christian, but Western culture: Many of these stories, like those about Noah, Dinah, and Joseph, have inspired classic Western literature.

Torah Study expands you. It reminds you of the whims of history, the power of personal commitment, and the challenges of family relationships. (Sibling rivalry and infertility are two vivid examples.) In our personal lives, we may be reluctant to address these topics openly, but we can begin to address them indirectly by focusing on the text.

Because Torah Study is usually done in groups, it provides regular, meaningful, and reassuring contact with others. For many, Torah Study provides a reliable social setting for intellectual and spiritual growth.

It can be healing and energizing to spend an hour (or more) weekly or monthly in the presence of nonmaterialistic ideas and nonsecular influences. For all its convenience and usefulness, technology can dull the senses and drain the spirit. Rabbi Elie Kaunfer explains how Torah Study provides a corrective:

> Torah study opens us up to the notion that there is something larger than ourselves in the universe. The more we learn, the more we feel there is to learn; we cannot know it all; we cannot control it all. This is a serious corrective to a contemporary culture that makes claims to being able to access every scrap of information. The Internet confers the illusion that everything is knowable. But Torah study is an exercise in humility.[1]

The stories, customs, rituals, and laws in the Torah have influenced millions of people for thousands of years. Unchanging but endlessly renewable, the Torah calls to each generation to find its own nuanced

---

1 *Empowered Judaism: What Independent Minyanim Can Teach Us About Building Vibrant Jewish Communities*, Woodstock, VT: Jewish Lights Publishing, 2010, pp. 152–3.

meaning, and to transmit those insights to succeeding generations. In
one sense, because the Torah was written thousands of years ago, it is
closed and finished. In another sense, because it continues to prompt
questions, conversation, and commentary, it is inexhaustible.

What Is the Torah About and Do I Have to Believe It Is Sacred?

The first five books of the Hebrew Bible (*Tanakh* in Hebrew) are
called the Torah, also known as the Five Books of Moses or the
Pentateuch. The Torah begins with a creation story and ends with a
death. The Torah records God's interactions with individuals, families,
and the Israelites, as they develop a covenant with their God. As part of
this covenant, God intervenes in Israelite history to earn their loyalty. In
turn, the Israelites are expected to show fealty to God. If they do so, they
are promised peaceful and prosperous lives in the Land of Israel.

For millennia, it was accepted that the Torah was written by God or
written by Moses who spoke for God. Some understood this to mean
the Torah was perfect. Others continued to believe in the divine origin of the Torah while questioning its anomalies and inconsistencies.
These questioners included even the great, medieval commentators,
like Rashi, Maimonides, Ibn Ezra, and Spinoza.

At the end of the 18th century, scholars began to analyze the Bible
not as a faith document but as an ancient Near Eastern text. By the early
19th century, biblical criticism had developed as a respected, secular
academic discipline. Scholars and theologians compared the Torah
with ancient writings from neighboring civilizations. These comparisons, along with archaeological discoveries, provided more knowledge,
though perhaps less certainty, about the origins of the Torah. Because
of these extensive studies, it is now generally accepted that the Torah
was composed by at least four or five redactors, who wove strands of
cherished stories into one narrative.

For many, these conclusions, based on secular scholarship, has
reduced confidence that the Torah is literally "the one true word of God."
Nevertheless, one can revere the Torah without calling it divine in every
aspect. Despite my love of the Torah, I recognize disturbing practices
and laws in it and I do not feel obliged to condone them. While continuing to venerate the Torah, I can nonetheless challenge it.

I am enlightened by secular scholarship, but the Torah as a secular anthology would not hold my interest for long. Something else keeps my interest: For me, the Torah is enduringly gripping because of its illuminating stories and spiritual teachings. For me, what makes the Torah holy is what it teaches about God, people, and the more just and unified world I dare to believe is possible.

How Is This Book Arranged?

This book does not provide a comprehensive survey of questions to ask of the text. There is no end to the ways in which each verse (often each word!) can be prodded and probed for insight and understanding. Many ancient and modern teachers have provided their own, extensive commentary on how to interpret and tease out meaning from the Torah.

I created this list of questions and reference points as a resource for contemporary Torah Study. For each Torah portion, I present the following sections:

First, a brief overview of the portion. Second, a selection of standout phrases and verses. Third, questions designed to illuminate the text ("Talk About"). Fourth, questions designed to prompt introspection ("Think About"). And finally, a focus phrase for reflection, prayer, or meditation.

Some of the questions in the Think About sections are of a personal nature and discussing them in a group might create discomfort for some participants. That is why I put them in the Think About section. But if you want to discuss any of these questions, I certainly encourage you to do so. Additionally, you may enjoy thinking privately about many of the Talk About questions.

In Jewish life, Torah Study is a uniquely powerful undertaking. It offers the rare opportunity to interact with texts that have informed conversations for centuries while remaining available for contemplation and discussion today. Studying Torah, we can get lost in the narrative and we can find ourselves as well. As much as Torah Study teaches you about Judaism, it can also help you learn about yourself. This may be the most valuable discovery of all.

I hope this work succeeds in presenting the Torah as a uniquely rewarding book. I hope you gain familiarity with Judaism's beloved stories, inspiring precepts, and troubling passages. I hope your Torah study will stretch you emotionally, spiritually, intellectually, socially, and religiously. There is an oft-cited Talmudic statement (*Pirkei Avot* 5:24) about the Torah: "Turn it and turn it for everything is in it." I agree with this—the Torah is vast, deep, and rich. But by changing one word in this sentence, an equally true notion is conveyed: "Turn it and turn it, for everything is in *you*." By this I mean that we each have the capacity to uniquely comprehend and manifest the messages and meanings of the Torah.

There is no word I treasure more than "Torah." May God find me worthy to continue to learn and teach Torah.

Rabbi Lenore Bohm

Rosh Chodesh Tevet 5782, December 2021

Why Study the Torah?

If the word "Torah" isn't inviting to you, maybe it's because you think it is only relevant to people who are observant, pious, or Jewishly literate. To engage with the Torah, you may think you have to pretend to believe things or that you have to know Hebrew.

This is not accurate. Torah Study is available to anyone who is interested, to people who want to learn and deepen their understanding of Scripture.

Why read a book filled with disturbing texts—stories that marginalize women, condone violence, reject homosexuality, and sanction slavery? By studying and discussing these stories, aren't we licensing them? The Torah and the Hebrew Bible do contain alienating and even odious ideas. These texts include stories that speak dispassionately about morally distressing incidents. But I believe there is great value in delving into these challenging texts.

The Torah can't be rewritten. But we can read it in an intellectually and morally honest fashion. We can respond to the objectionable sections by recognizing them as products of a different time and different world. We can decry misogynistic, xenophobic, and racist statements in the Torah that condone what we strongly believe to be unjustifiable behavior. The fact that the Torah contains these views should not prevent us from protesting them when they are used to disenfranchise or humiliate.

One can study the Torah (and Bible) and emerge rigid, punishing, and chauvinistic. But it is also true that a close, full examination will reveal the Torah's overarching mandates: justice, compassion, generosity, and responsibility. I believe that by studying the texts carefully and discussing them openly, we find that these noble mandates emerge as paramount.

What Is a Torah Portion and
What Is the Torah Cycle?

"Torah" is best translated as "guidance" or "instruction." The word "Torah" is formed from the three Hebrew root letters signifying "to direct" or "to aim." The same root letters form the Hebrew words for "parent" and "teacher." You may have heard Torah translated as "law," but this is not an adequate translation. Recognizing that Torah means "guidance" or "instruction," one can understand how the Torah is the foundation of many Jewish ideas and ideals.

The Torah consists of 54 sequential portions, each one called a *parashah* or *parsha* (from the Hebrew word meaning "portion"), or *sedra* or *sidra* (from *seder*, which means "order"). These words are used interchangeably. Their plural forms are *parashiyot* and *sidrot*.

Each Torah portion is named for the first word that stands out in the portion. The name may not offer clues to what the portion is about, but it is used as the standard identification of the chapters studied each week. In the Contents, I have listed the Torah portions by name, and have added a short phrase that lifts up one or more central themes in the portion. These descriptive phrases are not translations of the portion names.

Typically, one Torah portion is read each week. Because of the complexities of the Jewish calendar, a few portions are sometimes combined to enable the entire Torah to be concluded in a year. Each fall, on *Simchat*

Torah, we read the final portion in Deuteronomy (*V'Zot Hab'rachah*) and immediately begin again with the first portion in Genesis (*B'reishit*). This practice indicates that Torah learning is ongoing, continuous. As soon as we complete the reading cycle, we begin it again.

There are advantages to studying the Torah as a whole, from its opening verses describing the creation of the world to the concluding verses recording Moses' death. But there are also advantages to looking at each Torah portion as a unit, one week at a time, when it is studied by Jewish communities around the world.

If you want to find the weekly Torah portion, there are many resources along with this book to help you. Most Torah commentaries include the names and chapters of the 54 portions in order. Every Jewish calendar also displays the weekly *parashah*. Websites like HebCal.com readily provide this information as well.

There are several excellent translations of the Torah available to English speakers. The Orthodox, Conservative, and Reform movements have their own authorized translations with commentary, written by their rabbis and scholars. There are additional translations/commentaries available written by individuals or by groups of scholars not representing a particular denomination.

All translations are based on the Hebrew text, but nonetheless they vary. In your Torah Study, you may prefer a denominational or an independent translation. I enjoy using several *Chumashim* to gain multiple perspectives. *Chumash* is derived from the word for "five." The plural is *Chumashim*. All *Chumashim* include the printed Torah text, in Hebrew and English—or another vernacular.

Unless otherwise noted, all translations in this book are from *The Torah: A Women's Commentary*, Tamara Cohn Eskenazi and Andrea L. Weiss, eds., New York: URJ Press, 2008.

Torah Study Blessing

Studying is reading with a purpose, with some intensity, even with passion. To study is to inquire, search, examine, analyze, and review. Studying Torah means going beyond casual, superficial browsing. Torah Study is an invitation to reflect on and seriously ponder many of Judaism's central teachings and to locate the origins of many ideas central to Western civilization.

Torah Study is a *mitzvah* (usually translated as "commandment," but I prefer, "source of mandated or expansive connection"). Because of this, it is customary to recite a blessing before each Torah Study session. A blessing is a series of words that focuses attention on what we are about to do. To recite a blessing is to make a statement of intention, connection, and gratitude.

The traditional blessing for studying Torah is:

> Baruch atah, Adonai Eloheinu, Melech haolam, asher
> kid'shanu b'mitzvotav v'tzivanu laasok b'divrei Torah.

Blessed are You, Adonai our God, Sovereign of the universe, who hallows us with *mitzvot*, commanding us to engage with words of Torah.

If you have participated in Jewish religious gatherings, you will recognize the opening words: "*Baruch atah Adonai, Eloheinu Melech haolam asher kid'shanu b'mitsvotav v'tsivanu ...*" The closing phrase, "*laasok b'divrei Torah*" may not be as familiar. The word *laasok* means, "to occupy with." In modern Hebrew, *esek* is "business." We can extrapolate that "*laasok b'divrei Torah*" means "to occupy or busy one's self with words of Torah," or perhaps, "to make words of Torah one's business." This suggests that Torah Study is a kind of livelihood; it provides sustenance.

I enjoy thinking of the word *laasok* as connected to the English word "soak." (The English and Hebrew words are not connected—I'm being playful.) The blessing for engaging with Torah invites us to "soak" in those words, to be absorbed by them, to make them part of us.

Here are three interpretive translations of the Torah Study blessing:

1. Let us bless the source of life,
    source of the fullness of our knowing.

    May we learn with humility and pleasure,
    may we teach what we know with love,

    and may we honor wisdom
    in all its embodiments.[2]

2. Blessed are You, Breath of Life, Who makes us holy through connections, and breathes into us the wisdom to connect by breathing together with each other and with all life; by shaping our breath into words; and by shaping our words so that they aim toward wisdom, becoming words of Torah.[3]

3. *Nevareich et makor chayyeinu, ruach haolam, asher kid'shanu b'mitzvot ve'tzivanu laasok b'divrei Torah.* A blessing: In the presence of the Infinite, we honor the wisdom of our ancestors, engaging in words and deeds of Torah.[4]

Using any version of the blessing will distinguish Torah Study from other kinds of study or discussion. You may also want to speak your own introductory words of dedication ("I dedicate my study to the memory of ..." or "I'm participating today in honor of ...") before a session. In addition, some groups begin or end their Torah Study with songs or prayers of healing for people suffering in mind, body, or spirit.

May your Torah Study be rich and fruitful!

---

2 *The Book of Blessings: New Jewish Prayers for Daily Life, the Sabbath and the New Moon Festival*, Marcia Falk. New York, NY: HarperCollins Publishers, 1996, p. 168.

3 "Kaddish and Kavvanah: The Blessings over Torah Study," Rabbi Arthur Waskow, TheShalomCenter.org/node/279.

4 emanuelrochester.org/wp-content/uploads/sites/106/2020/07Blessing-for-Torah-Study_SJTS.pdf

Genesis/B'reishit

In Genesis, we meet God. Many people don't believe in God and resist contemplating what God could mean. Reading Genesis, I experience the Creator God and the God of Relationships. The Genesis creation stories increase my sensitivity to the mystery of life, the organic connection between people and other living things, and the prevalence of design and order in the universe. The Genesis characters display love, faith, and courage along with selfishness, brutishness, and questionable motives. All persons in Genesis are flawed. But these foundational stories dramatize that people have the capacity for moral and spiritual growth.

The narrative of Genesis plays out in the context of family connections. Both fierce loyalty and consuming hatred characterize kindred relations. Within this network, Genesis raises questions about human accountability. These timeless questions continue to vex us today.

B'reishit (Genesis 1:1–6:8) "Seize the Day"

Overview

A stirring account that makes us think and wonder, the creation story situates human beings as the pinnacle of God's handiwork. We are sui generis, and yet we are part of creation's peaceful and purpose-ful unfolding: light and darkness, sea and land, sun, moon and stars, vegetation, sea, sky, and land creatures. The early chapters of Genesis assert that order is superior to chaos, and that creation is intended, har-monious, and good. In Eden, there is no conflict. But when Adam and Eve yield to the desire to know more, they become both enhanced and tarnished by heightened awareness. Insight, desire, fulfillment, shame, deceit, pain, and struggle enter human life, and to this day, we are grat-ified and confounded by their hold on us.

Key to appreciating this portion is recognizing its revolutionary pronouncement: every person, created in the image of God, has innate worth and dignity. This is the central moral teaching of Judaism. On the small stages of our lives and the large stages of the world, this idea often remains an unrealized ideal, but its placement in the opening lines of the Jewish sacred canon cannot be over-appreciated.

STANDOUT VERSES

1:3 "Let there be light." Creation commences through language, not battles among the gods, as is common in contemporaneous ancient Near East creation stories. This initial light is not the light of the sun (announced in 1:16-17), so what is it? Perhaps this first light is spiritual or metaphysical, referring to the beginning of consciousness. Or, if you prefer, the Big Bang!

1:26-27 "God now said, 'Let us make human beings in our image, after our likeness' ... So God created the human beings in the divine image, creating them in the image of God, creating them male and female." We share biological urges, propensities, and limitations with animals, but the creation story posits that unlike animals, we also share qualities with God. How are we like God? The text doesn't elaborate. But these verses indicate that humans and God have a unique kinship. I believe we reflect God's nature through our capacity to be creative and intentional.

Additionally, self-consciousness and conscience develop in ways not available to other living things; only we can make choices guided by ethical precepts. These choices can deepen, enliven, and redeem our individual lives and humanity as a whole. We are makers-of-meaning; we are given opportunities to elevate our lives beyond mere existence towards personal significance and historical consequence.

In *Judaism: A Way of Being*, distinguished scholar David Gelernter concludes that in paganism, the gods are made in our image, which by definition culminates in our worshipping ourselves. In the Torah-Jewish view, we are modeled on something incomparably better, and must therefore struggle to exceed what we sense are our limits: "to be braver, nobler, more loving and forgiving, more just and honorable" than we would otherwise challenge ourselves to be.[5]

4:9 "Then YHVH said to Cain, 'Where is your brother Abel?' And he replied, 'How should I know; am I my brother's keeper?'" In 3:9, God speaks to Adam, using the interrogative WHERE to ask about Adam's moral/spiritual orientation in relation to God. The question to Cain highlights his responsibilities vis a vis another human being. Are we accountable for others' well-being? How broadly or narrowly do we define a brother or sister?

6:5-6 "When YHVH saw how great was the wickedness of human beings in the earth ... YHVH regretted having made human beings on earth, and was heartsick." Many have been taught that the Judeo-Christian God is infallible, all-knowing, and all-powerful. In numerous places, the biblical text does not bear this out. In the early chapters of B'reishit, God experiences regret, disappointment, and rage.

TALK ABOUT

1. There are two distinctive creation narratives in this portion. In 1:1-31, nature unfolds from less complex to more complex, culminating in the formation of a male-female being who is blessed, told to procreate, and to enjoy the paradise which is their home.

The second creation story begins in 2:4. The earthling (Adam) appears prior to trees, rain, animals, and nature as a whole, and the created woman is derived from man.

Why are there two creation stories? To me, each story instills its own sense of belonging, order, and relationship. The stories are not historical or factual. They are not "true," yet they contain many truths. In your reading of the creation stories, how does each enrich our understanding of human nature and the nature of the world?

---

5 David Gelertner, *Judaism: A Way of Being*, New Haven and London: Yale University Press, 2009, p. 178.

2. In Genesis 1:28, human beings are told to "... fill the earth and tame it ... hold sway over the fish of the sea and the birds of the sky and over every animal that creeps on the earth." Some have read this verse as granting permission to exploit nature. But that is not consistent with the creation story's tone or multiple additional Torah references to the natural world. Adam is instructed to "work and keep" his home environment. The Hebrew word for "keep" actually means "guard." The Torah values and respects nature. Our role is to serve as nature's custodians and stewards. Nowhere does the Bible give license to abuse nature.

3. This portion intimates that humans and animals are meant to be vegetarians (1:29). Only after acknowledging people's rapacious appetites does God concede to meat consumption (Genesis 9:3). Numerous commentators point out that the laws of *kashrut* (the dietary laws of keeping *kosher*) allow people to indulge their taste for meat, while never forgetting that eating meat involves animal death. Many Jewish thinkers observe that practicing *kashrut* inculcates sensitivity towards animals. Some reflect that in a perfect world, we will all be vegetarians again, just as the inhabitants of Eden were.

4. Death appears in this first Torah portion: In 2:17, Adam is told that if he eats of the Tree of All Knowledge, he will be "... doomed to die." This portion also includes the statement in 6:3 "Then YHVH said, "My spirit will not forever endure the humans ... their lifespan shall be only 120 years."

In Judaism, death is a natural part of life. Death is not a tragedy unless it is untimely (God forbid) or the result of devastating circumstances. Consider the Jewish funeral and mourning practices. How do they reflect the view that death is not an aberration and that mortality is a condition of existence? How do the stage-by-stage mourning practices (*shiva, sheloshim, yahrzeit*) encourage a healthy grappling with loss, and gradual re-entry into daily life on the part of mourners?

5. Eve took the fruit because she saw that it looked good to eat. The fruit was alluring and would provide knowledge and insight. Eve was curious, motivated, and bold. After eating the fruit, she "gave some to her man, who was with her, and he ate" (3:6). We can thus describe Eve as generous, or at least, kindly disposed towards her partner.

Many interpretations of this story cast blame on Eve for being disobedient, prideful, and the cause of "man's downfall." Reading the actual text, how do you assess Eve?

6. The Torah account of a first woman is unique among ancient Near Eastern texts. She is called a "helpmate," but this does not do justice to the Hebrew phrase in 2:18, *ezer k'negdo*. *Ezer* connotes "help," but *k'negdo* is a versatile word. The "*k*" implies "like," as in "similar." *Negdo* can mean "against him," "encompassing him," or "relational to him." This suggests that the man's partner is separate from but connected to him.

In thinking of your spouse or partner as a "helpmate," what aspects of your relationship come to mind? People use the verb "to husband" when speaking of conserving (as in "husbanding resources"). "To wife" is not a verb, but if used as a verb, what would it mean?

7. "Where are you?" God's question to Adam in 3:9 is not a request for location. It is an existential question posed to promote self-awareness in Adam. "Where are you in relation to Me?" God asks. "Where are you in relation to your partner, to your world?" "Where do your desire and discontent originate and where will they lead you?"

In *A Year of Sacred Moments: The Soul Seeker's Guide to Inspired Living*, thoughtful commentator Hanna Perlberger notes that 'why' questions often contain veiled accusations or criticism. By asking 'where are you?' instead of 'why did you do this?' God does not put Adam on the defensive; God gives Adam room to respond in multiple ways.[6]

Author Paolo Coelho suggests that implicit in the question "Where are you?" is the sentiment, "I miss you. I want to be with you."[7]

Could these sentiments be at the root of God's question to Adam?

Think About

1. Rabbi Elyse D. Frishman reflects on the fourth word of the first verse of Torah, the Hebrew word *et*.

"Perhaps the word suggests that what is on the surface is not obvious ... Perhaps *et* symbolizes all things; its two letters are the *alef* and the *taf*, suggesting the entire *alef-bet*; ... So we learn: God created everything

---

6 *A Year of Sacred Moments: The Soul Seeker's Guide to Inspired Living*, Bloomington, IN: Balboa Press, 2017, p. 2.

7 Paolo Coelho, *Aleph*, Translated by Margaret Jull Costa. NY, NY: Random House, Inc., 2011, p. 150.

at once. But that creation is too much for us, so we perceive it a bit at a time—through heaven and earth ... From the very first verse of Torah we learn: Look beyond the obvious."[8]

2. This first Torah portion introduces us to Shabbat: "Then God blessed the seventh day and made it holy" (2:3). Rabbi Abraham Joshua Heschel notes that many cultures and religions make space and place holy but in Judaism, we make time holy.[9]

Do you engage in or refrain from actions that set apart the seventh day? What are the outcomes of setting aside one day a week to interact differently with the world? What are the commercial/consumer implications of a day devoid of earning and spending money?

3. After describing various aspects of creation as "good," the first thing described as "not good" is in 2:18: it is "not good" that Adam be alone. This can be read as a repudiation of residing alone (un-partnered) or of living a solitary existence—with limited communal contact and engagement.

What are the advantages and disadvantages of a partnered and un-partnered life? What types of communities have you found most consequential—neighborhoods, political parties, academic affiliations, support groups, organized religious institutions, cultural associations, social justice advocacy groups, sports teams?

4. In the first Genesis creation story, a male God brings forth a male-female being, and in the second story, God forms a male person, Adam, and subsequently, God forms Eve. In "Blessing the Earth," feminist theologian Carter Heyward offers an unexpected account of the creation story in which God moans, labors, and give birth to the earth, which She then holds tenderly in her arms.[10]

What do you think of the earth being born from God's "body?" It's not a Jewish notion, but it can deepen our understanding of how we are connected to God and loved by God. Can you imagine God loving and

8 Rabbi Elyse D. Frishman, "The Power of God's Voice," in *Women Rabbis: Exploration and Celebration*, ed. Gary P. Zola, Cincinnati: HUC-JIR Rabbinic Alumni Association Press, 1996, pp. 83-91.

9 Rabbi Abraham Joshua Heschel, *The Sabbath: Its Meaning for Modern Man*, New York: Farrar, Straus and Giroux, 1951, p. 10.

10 *Our Passion for Justice: Images of Power, Sexuality and Liberation*, Cleveland, OH: Pilgrim Press, 1984, pp. 49-50.

wanting to protect the earth in the same way a mother or father loves and cares for their child?

5. For dubious reasons, Adam's (man's) superiority over Eve (woman) has been inferred from early in Genesis. In the first creation story, the created human being is both male and female (1:27) Adam is the first human creation in the second creation story (2:7). But being formed earlier in the creation sequence hardly suggests superiority: In the first creation story, living beings proceed from less to more complex: sea creatures, land animals, man, and finally woman. *Shabbat*, created on the seventh day, symbolizes fulfillment, even perfection. The human being closest on the timeline to Shabbat is woman. Plus, while Adam names the animals (2:26), Eve names their children, viewing herself as a partner with God, "Both I and YHVH ..." (4:1) Carefully reading the text, one does not encounter an initial hierarchical relationship between Adam and Eve.

6. Consider these examples of passing the buck: "The man said, 'The woman whom You gave me, she gave me the fruit of the tree, so I ate.' God YHVH then said to the woman, 'What is this you have done?' And the woman said, 'The serpent tricked me into eating it' (3:12-13). With regard to blaming others and deflecting responsibility, have people changed at all?

It is difficult to say, "I did it. I am responsible," regardless of extenuating circumstances. It takes courage to ask: "What is my accountability in personal, familial, and societal discord?"

7. "Where are you?" Answer this question in relation to your family, profession, citizenship, religion—or any other way you wish. If you are not where you want to be, can you think of small steps to lead you in the direction you desire?

FOCUS PHRASE (1:30, 2:7)

Nefesh Chayah, Nishmat Chayim—Breath of Life, Living Being.

Noach (Genesis 6:9–11:32) "Starting Over"

OVERVIEW

In the closing verses of the prior portion, God realizes that human beings cause seemingly insurmountable problems: People don't automatically obey God and some of their actions result in violence, even murder. In *Noach*, God's angry response to a willful and savage humanity is to release a flood that destroys the world except for one family and representatives of each animal species.

After the flood dissipates and the ark inhabitants return to dry land, God sends a rainbow as a covenantal sign that God will not destroy the earth again. God's expectations of humanity are lowered. The subsequent Tower of Babel story poses another example of human rebellion and Divine punishment. In the closing verses, we meet Abram and Sarai (later renamed Abraham and Sarah) who form a partnership, and become the founders of the Israelite nation, the Jewish people.

STANDOUT VERSES

6:9 "Noah was a righteous man: in his generation, he was above reproach; Noah walked with God." The Hebrew word for "righteous" here is *tzadik*, which shares root letters with the Hebrew word "justice." How do you define a righteous person? Is belief in God necessary to being a righteous person?

Righteous is an exalted designation. The word describes Noah, who isn't an Israelite. In the Hebrew Bible, there are numerous examples of individuals outside the Israelite community who are lauded for being exemplary in their character and actions. One example is Yitro, Moses' father-in-law (Exodus 18:5-27).

7:12 "Rain fell upon the earth for forty days and nights." There is a flood epic in the Babylonian Creation story, and similar flood accounts appear in diverse cultures. The raven and dove (mentioned in 8:6-10) also fill important roles in the Mesopotamian flood stories. But the Torah deluge account differs because it includes moral themes. In a Babylonian-Akkadian epic, gods send a flood as punishment because the people's noise disturbed the gods' rest. In the Babylonian epic, possessions and riches are saved along with the handsome heroes. In the biblical story, only a righteous family and animals are saved from destruction.

9:12 15 "Here is the sign I am giving you … I have placed My bow in the cloud—it will be a sign of the covenant between Me and the earth … and never again shall the waters become a flood to destroy all flesh." A rainbow is shaped like an archer's bow. In ancient folklore, gods used bows in battle. Whereas a bow (and arrow) were (and are) used to harm/kill, a rainbow isn't used for violence and isn't human-made.

11:4-6 "Then they said, 'Come, let us build a city with a tower that reaches the sky, so that we can make a name for ourselves … and YHVH said, 'Now, no scheme of theirs will be beyond their reach!'" Many commentators note that God disapproved of this building project because it was prompted by the people's arrogance.

TALK ABOUT

1. Both the creation story and the story of Noah take place prior to the appearance of Abraham and Sarah, the first "Jewish" people. Why does the Torah begin in a universal context? The Torah is given in the desert (Exodus 19:16-17), ownerless land. How would we be primed to understand ourselves, and Judaism differently if the Torah began with Abraham and Sarah or with Moses' birth, or with the giving of the Ten Commandments at Mt. Sinai?

2. Describing Noah as righteous 'in his generation' seems to diminish his value. Would he have been described as righteous if he had lived amongst less dishonest and less conniving people? On the other hand, the opening sentence, "This is Noah's chronicle: Noah was a righteous man," suggests that Noah was upright and decent.

3. "Noah walked with God" (6:9). Was Noah's primary relationship with God? Did he set himself apart from others? Do you know people about whom you would say, "They walk with God"? In our world, what does "walking with God" look like? Does it look like religious fanaticism? Piety? Integrity? Aloofness?

4. Here is a less adulatory assessment of Noah from penetrating scholar Avivah Gottlieb Zornberg in *Genesis: The Beginning of Desire*: "From the beginning to the end of the flood narrative, Noah says not a word. God talks to him twice before the flood telling of what is to come, telling him

how to build the ark, to enter it with his family and representatives of the animal world. And after each of God's long speeches (6:13-21, 7:1-4) the text tells us impassively, "And Noah did just as the Lord commanded him" (6:22 and 7:5). The impact of Noah's silent acquiescence in the destruction of the world is devastating."[11]

Do you agree with Zornberg's assessment of Noah?

5. The story of Noah's ark is a favorite for children, but the near complete destruction of the world is horrifying. The text says that God's anger and disappointment prompts the destruction. God is 'heartsick' (6:6), anguished at the people's degradation.

6. Following Noah and his family's return to dry land, Noah plants a vineyard and gets drunk. He lies naked in his tent. Noah's son Ham finds him and quickly tells his brothers, Shem and Japeth (9:22-23). The two walk backwards into the tent to avoid seeing their father exposed, and they cover him.

What do these actions reveal about the three brothers? Ham treats his discovery in a puerile fashion: He rushes to share his father's embarrassment with his brothers. Shem and Japeth, on the other hand, display empathy, and try to preserve their father's dignity. What makes a person want to shame or mock another? What contributes to a person responding with empathy? How else could the sons have handled this situation?

THINK ABOUT

1. This portion describes Noah as "walking with God." What does that mean to you? Perhaps that he was attuned to God and not to other people? Is this a virtuous, desirable way to live? Rabbi David Hartman specifically contrasts Noah's indifference to others' fate with Abraham's heroic confrontation with God regarding the inhabitants of Sodom and Gomorrah (Genesis 18:20-33).[12]

Other commentators chastise Noah for following God's directions in building the ark perfectly, but not warning others about the oncoming waters. Is this the response of a noble person?

---

11 Aviva Gottlieb Zornberg, *Genesis: The Beginning of Desire*, Philadelphia: Jewish Publication Society, 1995, p. 58.

12 Rabbi David Hartman, *A Living Covenant: The Innovative Spirit in Traditional Judaism*, Woodstock, VT: Jewish Lights Publishing, 1997, p. 39.

2.   In 6:14, God tells Noah, "Make yourself an ark." The Hebrew word
for "yourself" is *l'cha*. This phrase can also be understood as "make
of yourself an ark." Leaving aside the flood story, what does it mean
to make your self into an ark? Does it mean to try to shield your self
against life's vicissitudes? Does it mean to separate from others? Does it
mean to provide shelter?

   The only other use of the word for "ark" (*teivah*) in the Torah is in
Exodus 2:3 (where it is often translated as wicker basket). Moses' mother
places him in a *teivah*. She deposits it on the river to save her son's life.
With both Noah and Moses, the arks hold individuals who represent
hope in the future.

3.   The first thing Noah does when he leaves the ark is offer thanks by
sacrificing animals (8:20), the accepted method of thanksgiving at that
time. How do we offer thanks today? Are there ways to express gratitude
besides speaking words of thanks?

4.   In Genesis 9: 8-17, we first encounter the concept of covenant. How is
a covenant different from a contract? One difference is that a covenant
is not transactional. Marriage is a covenantal, not a contractual
relationship. The Hebrew word for covenant is *b'rit*, the word for
circumcision (also called *bris*). How have you heard the word "covenant"
used, in Jewish life or in a broader context? Would you describe any
relationships in your life as "covenantal"?

5.   At some point after returning to dry land, Noah gets drunk. It's
possible Noah was a guilt-ridden survivor, a man suffering from PTSD.
Getting drunk may not have been Noah's wisest choice, but many of us
know people who, shortly or belatedly following a trauma, engage in
risky, self-destructive behavior. What can family, community or society
do to protect individuals from harming themselves or others when they
are trying to recover from devastating events?

   Wine accompanies every Jewish holiday and celebration. Because
of appropriate concern for those who struggle with alcohol addiction, grape juice is an accepted substitute. When synagogues or other
Jewishly identified buildings offer space to AA or similar groups, they
are sending important messages of support for those who commit to
managing their alcoholism.

6.   The story of the Tower of Babel (Genesis 11:1-9) is a familiar biblical
story but it is inexplicable on many levels. Why do the people want to

erect the tower? Why is God so aggrieved by this endeavor, which seems to reflect a reasonable attempt at cooperation? Why is God's response to confuse the languages of the people?

FOCUS PHRASE (6:9)

Et HaElohim hitalech—With God (toward God), walk.

Lech L'cha (Genesis 12:1–17:27) "Finding Yourself"

OVERVIEW

Now the story of the Jewish people begins. Abram responds to God's invitation to leave his homeland. With his wife, Sarai, and his nephew Lot, Abram undertakes a journey of mind, body, and spirit. God indicates a promised land that would, ever after, remain part of Jewish history and destiny.

In this portion, Abram and Sarai experience the complexity of survival as outsiders and the vying of disparate needs within a family setting. By the end of this *parsha*, Abram and Sarai are promised offspring and national territory. Circumcision makes a symbolic and physical mark of the covenant with God, and Abram grows in stature and faith as his ongoing dialogue with God continues.

STANDOUT VERSES

15:7 "I am YHVH ..."

17:1 "I am El Shaddai ..."

With these new names, God self-identifies in new ways. YHVH is God's unpronounceable name. It is composed of the letters comprising three tenses of the verb "to be"—was, is, and will be. Other understandings of YHVH include Eternal One, Potentiality, and Fullness of Being.

El Shaddai means "God of the mountains" or "God of my breasts." Many ancient Near Eastern deities bear names identified with mountains. It seems plausible to link God with the nourishing capacity of female breasts.

15:13 "God said to Abram, 'Know now that your descendants shall be strangers in a land not theirs; they shall be enslaved and afflicted for four hundred years.'" This foreshadows the Israelite bondage in Egypt.

16:1-2 "Now Abram's wife Sarai, who had not borne him a child, had an Egyptian slave named Hagar ... maybe I will have a son through her." In the first two *parashiyot* of Genesis, fertility is abundant. In *Lech L'cha*, Sarai's story centers on her barrenness. The challenge of infertility is a heartbreaking theme in Rebekah and Rachel's lives as well. In ancestral times (and in many cultures to this day), producing descendants is singularly important. Infertility had (and has) social and psychological consequences beyond the biological.

16:6 "Sarai then so afflicted her that she ran away, and an angel of YHVH found her ..." It is deeply unfortunate that the Torah story recording the first interaction between two women shows a fractured and abusive relationship. Sarai and Hagar live in the same household but they don't speak to each other or say each other's name. In contrast, God calls Hagar by name (16:8).

A later biblical tale of women's relationships, the story of Rachel and Leah, highlights the sisters' competitive interactions (30:8). Later, they collaborate, calling for their appropriate inheritance. In Numbers 27:1-8, the daughters of Zelophehad (individually named in Numbers 27:1), also request their family inheritance. They work together to achieve a common goal.

TALK ABOUT

1. The words *lech l'cha* translate to "Go forth." But the words actually mean "Go for yourself," or "Go to yourself." Medieval commentator Rashi explains: "Go for your own benefit, for your own good." Many commentators and rabbis use these words to encourage inward personal exploration and spiritual growth. What have you learned about yourself as a result of leaving what is familiar? Why do the words appear in this order—leave your "land, birthplace, father's house"? Do these represent stages of breaking away? Some journeys are geographical and others are psychological or spiritual. "*Lech l'cha*" can be a command. I read it as an invitation. What do you think?

2. In 12:2, God tells Abram that God will bless him and make his name a blessing. The text does not say that Abram will *amass* blessing in terms of riches or power. Rather, Abram will BE a blessing. How does a person become a blessing? When you say you are blessed, or you speak of someone's memory as a blessing, what do you mean? People who express gratitude sometimes say they count their blessings. In 12:7-8, Abram expresses gratitude.

3. The first time Abram speaks to God is in 15:2, "God YHVH, what can You give me, when I am going to die childless ..." Is it surprising that Abram doesn't speak to God when he is told to leave his home and journey for an unknown destination? Or that he doesn't question

God during the dicey circumstances in Egypt, or when his nephew is kidnapped? What does it say about Abram that his first query of God is about having a child, and he notes that any other blessing pales in comparison?

4. We are not told why Abram was chosen. But aspects of Abram's character appear in this portion and they draw a picture of man who primarily has family, peace, and justice on his mind:

13:8-9 Abram to Lot, "There should be no quarrel between you and me ... if you go north, I will turn south; and if you go south, I will turn north."

14:14-16 Hearing that his kinsman had been taken captive, Abram mustered his retainers ... going in pursuit ... He then brought back all the possessions; his nephew Lot, too... and the other people.

14:22-23 But Abram said to the king of Sodom, I have raised my hand to YHVH Most High, maker of heaven and earth, that I would take nothing of yours, not even a thread or a sandal strap...

15:2 Abram then replied, "God YHVH, what can You give me, when I am going to die childless?"

What do these verses indicate about Abram's character and priorities?

5. In 12:13, Abram asks Sarai to call herself his sister (not his wife), in order that "it may go well for me, and that my life may be spared because of you." What does this incident say about Abram's character? Because of Sarai's beauty, she is taken to Pharaoh's palace, where she would be expected to sleep with him. The text suggests that God intervenes to protect her (12:17-20). The couple leaves intact.

What are we to make of a husband who puts his wife in such a precarious position? Abram is dismissive of Sarai's safety here, and his actions in next week's portion regarding the near-sacrifice of Isaac are similarly reprehensible (Genesis 22:1-14). Yet, Abraham is lauded for his defense of Sodom and Gomorrah (Genesis 18:23-33). Why does Abram speak up on strangers' behalf but not for his wife and son? Can you reconcile these asymmetrical responses?

6. Circumcision is instituted in 17:10-12. "This is My covenant that you and your descendants after you are to observe. Let every male among you be circumcised ... Let every eight-day-old boy among you be circumcised ..." Circumcision is an ancient tribal ritual. In the biblical

account, circumcision moves from an adult practice to an event in infancy, removing its sexual and fertility associations.

Rabbi Elyse Goldstein explains that the biblical focus of *brit milah*, the covenant of circumcision, is the releasing of blood that follows removal of the foreskin. In the Torah, blood atones. Blood is an offering. An animal cannot be sacrificed before the eighth day of its life, so male Israelites must be circumcised precisely on the eighth day, when their blood will be reckoned as a sacrifice.

In *ReVisions: Seeing Torah through a Feminist Lens*, Goldstein further notes that Sarah is not commanded to circumcise nor to be circumcised. She suggests that, "We can also see *brit milah* as a male birthing experience ... ritual rebirth by males is almost a universal religious phenomenon ... But on another level, it offers proof of men's deep longing to be able to give birth themselves."[13]

How do you respond to Rabbi Goldstein's ideas?

Think About

1. *Lech L'cha* presents Abram's journey as a combination of leaving behind and moving toward. For some, it's easy to leave a familiar place/ job/relationship when it no longer satisfies. For others, "leaving behind" is anxiety producing. Leaving what is comfortable, safe, and predictable, even if it no longer deeply satisfies, takes courage.

Do you welcome or resist new opportunities? It's possible to grow from navigating a new environment; it's also possible to grow by adapting to or refining one's self within a familiar environment. Have you grown in both kinds of circumstances?

2. We associate Abraham with Sarah for obvious reasons, but look at the common experiences shared by Abraham and Hagar. Both experience physical dislocation and both respond with strong spiritual resources (Abraham in 12:4, and Hagar in 21:14-19).

In 13:16 and 15:5 God tells Abram that he will have numerous offspring, and God makes the same promise to Hagar in 16:10. Hagar calls God "One Who Sees" in 16:13 and Abraham names a mountain "God Will Be Seen" in 22:14. Can you think of other commonalities between Abraham and Hagar, between Abraham and Sarah, between Sarah and Hagar?

---

13 Rabbi Elyse Goldstein, *ReVisions: Seeing Torah through a Feminist Lens,* Woodstock, VT: Jewish Lights Publishing, 1998, p. 118.

3.   Hagar is the only person in the Torah to give God a name! *So she called YHVH who had been speaking to her, "You are El Ro'i"—which means—"I have seen the One who looks upon me!"* (16:13) God speaks to Hagar, a slave, and she claims the encounter by naming the Deity.

   What names of God do you use? Can you create a name for God based on how you experience The Holy One?

4.   In this portion, Abram's name is changed to Abraham, and Sarai's name is changed to Sarah (17:5 and 17:15). In both cases, the addition is the Hebrew letter *hey*, which is one of the letters associated with God. Read the sections following the name changes (17:6-16). What else changes as a result of the altered names?

   Does your given name suit you? If you are named for someone, have you tried to emulate them? If you have changed your name, how long did it take to recognize yourself in your new name? If you've returned to a name, did it feel like a homecoming?

5.   Many oral and written discussions of infertility in the *Tanakh* (the Hebrew Bible) draw attention to the status biblical women gained by giving birth, thus contributing to the family's or clan's growth. Some portray this association of having children with an increase in value as a relic of the past. Yet even in the early decades of the 21st century, some people have misgivings about women who choose not to have children (biologically or through adoption). They may be judged as selfish or treated as if they are not fully actualized women.

   Are men who choose not to become fathers (or husbands) held to the same standard? In an overpopulated, resource-hungry world, what are your thoughts about having children? Does the shrinking Jewish population impact your opinion? Does a shrinking Jewish population concern you?

6.   Several decades ago, when 20th century Jewish feminism emerged, many women and men created new prayers and rituals to recognize female equality in the spiritual dimension of Jewish life. To correspond to the *brit milah*, ceremonies of welcome for girls have flourished. Families welcome female infants with songs, prayers, and blessings. Some ceremonies include sprinkling or caressing the baby's face, hand, or limbs with water, adding a physical dimension to the ritual. The baby receives a Hebrew name.

   You can find many *Simchat Bat* (Rejoicing in a Daughter) ceremonies and other creative rituals for various life events on the website

Ritualwell.org. Why is it important to have Jewish prayers and rituals for menstruation, pregnancy, fertility treatments, abortion, birthing, weaning, and menopause?

FOCUS PHRASE (12:1)

Lech l'cha—Go forth; go for yourself.

Vayeira (Genesis 18:1–22:24) "Finding God"

OVERVIEW

This portion is packed with incident, including some of the most recognized and controversial narratives in the Torah. Lot offers his daughters to satisfy hostile and aggressive neighbors and Abraham nearly sacrifices Isaac. These stories make us shudder. What are these stories intended to teach?

When Abraham confronts God about destroying Sodom, he stands out as an example of moral courage, but Abraham's willingness to take his son to be sacrificed staggers the mind. The portion closes with a genealogical list that demonstrates growth and succession in Abraham and Sarah's family.

STANDOUT VERSES

18:1-2 "YHVH appeared to him by the oaks of Mamre as he was sitting at the entrance of the tent ... Looking up, he saw—lo—three men standing opposite him!" These verses immediately follow the announcement of Abraham's circumcision. The Talmud explains that these visitors are engaging in "*bikkur cholim,*" the *mitzvah* of visiting the sick. This *mitzvah* speaks to the healing properties of connection to decrease a person's feelings of isolation and fear of abandonment. I heard *bikkur cholim* described as "the most delicate *mitzvah.*" What is "delicate" about visiting an ailing friend or relative?

18:25 "Must not the Judge of all the earth do justly?" Abraham's audacious challenge gives voice to a singular moral standard for God and for us: Justice is the standard. Abraham's plea suggests that he believes God has a conscience.

19:26 "And his wife looked behind him and became a pillar of salt." Why did she look back? She is often blamed for being disobedient, reckless, and even voyeuristic! To me, her glance backwards is not an act of disobedience, but a gesture of compassion. She was leaving her home, family, and friends. As agonizing as it must have been to see the destruction, it was a profoundly human response to take one last look.

22:2 "Take your son ... the one you love ..." In "Bound to the *Akedah*: Some Teachings for Our Time," Rabbi Susan Laemmle writes, "I have not domesticated the *Akedah*, but decided to make an uneasy peace with it ... Filled with beauty and pleasure and sensation as it is, life is essentially serious and scary. We understand more and more scientifically, but at its core, life remains mysterious and filled with terror ... Because we cannot and should not keep death and life's terror always in our minds, art and religion crystallize their recalcitrance into enduring forms whose beauty enables us to stretch our capacities for acceptance ... Abraham of the *Akedah* carries on, decides, and acts in the face of imperfect knowledge. He and we may not understand God's demand of him, but Abraham does not buckle or run away or go mad— all likely possibilities. He confronts life's rigor and, in some sense, goes forward."[14]

TALK ABOUT

1.   Hospitality is a well-recognized virtue in the ancient Near East and in current Middle Eastern countries. When Abraham rushes to greet the wayfarers (18:2-8, 16), he invites them to refresh themselves, provides food for them, and accompanies them when they depart. What are additional ways Abraham epitomizes gracious hospitality?

2.   In 18:9, the travelers ask for Sarah with the Hebrew word, *ay-yeh*. This is a variation of the word used by God in 3:9 "Where are you, Adam?" and, again in 4:9, "Where is your brother Abel?" In Question 7 in the chapter on the portion *B'reishit*, I explain that the word *ay-yeh* does not ask about a physical location, but a more profound, existential location. On a hot afternoon in the desert, the visitors probably surmised that Sarah was in the tent. Inquiring about her whereabouts with the word *ay-yeh*, what else could the visitors have been asking?

3.   What does the Torah tell us God wants? 18:19 suggests a clear answer: *doing what is right and just.* How do we know what constitutes 'right and just'? We know what *isn't* right and just because of God's response to Sodom's callousness and cruelty. The text reports God heard the citizens' outcry, using the same word describing the Israelites' pained

---

14 Rabbi Susan Laemmle, "Bound to the *Akedah*: Some Teachings for Our Time" *CCAR Journal: A Reform Jewish Quarterly.* Fall, 2003, pp. 7-18.

response to Egyptian slavery (Exodus 3:7). In Exodus 22:21-22, God hears this outcry again from the mistreated widow and orphan.

What do you think are right and just acts? Is this a high enough standard for what God wants? What else could God want?

4. In the story of Lot and his family in 19:4-26, Lot extends hospitality (19:1-3), as did Abraham earlier in this portion. But then events take an ugly turn. The men of Sodom demand access to the guests, presumably for the purpose of rape. Lot tries to protect his guests, but quickly falls into a moral abyss by offering his daughters to satisfy the townsmen's lust. This story is mentioned in Professor Phyllis Trible's *Texts of Terror: Literary-Feminist Readings of Biblical Narratives*. In this book, biblical scholar Trible uses literary criticism to fully expose the tragic stories of several women in the Bible. These women are each terrorized through manipulation coupled with cruel disregard for the women's lives and well-being.[15]

5. Lot's wife is not named. In the *Tanakh*, less than 10% of names are women's names. Rabbinic literature calls Lot's wife Idit, from the Hebrew word for witness. The name makes sense: Watching her city burn in the distance, Idit witnesses massive destruction. When Lot tried to protect the visitors (19:4-11), what does Idit witness? Poet Merle Feld's wrote a dramatic *midrash* called "Lotswife" in which she imagines Idit ascertaining her fate as a "bit player" in the scene after Abraham converses with God in a commanding performance. Feld describes Idit's turn to look back at her burning neighborhood as a mother's compassionate response, not a disobedient act, but an act of desperation and love.[16]

6. Perhaps because the ancestry of the Jewish people is traced through Isaac, or perhaps because we read this disturbing text annually during *Rosh HaShanah*, we are riveted by the near-death of Isaac at the hands of Abraham. In 21:14, Abraham is also complicit in the near-death of his first son, Ishmael.

The introductory Hebrew words are the same in these parallel events: "*V'yash'keim Avraham ba'boker*," "And Abraham arose in the morning" (21:14 and 22:3). The use of identical language in both stories

15 Phyllis Trible, *Texts of Terror: Literary-Feminist Readings of Biblical Narratives*, Minneapolis, MN: Fortress, Press, 1984.

16 Merle Feld, *A Spiritual Life: A Jewish Feminist Journey*, New York, NY: SUNY Press, 1999, pp. 273-74.

invites us to notice how the stories mirror each other. Additionally, in both stories, an angel of God intervenes. How else are these accounts similar and how do they differ?

7. Isaac's first word in the Torah is "Father!" in 22:7. Knowing that Isaac says this while Abraham's ascends a mountain presumably to sacrifice him makes this a heart wrenching moment. What emotions do you experience when you read this portion?

How does the Torah portray fathers? Consider Noah (9:24-27), Abraham (17:18, 17:26, 21:14, 22:3-12), and Lot (19:8). As your read further in Genesis, keep this question in mind when you encounter Isaac, Jacob, Laban, and Joseph.

THINK ABOUT

1. Many biblical characters are depicted sparingly, but we are treated to somewhat fuller development of Abraham and Sarah. For example, we read that they both laugh: Abraham in 17:17 and Sarah in 18:12. These occasions of laughter are in response to hearing they will have a child together at their elevated ages.

Becoming pregnant and bearing a child are occasions for rejoicing. (Pregnancy as a result of rape and when a woman is ill-equipped to appropriately care for the child are exceptions.) Tears and laughter often accompany the happy announcements of new life. How do you and your loved ones respond to news of a pregnancy? What kind of prayer or blessing give words to the deep emotions experienced at that time?

2. In 18:25 and following, Abraham argues to save Sodom from God's wrath. Virtually all commentaries praise Abraham for his defense of the city. Have you argued on behalf of people who are vulnerable? Have you engaged in acts of civil or moral disobedience? What was the experience like? What is your reaction to people who stand up for noble causes? Consider Idit's (Lot's wife) pivot to look at her city's devastation as an act of dissent. Does that change your assessment of her backward glance?

3. In 21:19 it says, "God then opened her eyes, and she saw a well." For a second time (the first time was in 16:6), Sarah displaces Hagar. God speaks to Hagar in the wilderness, reassuring her that her son will

prosper. Was the lifesaving well always there but Hagar was unable to see it in her distress?

Similarly in 22:13, Abraham is caught in a desperate situation, but when he lifts his eyes, he finds a solution. Had the ram been present all along but Abraham could not see it in his desperation? Sometimes we can create opportunities to impart confidence or affirmation to someone unable to see beyond momentary despair. Our words or gestures can give hope and courage.

4.   God tells Abraham to offer Isaac as a sacrifice in 22:2. An appalling notion! When God tells Abraham to undertake this desperate mission, God says, "*Lech l'cha.*" These are the same words spoken by God to separate Abraham from his home and homeland in 12:1. In some ways, Abraham's journey was successful: God blessed Abraham in every way (24:1). He died in good old age and was gathered to his people (25:7). His sons, Isaac and Ishmael, buried him (25:9).

Perhaps using the phrase "*Lech l'cha*" early in this story is designed to reassure us in advance that this incident won't end in tragedy. This story marks the first time the word "love" appears in the Torah, describing Abraham's feelings toward his son (22:2).

5.   The *Akedah* story does not end in tragedy; it does however end in silent animosity and estrangement. Isaac doesn't speak to his father following the events of 22:3-19. The text specifically tells us that Abraham returns alone to his servants and relocates to Beersheba (22:19). We next encounter Isaac in a different location entirely (24:62). There is no contact between father and son until Abraham's burial.

Also, Sarah and Abraham no longer reside together after the *Akedah*. Abraham moves to *Beer-Sheva* (22:19). Sarah dies in Hebron (23:2). Abraham and God don't speak after the *Akedah*. They had communicated frequently prior to the events on the mountain, but no words pass between them after this devastating encounter.

6.   One of the most well-known declarations in this portion, *Hineni*, appears three times: 22:1, 7 and 11. In the first instance, it is Abraham's response to God. In the second, it is Abraham's response to Isaac, and in the third, it is Abraham's response to an angel. *Hineni* means, "Here I am." Imagine if Adam had responded with *Hineni* when God asked him in the Garden, "Where are you?"

7. What do we learn about Abraham, who responds with *Hineni* in three different situations? Do you speak the same way to people in authority over you and to those over whom you have authority? Do you use the same tone with close family members and with friends and colleagues? When you say, "I am here," are you communicating more than a physical meaning? In which situations are you most present?

FOCUS PHRASE (22:1, 7, 11)

Hineni—I am here, present, and ready.

Chayei Sarah (Genesis 23:1-25:18) "Finding Others"

OVERVIEW

This *parsha* begins with the death of Sarah, and includes the deaths of Abraham and Ishmael. Some commentators attribute Sarah's death to the trauma she suffers when she discovers that Abraham took their son as a would-be sacrifice. Abraham purchases a burial plot for Sarah in the Promised Land, and he mourns her. Since biblical times, respect for and proper burial of the dead have been characteristic of Israelite/Jewish norms. The Israelite family grows through Isaac's marriage to Rebekah.

STANDOUT VERSES

23:1-2 "Sarah lived ... Sarah died." The only Torah portion that carries a woman's name, *Chayei Sarah* means "the life of Sarah," although the portion devotes significant attention to her death and burial. Learning of a death, it is common to hear, "How did they die?" A more illuminating question might be *"How did they live?"*

24:1 "Abraham was old, well advanced in years." The Torah records improbable ages for many people who lived prior to Abraham (e.g., Genesis 5:3-32). But Abraham is the first to be described as old. The Torah and Judaism teach honor and reverence for the aged in statements such as Leviticus 19:32, "You shall rise before the aged and show deference to the old."

24:18-19 "Drink ... Quickly she lowered her pitcher... And she said, 'I'll draw some for your camels, too, till they are done drinking.'" In many places, the Torah prescribes compassion and protection for animals. A law in the Talmud instructs people to feed their animals before feeding themselves. It is permissible for a person to drink before their animals (because drinking happens quickly), and that is what is described here—Abraham's servant drinks and then Rebekah offers water to the camels. This is not a trivial offer on her part; camels consume large quantities of water.

25:9 "His sons Isaac and Ishmael buried him ..." To me, this is one of the most hopeful sentences in the Torah. It presents a powerful image of reconciliation between brothers (who are competitive and confrontational throughout Genesis), and between nations. This portion is the first and only one in Genesis without conflict. Although *Chayei Sarah* includes death, mourning, and weeping, there is no jealousy, bitterness, deceit, or expulsion in this portion. A welcome change!

TALK ABOUT

1. Why is this portion called *Chayei Sarah*? Rabbi Rona Shapiro wonders whether Abraham became old and tired, or has the trauma of the *Akedah* "broken open his heart to care for his family members and live out his life on a human plane."[17]

2. Sarah is the only woman in the Torah whose age at time of death is mentioned (23:1). Why are some women reluctant to reveal their ages?

3. Although death is mentioned in prior *parashiyot*, the first account of mourning appears in *Chayei Sarah*, "Abraham proceeded to mourn for Sarah, and to bewail her" (23:2). The Hebrew verb "to mourn" shares a root with the Hebrew word "to eulogize," that is, to verbally lament one's loss. The Hebrew verb for "to bewail" simply means to cry.

This suggests two critical aspects of facing a loss/death: speaking about it and grieving it in additional expressive ways. Later in the portion Rebekah comforts Isaac following his mother's death. This is a third critical aspect in healing: receiving support from loved ones.

4. The Hebrew word *chesed* is used in 24:12, 14, 27, and 49. It is translated as kindness, graciousness, faithfulness, and lovingkindness. You may be familiar with the phrase *Gemilut Chasadim*, which refers to kind deeds or acts of generosity. *Gemilut Chasadim* is different from *Tsedakah*. *Tsedakah* refers to financial support. *Gemilut Chasadim* are done in person or with one's body—cooking, visiting, calling, fixing, etc.

Gemilut Chasadim widens the scope of giving because it benefits people regardless of their material well-being; every person at one time or another needs acts of lovingkindness to sustain them.

D'var Acher (another thing): The word *gemilah* means to "deal fully with something," to "close a circle" or to "pay back." Any act of

---

17 Rabbi Rona Shapiro, *The Women's Torah Commentary: New Insights from Women Rabbis on the 54 Weekly Torah Portions*, Elyse Goldstein, ed. Woodstock, VT: Jewish Lights Publishing, 2000, p. 74.

lovingkindness enables us to give back in a way that brings closure. When we engage in *Gemilut Chasadim*, there is no consideration of whether or not the recipient is deserving of the support. We ennoble and complete ourselves—we fulfill and elevate *ourselves* through building others up. In Modern Hebrew, *gemilah* means "recovery" or "rehab" (from addiction). We recover and rehabilitate *ourselves* when we give of ourselves; both the giver and recipient are beneficiaries of these actions.

5. In 24:12-14, Abraham's servant creates a test to find a suitable wife for Isaac. What qualities does he seek? What kind of "test" would you use to find a desirable partner for a person you care about? Was there one thing your chosen partner said or did that convinced you that they were "the one"? Rebekah's brother and mother ask if she wants to marry Isaac (24:57-58). Rabbi Dr. Tamara Cohn Eskenazi points out, "Rebekah's decision to leave her homeland and her family, go to a new place, and live with a man unknown to her, is reminiscent of Abraham, who left everything behind him in order to fulfill a divine command (12:1). Women's contribution to the fulfillment of national destiny finds its expression not only in their role as child bearers but also in their ability to take bold and vital action at critical moments."[18]

What were Sarah's bold and vital actions? Keep this description in mind as you encounter Rachel, Leah, Miriam, and other women in the Bible.

THINK ABOUT

1. In 23:4, Abraham describes himself as a *ger v'toshav*. *Ger* means stranger (implying an outsider); *toshav* means resident (implying an insider). Why does Abraham refer to himself as both an outsider and an insider? How does this description reflect the experience of Jews in the Diaspora? In what situations have you felt like a *ger v'toshav*?

2. Why does Abraham send a representative to find a wife for Isaac? Israeli author Meir Shalev reflects that in contrast to prior years of obedience to God and Sarah, Abraham finally does something of personal significance without getting instructions from his God or his

---

18 Rabbi Tamar Cohn Eskenazi, PhD and Rabbi Andrea Weiss, PhD, eds., *The Torah: A Women's Commentary*, New York, NY: URJ Press, 2008, p. 122, n. 58.

wife. Abraham's concern for his son in this instance stands in contrast with two prior actions he took: banishing Ishmael and binding Isaac.[19]

3. Abraham's servant utters the Torah's first prayer of supplication (24:12-14). He asks for success in determining a suitable wife for Isaac. He does not ask for a miracle or divine intervention. This is similar to praying to do one's best, not praying to win, or praying for the strength necessary to withstand painful situations, not praying to be spared any pain. About what have you prayed? Did anything *in you* change as a result of your prayers?

4. In 24:67 the text reports, "And he took Rebekah, and she became his wife and he loved her." The more natural progression would be that Isaac loved Rebekah and then she became his wife. This is certainly the case in most Western marriages today, where arranged marriages are largely rejected.

Do you know people whose marriages were arranged? How do they describe the positive and negative aspects of this practice? Many people imagine they can't love their spouse more than on their wedding day, only to find that love deepens over time. How do you love your partner differently from how you loved them when you first made a formal commitment?

5. There isn't a lot of romance in the Bible, but Isaac and Rebekah's first meeting (24:62-67) displays some sizzle. The phrase "looked up," describes each of their reactions on seeing the other (24:63 and 64), indicating a parallel response. The word "love" is used. Of the three patriarchs, Isaac appears the weakest and least charismatic. Are you surprised there is romance in his love story?

6. In 25:7, the Torah mentions Abraham's age in terms of "the days of the years." Jacob uses this phrase when talking about his life (Genesis 47:9), and repeats it when he is dying (47:28). This draws our attention to the incremental passage of time and daily interactions that contribute to a complete life story. If you selected any day of the year to think about, would it give you insight as to the character of the entire year? When

---

19 *Beginnings: The First Love, the First Hate, the First Dream ... Reflections on the Bible's Intriguing Firsts,* New York, NY: Random House, 2011, p. 14.

you think back on your life until now, are there years and days that stand out or do specific experiences and events stand out? Or all of the above?

FOCUS PHRASE (24:21)

Ma'cha'rish la'da'at—Be silent in order to know.

Tol'dot (Genesis 25:19–28:9) "Confusion"

OVERVIEW

Tol'dot begins with Rebekah's barrenness, but moves quickly to the twins she bears, Esau and Jacob. The brothers have different temperaments. Isaac favors Esau, a hunter and "man of the field," and Rebekah favors Jacob, an indoor (inward, mild) person. Jacob connives to secure Esau's firstborn birthright. Later, Jacob (with Rebekah's strategic help and encouragement) tricks a sight-impaired Isaac into bestowing his primary blessing on his younger son. Jacob flees from an enraged Esau to seek a wife for the next stage of his life.

STANDOUT VERSES

25:19 "This is the line of Isaac son of Abraham. Abraham begot Isaac." Although Isaac's name appears in the portion's opening line, it is Isaac's father, wife, and son who dominate in Tol'dot and in the patriarchal-matriarchal narratives as a whole.

26:18-19 "Isaac then turned to digging anew the water wells they had dug in the time of his father Abraham ... and they discovered a well of living waters." Each generation seems to have to relearn the lessons and refight the battles of the prior generation(s). Do we make any progress at all?

27:22 "The voice is the voice of Jacob, but the hands are the hands of Esau." This verse refers to Isaac's confusion about which son stands before him, and these words also describe deception. Deception results when words and deeds don't match; when something is positioned to appear one way, but in reality, is something else.

27:32 "But his father Isaac said to him, 'Who are you?'" This is a straightforward question from father to son, and an important question to ask young people as they approach and achieve adulthood. We can't assume we know who our children are becoming unless we pose searching questions. Asking people we love about their important decisions, doubts, and desires (instead of simply where they are going, who they are seeing, and similarly superficial plot questions) cultivates lasting connections.

TALK ABOUT

1. Although the Hebrew Bible is patriarchal—meaning, men predominate and social structures support their authority—Rebekah, resourceful and self-directed, takes center stage in *Tol'dot*. In 25:22, she displays spiritual acumen, asking: If pain is a companion to blessing, what is the point of pursuing blessing (life)? She tries to find meaning in her suffering, and questions God directly. Her questions are reminiscent of Abraham's query in 18:25: Why are Your (God's) ways inscrutable? Why isn't life "fair"?

2. Esau gets a bad rap in most Torah commentaries. Throughout rabbinic literature and in some contemporary appraisals, he is denigrated. But based on the actual Torah narrative, it is not clear why. Esau's actions toward his father reveal respect. When his father calls him in 27:1, he quickly responds, "*Hineni*" (Here I am), employing the phrase we associate with Abraham (Gen. 22:1, 7, 11). It is Jacob who manipulates Esau out of his birthright, and then cheats him of his blessing.

It is not surprising that Esau harbors resentment. Nevertheless, he doesn't actively pursue Jacob to exact revenge. When they finally meet in 33:4, Esau approaches his brother peacefully: "Esau runs to meet him, embraces him, falls on his neck, and kisses him." Once again, Jacob is devious, telling Esau they will meet in Seir, only to travel elsewhere (Gen. 33:14-15). Even if we agree that Rebekah chose correctly in promoting Jacob as the covenantal heir, why do so many commentaries present Esau as villainous?

3. On the other hand, in 25:32, the text indicates that Esau spurned his birthright. The Torah frequently associates the firstborn with inheriting the choicest material and spiritual inheritance. Why was Esau so casual about this inheritance, thoughtlessly exchanging it for a bowl of lentil stew?

Although Esau is not young during this exchange, he is not yet a husband or father. Can we cut Esau some slack for not appreciating his heritage in a mature and heartfelt manner?

At what age did you start to appreciate family history? Different kinds of maturity come at different times in life. Is there something in your past that you have only recently begun to appreciate? Unlike Esau, do you see Judaism as a precious legacy? Imagine Esau saying to himself at a later date, "If only ..."

4. It is with a tormented cry that Esau entreats his father, "Bless me. Me too, Father" (27:34). He repeats this plea in 27:38, "Do you have but one blessing, Father? Bless me. Me too, Father."

About Esau's despair, psychotherapist and Bible teacher Naomi H. Rosenblatt writes: "... all too often, the first lesson we learn from family life is there is never quite enough love to go around."[20]

Do you agree with Rosenblatt? Do you feel empathy for Esau? What is the difference between receiving the same blessing/treatment and receiving equal blessing/treatment in any given situation?

5. In the questions posed for *Lech L'cha*, in an earlier chapter, I ask how Abraham's character is revealed by his actions. Did his qualities of loyalty, kindness, and responsibility prompt God to choose him as progenitor of a new faith? What about his willingness to abandon Sarah to Pharaoh and Isaac to a woodpile? Similarly, in this portion, Jacob reveals aspects of his character: He cheats his brother (25:29-34), and he deceives his father (27:19-35). Is it not surprising that Jacob is deceived himself when Laban promises Rachel but delivers Leah as a wife (29:20-25)? Years later, Jacob's sons imitate their father (34:13), "The sons of Jacob answered Shechem and his father Hamor deceptively."

Are Abraham, Isaac, or Jacob admirable role models? What qualities do you look for in a role model or mentor? The Torah is praised for not presenting our founding ancestors as perfect, but do you think they could be a little less imperfect?

6. In these same closing verses, Isaac invokes Abraham's name twice; his father's name is among the last words Isaac speaks before death. Has Isaac forgiven his father for the *Akedah*? Does Isaac reconcile himself to the idea that while Abraham failed as a father in some ways, he also left a valuable legacy? If Isaac could forgive his father, perhaps he is owed more respect and appreciation than he is generally given.

THINK ABOUT

1. In the Torah, rabbinic literature and beyond, Isaac is not treated deferentially as is his father, Abraham, or his son Jacob. Yet I am particularly moved by Isaac's response to his wife's unfulfilled desire

20 Naomi H. Rosenblatt, with Joshua Horowitz, *Wrestling with Angels: What Genesis Teaches us About our Spiritual Identity, Sexuality and Personal Relationships,* New York, NY: Dell Publishing, 1995, pp. 240-241.

for a child. In 25:21, the Torah says, "Isaac pleaded with YHVH on behalf of his wife." Compare this with Jacob's response to his beloved wife, Rachel, when she bemoans her barrenness (30:2). He chastises her!

I credit Isaac for sharing his wife's despair at remaining childless. He supports her in a loving and respectful manner by adopting her desire as his own. Look at how prayer functions here as a tool. Some people are uncomfortable with the notion of praying for someone or someone praying for them. When Isaac prays for Rebekah, he shows commitment to her and a willingness to reach out and be vulnerable. To me, this is very touching. How does it strike you?

2.   In Gen. 27:1 Isaac has aged and his sight is failing. This sets the stage for Jacob fooling Isaac by pretending to be Esau. 'Seeing' occurs through one's eyes and also through emotional or intellectual understanding. To see something is to figure it out. Which kind of sight did Isaac lack when Jacob came to his bedside? It is not clear what he was able and unable to see and what he chose and chose not to see.

Isaac's eyes are mentioned again at the end of this portion. Verse 28:8 is translated as, "... Isaac *looked* with disfavor at the daughters of Canaan ..." The Hebrew says that these women were undesirable "in Isaac's *eyes*." So, regardless of whether or not Isaac's eyes were weak, in this second instance, he uses his eyes to judge.

Most of us have experienced our eyes "opening" when we suddenly realize something is important. Some of us have reliable insight. This does not refer to optical vision. What are the different meanings of look, behold, notice, vision, blind, dim, shortsighted, myopic, and other words connected to seeing?

3.   Rebekah makes a "tasty dish," in 27:14. Almost thirty years ago, Dr. Ellen Frankel authored a creative Torah commentary in which she interwove biblical women's voices with women's voices of later generations. In the chapter on *Tol'dot*, Frankel includes a recipe for the stew Rebekah made for Jacob to give his father.[21]

The Torah portion refers to goat meat as a key ingredient. Deferring to the rarity of goat meat in some regions, Frankel suggests lamb, "or if you are a vegetarian, turnips or potatoes." If women had made contributions to the Torah, it might have included recipes, birthing and lactating techniques, and other examples of women's lore to be passed

21 Ellen Frankel, PhD, *The Five Books of Miriam: A Woman's Commentary on the Torah*, New York, NY, 1996, p. 46.

down through the ages. How would the Torah have been different if a significant number of women had been among the authors and redactors of it?

4. "Esau now bore a grudge against Jacob ... I will kill my brother Jacob" (27:41). Sibling enmity resulting in violence is a familiar theme in the early Genesis families, and the theme continues into the next generation with Joseph and his brothers. But fraternal relations gradually become less violent. In the first family, Cain kills Abel. A few generations later, Esau fantasizes about killing Jacob, but over time, his vengeful thoughts dissipate. Later still, Joseph's brothers also consider killing him but instead sell him to traveling merchants. Ultimately, the brothers reconcile (Gen. 45:8-15).

By the end of Genesis, fraternal relations have progressed from deep hatred to peaceful and supportive concern. A key element in this evolution is forgiveness. Has forgiveness changed your family dynamics? Why is it hard to forgive?

FOCUS PHRASE (25:22)

Lamah zeh anochi—For what purpose do I exist?

Vayeitzei (Genesis 28:10-32:3) "Spiritual Growth"

OVERVIEW

En route to Haran to find a wife, Jacob rests his head atop a pillow of stones. Dreaming of a ladder reaching to heaven, with angels ascending and descending, he awakes awestruck, and confirms he is in God's presence. Continuing on his way, Jacob displays new confidence and connection to God.

Shortly, Jacob falls in love. He agrees to work seven years for Laban, Rachel's father, to earn her as a wife. On the wedding night, Laban substitutes his older daughter, Leah, for Rachel. Jacob balks at the deception, but commits to working another seven years in order to marry Rachel. Leah, Rachel, and their handmaids give birth to eleven sons and one daughter, Dinah. After twenty years, Jacob departs with two wives, concubines, many children, and substantial riches.

STANDOUT VERSES

28:12 "A ladder was set on the ground, with its top reaching to heaven, and lo—angels of God going up and coming down on it." This image has evoked many spiritual interpretations. Among them is our capacity to get closer to God by striving for higher levels of consciousness. For centuries, distinguished artists, including William Blake, Marc Chagall, and Helen Frankenthaler have depicted this richly symbolic biblical scene.

28:16 "Waking from his sleep, Jacob said, 'Truly, YHVH is in this place, and I did not know it!'" Acclaimed biblical scholar Nahum Sarna notes Jacob's surprising emotional response: "This reaction of amazement is unprecedented in the patriarchal stories. Neither Abraham nor Isaac exhibits any surprise at their initial experience of God's sudden self-revelation."[22] Why is Jacob surprised? Did he think God was no longer part of his life? Did he suspect that the baseness of his behavior toward his father and brother precluded an ongoing relationship with God?

30:1 "She said to Jacob, 'Let me have children; otherwise I am a dead woman!'" For many women, having a child is a deep and profound

22 Nahum Sarna, PhD, *The JPS Commentary: Genesis*, Philadelphia: The Jewish Publication Society, 1989, p. 199, n. 16.

desire, unmatched in intensity. In this verse, Rachel responds to her barrenness with desperation. Each of the Genesis matriarchs knew that having children was critical to their influence and standing within their families. How much is this true in our world today?

30:33 "My honesty shall answer for me on the morrow." Until now, Jacob has been anything but honest. For the first time, perhaps because he has encountered God in his dream or perhaps because he has fallen in love, Jacob grows in accountability.

Talk About

1. Many people see Jacob's dream (28:12-15) as a spiritual awakening. Realizing the revelatory nature of his dream, he admits in 28:16 "I did not know." These are difficult words to say. We pride ourselves on what we know and hesitate to reveal vulnerability by admitting all we don't know. Many people who pursue a spiritual path say that embracing an attitude of "I don't know" supports spiritual growth.

What is your experience with saying "I don't know"? Does it get easier to say over time? Do you feel any relief in admitting, "I don't know"?

2. The angels ascend and descend in Jacob's dream (28:12). Is this sequence incorrect? Angels live in heaven, so they should descend to earth. Do you think there is an explanation for this anomaly?

In his searching spiritual classic on Jacob's dream, Rabbi Lawrence Kushner offers this interpretation, "The angels did not reside in heaven at all. They lived on earth. They were ordinary human beings. And, like ordinary human beings, they shuttled back and forth between heaven and earth. The trick is to remember, after you descend, what you understood when you were high on the ladder."[23]

Does Kushner's interpretation speak to you? In the title of this book, what was Kushner trying to express by writing the first "I" in upper case letters and the second "i" in lower case letters?

3. In 29:35, Leah gives birth to her fourth son and names him Yehudah, formed from the Hebrew word "to give thanks." Leah explains, "This time I give thanks to YHVH." The names of her first three sons—*Reuven*,

---

23 Rabbi Lawrence Kushner, *God Was in This Place & I, i Did Not Know: Finding Self, Spirituality and Ultimate Meaning*, 25th Anniversary Edition. Woodstock, VT: Jewish Lights Publishing, 2016, p. 15.

Simeon and *Levi*—indicate Leah's desire to get her husband's attention. Giving birth to Yehudah, Leah expresses gratitude.

One of the names of the Jewish people is *Yehudim*, from the name Yehudah. This suggests that we are a people who give thanks and show appreciation. Compare this name to two others: *Ivrim*, "those who pass" and *Yisrael*, "one who struggles with God." Do you think these are all apt names for the Jewish people?

4. 29:17 reports that Leah has "weak eyes." Some commentators note that Leah's eyes are weak as a result of frequent crying. Why does she cry so much? Some imply it is because she isn't as attractive as her sister! Others say it refers to her gentle or tender eyes. Could the phrase mean that Leah doesn't see well or that her appearance isn't bright-eyed?

What are current societal norms relating to women's appearances?

THINK ABOUT

1. Talmud teacher and Maharat rabbinical student Dr. Liz Shayne begins one of her teachings on this portion: "Parashat Vayetzei is the story of a man in search of his identity."[24]

Most people think that an identity is not earned, but is something *given* by parents, profession, religion, and other external entities. How have you pursued your identity? Have you earned it?

2. 29:1 is usually translated as "Jacob moved on," or "resumed his journey." But the words in Hebrew actually mean, "Jacob lifted his feet." To me, this is reminiscent of the phrase "walking on air," and depicts a more optimistic and less burdened Jacob. We can all identify with feeling relief when a serious worry or plaguing doubt is put to rest.

The text reports that Jacob sees a well, representing life and sustenance. He appears to single-handedly remove the stone from the well so Rachel's flock can drink. When we first meet Jacob, he is described as preferring indoor (in tent) living, in contrast to his brother—a hunter; an outdoor, physical person. Look at Jacob in this portion: traveling outside, sleeping under the stars, using his physical strength to make an impression.

Have your comfort zones expanded over time? Are you surprised by your capabilities when attempting something new or difficult?

---

24 Yeshivatmaharat.org "Losing Yourself, Finding Yourself: Jacob's Psychological Journey," 2017/5778.

3. The Talmud asserts that Leah's words of thankfulness on giving birth to her fourth son are exceptional: They stand out as the Torah's first intentional words of gratitude (29:35). Gratitude is an important component of many religions, including Judaism. Rabbi Jonathan Sacks recognizes that part of the essence of gratitude is acknowledgement that we are not the sole authors of what is good in our lives. Gratitude "protects us from resentments and the arrogance of power."[25] It reminds us that we are dependent on others and on forces beyond our control.

Does gratitude protect us from resentment and arrogance? Gratitude's opposite is not simply ingratitude: Indifference, selfishness, greed, and envy are also contrary to gratitude. How do (grand)parents and teachers instill gratitude in children? How does a religion or society foster gratitude? Why is Thanksgiving called the most Jewish of American holidays?

4. Gratitude is one highlighted *middah* (quality) in *Vayeitzei*. Patience (*savlanut* in Hebrew) is another. Jacob is forced to wait fourteen years to marry Rachel, the woman he loves. Rachel also waits—for a child. Years pass before she gives birth to Joseph. Patience is the capacity to tolerate delay, suffering, or hardship with calmness. Patience requires acceptance of situations beyond our control. Patience benefits from trust and faith.

FOCUS PHRASE (30:6)

Elohim shamah b'kolee—God listened to my voice.

---

25 Rabbi Jonathan Sacks, *Essays on Ethics: A Weekly Reading of the Jewish Bible,* Jerusalem: Maggid Books, 2016. pp. 290-291.

Vayishlach (Genesis 32:4-36:43)
"Actions and Reactions"

OVERVIEW

Twenty years have passed since Jacob stole Esau's blessing and fled his home. Now, with a large family, flocks, herds, servants, and material goods, Jacob returns to his birthplace, Canaan. To get home, Jacob must pass through his brother's land. Jacob fears Esau's retribution, but hopes for the best. He secures his family and most of his goods, and attempts to appease Esau with gifts. The night prior to the brothers' meeting, a "man" wrestles with Jacob, wrenching his hip and leaving him limping. Physically weakened, Jacob emerges spiritually strengthened. He receives a new name, *Yisrael*, because he "wrestled with God and with men and overcame." When Jacob and Esau come face-to-face, they speak to each other deferentially and part peacefully.

Dinah, Jacob's only named daughter, attracts the attention of Shechem and he abducts her. Her brothers Simeon and Levi seek to avenge her. They promise the Shechemites a peaceful alliance between their peoples if the Shechemites undergo circumcision. The Shechemites agree. While they are recovering, Dinah's brothers murder the males in the city and plunder their goods. En route back to Canaan, Rachel dies giving birth to Benjamin and is buried in Efrat. Isaac dies and is buried with Abraham and Sarah. Jacob and Esau come together one last time to bury their father.

STANDOUT PHRASES

33:9 Esau: "I have an abundance." 33:11 Jacob: "I have all that I need." Is Jacob trying to one-up Esau here? Is he referencing the birthright he stole from his brother (the birthright is all he needs)? Is there a quantitative and/or qualitative difference between "abundance" and "everything I need"? At the end of Genesis, in 47:9, Jacob sums up his life with these words, "Few and miserable have been the days of the years of my life." This is quite a different from "I have all that I need."

34:1 "Dinah, Leah's daughter ... went out to see the women ..." Most traditional sources condemn Dinah for venturing out beyond her immediate surroundings.

35:10 "Jacob is your name; but Jacob are you called no more, for Israel is your name!" After Abram's and Sarai's names are changed, they are exclusively known as Abraham and Sarah. The name Jacob appears many times following his name change to Israel.

35:29 "Isaac then breathed his last and died ... and his sons Esau and Jacob buried him." Just as Abraham's sons Isaac and Ishmael came together to bury him (25:9), here Isaac's sons together pay last respects to their father.

TALK ABOUT

1.   Jacob prays for the first time in 32:10. This prayer follows a description of Jacob in 32:8, where he is described as terrified, and anxious. Are these the emotions that prompt his prayer? Which emotions prompt your prayers?

2.   The story of Jacob wrestling with a "man" (32:25-30) is among the best known stories in the Torah. But who is the "man"? God? An angel? Jacob's conscience? Esau disguised?

Esteemed scholar Rabbi W. Gunther Plaut teaches, "Since ancient days, crossing a river has been symbolic of overcoming hazard and going forward to new experience (note such expressions as "crossing the Rubicon"). In this sense, Jacob passing over the Jabok to meet Esau crosses the watershed of his life. Everything that has happened to him since he obtained both birthright and parental blessing by doubtful means has been tainted with his own guilt and his brother's enmity. Jacob cannot fully face his own past unless he seeks reconciliation with Esau ... Some interpreters say that Jacob struggled with no one but himself ... However, this complete internalization of the struggle does not reflect the biblical intent. The text tells of God's role in Jacob's renewal ... God's name is embedded in the cognomen that the forefather now bears and that his descendants will bear after him."[26]

3.   Jacob receives the name "Israel" in 32:29. On May 14, 1948, David Ben-Gurion declared statehood in the old Tel Aviv Museum, now Independence Hall. The climax was this sentence: "We hereby declare the establishment of a Jewish state in *Eretz Yisrael*, to be known as the State of Israel."

26 Gunther Plaut, ed. *The Torah: A Modern Commentary,* Revised edition. New York, NY: URJ Press, 2005, p. 233.

The next stage of Jewish history had begun. Why was "Israel" chosen as the name of the Jewish state? It includes a reference to God—"*el*"— but not a reference to the Jewish people. The Israeli national anthem, *HaTikvah*, doesn't mention "*Yisrael*" or God.

4. There are two main sections in the Torah that address *kashrut* (keeping *kosher*), Leviticus 11 and Deuteronomy 14:3-21. *Vayishlach* includes the purported origin of an aspect of *kashrut* not mentioned in Leviticus and Deuteronomy: "To this day that is why the people of Israel do not eat the thigh muscle that is in the socket of the hip, because he struck Jacob's hip-socket at the thigh muscle" (32:33).

Therefore, *kashrut*-observant people do not eat the hindquarters of a kosher animal. It is unusual for a *mitzvah* to be included as part of a story, and not as a commandment per se. Knowing the origin of this prohibition, is it more or less relevant to you? When you hear the term "keeping *kosher*," which eating practices come to mind?

5. Chapter 34 is a frightening text. Dinah is abducted and possibly raped. Her brothers respond with a massacre of all the males in the town where Dinah had been taken. This vengeful response reveals that violating a woman is viewed primarily as damaging family honor, and only secondarily (if at all), as a violent act against the woman.

There are no winners in this story. Violence leads to more violence. Dinah's name only appears one more time in the Torah after this abhorrent series of events (46:15), and no clue is given about how she weathered this storm.

Biblical scholar Richard Elliott Friedman asks us to consider whether Shechem's act was indeed rape. "The nature of the act is not in fact clear from this wording. The three key terms here (took, lay, degraded) appear to suggest force, but all three are used without such a meaning in the Torah's laws concerning marriage ... It may be a rape, but we cannot be sure. What we can say, at a minimum, is that Shechem's act, taking place before the request for marriage, is regarded as disgraceful by Dinah's family."[27]

Anita Diamant brought Dinah to life in her award-winning and wildly popular novel *The Red Tent*. Whereas in the biblical story, what happens to Dinah is reported by her brothers, in Diamant's modern *midrash*, Dinah speaks for herself. *The Red Tent* portrays Dinah as in

---

27 Richard Elliot Friedman, *Commentary on the Torah*, New York, NY: HarperCollins, 2001, p. 116.

love with her abductor. She is horrified when her brothers kill him and she returns to her family heartbroken and outraged.[28]

Another contemporary *midrash* about Dinah that imagines her and Hamor equally desiring each other is found in *Joseph and the Way of Forgiveness* by Stephen Mitchell.[29]

THINK ABOUT

1. Jacob prepares to meet Esau in three ways. First, he prays (32:10-13). Then he strategizes by selecting gifts to send (32:14-22) and securing the well-being of his family and possessions (32:23-24). Finally, Jacob secludes himself to mentally and spiritually prepare for their meeting (32:25). Do you think these are adequate preparations? How do you prepare for a difficult encounter?

2. In 32:25, we read that Jacob was "alone." The Hebrew word *l'vado* also carries the connotation of lonely. As part of the second creation story, in Genesis 2:18, God says (thinks?), "It is not good for Adam to be alone (*l'vado*). The Torah favors relationships and community, not solitude and independence. How are being alone and lonely different?

3. Jacob emerges wounded from his nocturnal struggle (32:32), "He was limping on account of his thigh." Does this impairment humble him? In 33:12-14, Jacob tells Esau that the children and animals need to journey at a slower pace, and that he, Jacob, would continue with them. Was Jacob trying to camouflage his disability and his need to walk at a slower pace from his brother? Did he not want to reveal any weakness?

When you have revealed weaknesses to a close friend or family member, how have they responded? How do you respond when someone reveals a weakness to you?

4. The name Dinah comes from the Hebrew root for "judge." How do you judge Dinah, her brothers, her father, and Shechem? In one Jerusalem neighborhood, streets are named for 11 of Jacob's sons. Recently, a new street in the area was named "Dinah."

Many commentators are disappointed that Jacob, Dinah's father, did little in response to her rape and to his sons' vengeful acts. He simply says in 34:30: "You have made trouble for me by making me odious to

---

28 Anita Diamant, *The Red Tent*, New York, NY: St. Martin's Press, 1997.

29 *Joseph and the Way of Forgiveness: A Biblical Tale Retold*, Stephen Mitchell. New York, NY: St. Martin's Publishing Group, 2019, pp. 21-22.

the land's inhabitants ... they will gather themselves against me and strike at me, and I and my household will be destroyed." Should we expect more of Jacob by now? After all, his name had already changed after struggling with his demons, he reconciled with his brother, and he arrived home safely in Canaan with family unscathed. How might Jacob have responded differently to Dinah's abduction and her brothers' murderous plans?

Others point to Jacob's chastisement of the brothers, in 49:5-6, as appropriate penalty for their misdeeds. Jacob is on his deathbed and projects the future entitlements of each son. Simeon's and Levi's inheritances are diminished because of their actions in Shechem. Does this culmination seem adequate to the brothers' actions?

5. Rachel, Jacob's beloved wife, dies in childbirth (35:18) and, Isaac, Jacob's father dies of old age (35:28-29). Judaism makes no excuses for death; Judaism's focus is on life, encouraging us to celebrate and value life.

FOCUS PHRASE (33:9)

Yesh li rav—I have an abundance.

Vayeishev (Genesis 37:1–40:23) "Misadventures"

OVERVIEW

In this portion we meet Joseph and his brothers. Their story contin-ues for four *parashiyot*. Joseph is his father's favorite child. Jacob gives Joseph an ornamented tunic, which cements his lofty status. The other brothers work hard as shepherds while Joseph dreams. When Joseph brazenly shares his self-aggrandizing dreams with his brothers, they fume, waiting for a moment to get revenge (a familiar theme in Genesis!). The moment arrives when Joseph is alone with his brothers, away from their father's watchful eye. After discussing whether or not to kill him, the brothers decide to sell Joseph to passing merchants. Joseph is trans-ported to Egypt where he becomes a slave. *Vayeishev* also includes the story of Tamar, who tricks Judah, her father-in-law, into impregnating her so that she can continue the family lineage.

STANDOUT PHRASES

37:2 "This is the family history of Jacob, when Joseph was 17 years old ..." In Hebrew, the name "Joseph" immediately follows "Jacob," ensuring that when we hear Jacob, we quickly think of Joseph. This sequencing of names also occurs in *Tol'dot*, which begins, "This is the line of Isaac, son of Abraham: Abraham begot Isaac" (25:19). The subject of this verse is Isaac, but Abraham's name follows quickly, and twice.

37:3 "Yet Israel loved Joseph better than his other sons, for he was to him the son of his old age; he therefore made him a coat of many colors." The image of the many-colored coat is unusual. Except for the adorned Tabernacle and the priests' ornate clothing (described in Exodus and Leviticus), there is no other mention of eye-catching color in the Torah.

37:19 "Here comes that master of dreams." A few other Torah characters have dreams, but dreams are central to Joseph's life and so he is called Joseph the Dreamer. Later Jewish tradition renames him: Joseph *HaTzadik* (the Righteous One). Some say this is because he refused Potiphar's wife's sexual advances. Others say it is because he wholeheartedly forgave his brothers in the closing chapters of Genesis. Which epithet do you think better describes him, Joseph the Dreamer or Joseph the Righteous One? Do you think refusing ill-conceived sexual advances is a sign of righteousness?

38:26 "She is more in the right than I." Judah admits this when he realized he unknowingly impregnated his daughter-in-law, Tamar. Judah publicly confesses he was wrong, in deference to a young widow, with considerably less status than he in the ancient world. Later in Genesis, Judah becomes an exemplar of *t'shuvah* (repentance and repair) and moral responsibility (43:8-9, 44:18-34). In *Vayeishev*, we can identify the beginning of Judah's moral growth.

TALK ABOUT

1. The man asked him: 'What are you looking for' He said, 'I'm looking for my brothers' (37:15). Rabbi Jeffrey Salkin probes the meaning of masculinity in Judaism in a book based on this exchange between Joseph and this man who directs him to his brothers. Salkin explains, "The American definition of masculinity has classically been: toughness, a preference for solitary action, a lack of emotion, a fondness for sports, a respect for military strength, a disdain for eggheaded intellectualism ... Throughout history, Judaism has been quietly teaching the world a radically different view of masculinity...."

"The Jewish critique of macho culture began early ... Men celebrated Torah not toughness. Western culture said, "Be a man." Jewish culture said, "Be a mensch."[30]

What do you think characterizes masculinity in Judaism? Do you discuss this with your father or son or friends? Is this an important discussion to have?

2. When we first meet Joseph, he is spoiled and narcissistic, indifferent to others and oblivious about the impression he makes. He taunts his brothers and flaunts his role as their father's favorite. It takes a lot of life to lower Joseph from his high perch. But a near-death experience in the pit, slavery, and alienation finally make an impact. With trials and tribulations, Joseph matures.

One sign of his growing maturity is his new awareness that he is not in complete control of what happens to him. Joseph says in 39:9, "How then could I do this great evil, and thus sin against God?" He says in 40:8,

---

30 Rabbi Jeffrey Salkin, *Searching for My Brothers: Jewish Men in a Gentile World*, New York, NY: Penguin Putnam Inc., 1999, pp. 2-4.

"Surely God's interpretations are in God's domain." Acknowledging others' help, sharing success, being accountable: These are all signs of maturity. What are other signs of Joseph's maturation? Why was he silent when his brothers were arranging his sale to passing merchants?

3. "Couple with your brother's widow ... and raise up offspring for your brother!" (38:8) refers to levirate marriage, a well-documented practice in the ancient Near East. When a man left no heir, the oldest unmarried brother insured the dead man's name and posterity by marrying and impregnating the childless widow. This obligation preserved biological continuity.

This scenario is quite foreign to us, but can you understand its purpose in biblical times? In Jewish law, levirate marriage was rare and occurred only under strictly circumscribed conditions. Plus, a ritual to release the widow from this obligation was always available. You can read more about levirate marriage in Deuteronomy 25:4-6.

4. Two stories of sex stand at the center of this portion: Judah and Tamar (38:6-26) and Joseph and Potiphar's wife (39:7-19). Mieke Bal notes that Tamar sees what Judah does not see: the injustice done to her. She also recognizes that Judah is untrustworthy. Judah, in his turn, sees a whore instead of a relative. Tamar teaches Judah discernment, which is to see into, and not just to look at.[31]

Naomi Rosenblatt describes Potiphar's wife's failed tryst with Joseph as a "tale of sexual harassment in the workplace." She points out that the Bible consistently frowns upon abuse of power, be it in political, economic, or social realms.[32] Are you surprised that shaming, sexual coercion, infidelity, and prostitution all have a place in the Torah? Do you think the Torah/Bible consistently condemns abuse of power?

5. Joseph embodies the challenge of Jewish distinctiveness versus assimilation. This is a particularly relevant theme at Chanukah time, which annually coincides with the reading of the Joseph saga. The holiday of Chanukah emerged from the Jewish victory over the Syrian-Greeks, who sought to assert religious and cultural rule. The (Jewish) Hasmoneans rejected (Greek) Hellenism and fought to maintain Jewish separateness. Chanukah celebrates the right to be different.

---

31 Mieke Bal, *Lethal Love: Feminist Literary Readings of Biblical Love Stories*, Bloomington and Indianapolis: Indiana University Press, 1987, p. 102.

32 *Wrestling with Angels: What Genesis Teaches Us about Our Spiritual Identity, Sexuality and Personal Relationships*, New York, NY: Dell Publishing, 1995, pp. 332-33.

Joseph had an Egyptian wife and lived comfortably in Egyptian culture. Does the text indicate to what extent he remained loyal to Israelite customs? He asked for his final resting place to be in his ancestral land, but he didn't choose to live there. Do you find it challenging to maintain a Jewish identity in the United States? Did you ever consider moving to Israel? Do you think it is easier to live a fully Jewish life in Israel? How did you feel as a child about being Jewish at Christmastime? Is this a topic of conversation with your (grand)children today?

THINK ABOUT

1.   The text tells us that Jacob loved Joseph "better" or "more than" his other sons (37:3). What does it mean to love a child better? Does it mean giving them more or appreciating that they bring you more satisfaction (*naches*)? Does it mean having a more natural affinity toward the child? Does it mean having higher hopes or expectations for the child? Many parents today understand the importance of expressing love for each child appropriate to their uniqueness.

2.   Jacob used a slaughtered goat and a garment to fool his father into giving him the blessing intended for Esau (Genesis 27:16-19). In 37:31, Jacob is the victim of a deception with the same props: a goat and a garment. Jacob is deceived several times in his life. The Torah seems to suggest that a person's past will catch up to them. The purpose of *t'shuvah* (repentance, repair) is to *alter* the past; that is, to change the trajectory of where past actions seem destined to culminate. Perhaps being wounded and limping was part of Jacob's *t'shuvah*. What else could Jacob do to redeem his past? Apologize to his father and Esau? Treat his children with transparency and even-handedness?

3.   Joseph loses his clothes twice in this portion. In 37:31, he loses his colorful tunic to his brothers, and in 39:12 Joseph loses his coat to Potiphar's wife. Who are we without our clothes? I am not referring to nakedness; rather, to the type of clothes we wear to demonstrate our professional standing, our financial resources, or social status. How hard is it *not* to make assumptions about someone based on their attire? What message do you try to communicate by how you dress?

4.   Why is the Joseph story interrupted with the tale about Judah and Tamar? Some see no connection to the narrative preceding or following. Others notice similarities including repeated words and themes. Does

the Judah and Tamar story seem like an artificial intrusion into the Joseph saga, or does its placement make sense?

5. An unlikely character plays an important role in this portion (40:9-15). While in jail, Joseph interprets Pharaoh's chief cupbearer's dream, telling him the dream signifies that the cupbearer would be released and restored to Pharaoh's good graces. In exchange for this good news, Joseph asks the cupbearer to mention him to Pharaoh so that Joseph might also be freed. Once liberated, however, the cupbearer forgets Joseph, who continues to languish in prison.

Later, Pharaoh has a disturbing dream. The cupbearer recalls the Hebrew slave who had accurately interpreted his dreams in prison. He apologizes to Pharaoh for not having mentioned Joseph before, saying, "This day I acknowledge my sins" (41:9). Admitting his own lapse publicly, the cupbearer practices *t'shuvah*. Acknowledging mistakes and taking responsibility for them are the first steps in repairing what is broken and forging an unexpected outcome.

6. The only place in the *Tanakh* that mentions a birthday is in this portion—40:20. It is Pharaoh's birthday and he celebrates it by throwing a party. Ecclesiastes 7:1 says, "The day of one's death is better than the day of one's birth." What could this possibly mean? Think about the difference between the Israelite and Egyptian approach to death as a way to shed light on this.

FOCUS PHRASE (37:15)

Mah t'vakesh—What are you looking for?

Mikeitz (Genesis 41:1-44:17) "Final Exam"

OVERVIEW

Joseph remains in captivity until he successfully interprets Pharaoh's two dreams. Pharaoh rewards him with responsibility for food collection and distribution for the following fourteen years—seven years of prosperity and then seven years of famine. Joseph marries Asenath, an Egyptian priest's daughter, and they have two sons, Manasseh and Ephraim.

At Jacob's request, Joseph's brothers, minus Benjamin, travel to Egypt to obtain food. Joseph recognizes his brothers, but they don't realize that he is Joseph, their long-abandoned brother, who stands before them as a powerful Egyptian viceroy. Intent on discerning whether his brothers have changed, Joseph arranges for Simeon to be kept hostage while the remaining brothers return to Canaan to retrieve Benjamin. When they return with their youngest brother, Joseph continues testing them. He falsely accuses Benjamin of stealing and demands that he remain as Joseph's slave. The other brothers are granted permission to return to their father, but Judah refuses to leave Benjamin behind.

STANDOUT PHRASES

41:33 "Discerning and wise." How do discernment and wisdom differ? Pharaoh appoints Joseph as viceroy because he observes these qualities in him. Do you see these attributes in Joseph?

41:51-2 "Joseph named the first-born son Manasseh, 'For God has made me forget all the troubles I endured in my father's house.' And he named the second one Ephraim, 'For God has made me fruitful in the land of my affliction.'" The first son's name reflects Joseph's acceptance of past trials and the second son's name expresses Joseph's hope in a better future.

41:53-54 "The seven years of plenty that prevailed in the land of Egypt came to an end, and the seven years of famine began, as Joseph had foretold." Things change. Even without a portentous dream and an inspired dream-interpreter, we know that fortunes, health, relationships, and luck ebb and flow. Joseph acts wisely by preparing for the years of famine during the years of plenty. Planning ahead is always a wise course of action.

42:24, 43:30, 45:2, 45:14-15, 46:29 Joseph weeps five times. The first time his tears are in response to seeing his brothers after twenty years separation. The brothers are humble and Joseph is moved. The second time Joseph cries when he sees Benjamin, the only brother born to Rachel. Look ahead and see what moves Joseph to tears in chapters 45 and 46.

TALK ABOUT

1. This portion is almost always read on the Shabbat during *Chanukah*. What themes do *Mikeitz* and *Chanukah* share? Both are stories of unlikely triumph. Rabbi Dr. Erin Leib Smokler makes the connection that the story of *Mikeitz* (the end of Joseph's darkness) shares the message and the imperative of Chanukah: During the darkest part of the year the darkest part of the night, we continue to believe in light.[33]

2. Asenath, Joseph's wife appears three times in the Joseph story: 41:45, 41:50, and 46:20. *The Torah: A Women's Commentary* suggests that because Jacob adopts Ephraim and Manasseh (48:5), Asenath (the boys' mother) becomes, by proxy, a seventh matriarch![34] (Sarah, Rebekah, Rachel, and Leah are the four predominant matriarchs. Some people add Bilhah and Zilpah, whose sons are counted among the twelve tribes of Israel.)

3. Imagine including Asenath in the daily prayer that honors our ancestors (*Avot/Imahot*)! How would that impact our appreciation of families in which a partner of another faith actively nurtures and preserves the family's Jewish identity? In 43:8-9 and 44:16, Judah shows consideration for others and not only himself. Poet and professor Jacqueline Osherow notes that Judah's story signals a shift in the book of Genesis from being primarily a narrative of human beings in relation to God to becoming a narrative of human beings in relation to one another. She points out that Abraham, Isaac, and Jacob are the great patriarchs, but that Judah becomes a great human being, "the ideal of a brother's keeper."[35]

33 Yeshivatmaharat.org "Dreaming in the Dark: Miketz and the Menorah," 2015.

34 Eskenazi and Weiss, p. 269, n.20.

35 Jacqueline Osherow, "That We May Live and Not Die: Judah as Life Force of Genesis," *Reading Genesis: Beginnings*, ed. Beth Kissileff. London, UK: Bloomsbury Publishing Plc, 2016, p. 225.

4. Do you think Genesis moved from being a narrative about people and God to a narrative about people interacting with each other? Do you think Judah's encounter with Tamar (38:12-26) was the impetus for his development? Can you attribute growth in your life to specific, transformative events?

THINK ABOUT

1. Most commentaries translate 42:1 as "Why are you staring at each other?" The Stone Chumash Commentary translates the verse as "Why do you make yourselves conspicuous?" This understanding suggests that Jacob's rhetorical question is based on fear that Jews who flaunt their wealth and success encourage antisemitism.[36]

What do you think of this notion? Are you uncomfortable or concerned when Jewish people dress or behave conspicuously?

2. Joseph asks his brothers where they come from (42:7). They respond, "Canaan." But the question of where a person is from can also have a broader, non-geographical meaning. Do you come from a place of tolerance or judgment, from an orientation of abundance or scarcity? From empathy or indifference? Perhaps Joseph wanted to know if his brothers came from a place of regret, or if their resentment towards him had lingered.

3. When Jacob reluctantly agrees to let Benjamin return to Egypt with his brothers, Jacob says (43:14), "And as for me—if I am bereaved, I am bereaved." Jacob uses the same Hebrew word, "*shacolti*," when speaking of his presumed dead son Joseph. (42:36) *Shacolti* specifically refers to bereavement when someone loses a child, the most painful and cruel loss imaginable.

4. *Hineni* (I am here) is the word Abraham uses in the *Akedah* story when he responds to God and Isaac (22:1, 22:7, 22:11). *Hineni* expresses a state of preparedness to respond quickly and fully. In 44:16, Judah says on behalf of himself and his brothers, "*Hinenu* (We are here)."

In this instance, Judah offers himself and his brothers as slaves. Surely this was not the outcome Judah wanted but he recognizes his responsibility. *Hineni* is not a response to an easy task. It is a willingness

36 Rabbi Nosson Scherman, *The Stone Edition of the Chumash*, Brooklyn, NY: Mesorah Publications, Ltd., 1993, p. 232, n. 1.

and readiness to do what needs to be done. What have been some of your *hineni* moments?

FOCUS PHRASE (41:33)

Na'von v'cha'cham—Discerning and wise.

Vayigash (Genesis 44:18-47:27) "Revelation"

OVERVIEW

Judah asks Joseph to be Benjamin's replacement as a slave in Pharaoh's court. Judah's display of loyalty and selflessness moves Joseph and he reveals his true identity. He assures his brothers he forgives them for having sold him into slavery decades earlier. Joseph's family, including Jacob, travel to Egypt to "live off the fat of the land." Under Joseph's leadership, provisions were made to survive the famine. The Israelites remain in Egypt.

STANDOUT PHRASES

44:18 "Judah now approached him ..." The same Hebrew word— *Vayigash* (he approached)—is used when Abraham approaches God to argue on behalf of Sodom (18:23). *Vayigash* indicates trepidation, and uncertainty about outcome. *Vayigash* is also used when approaching battle or prayer. Perhaps Judah saw himself as doing battle with Joseph or perhaps he was beseeching him in a prayerful way.

45:3 "I am Joseph. Is my father really alive?" There is urgency in Joseph's question. It appears that he has not forgotten his father.

46:4 "Joseph will lay his hand upon your eyes." It is a Jewish custom and an act of *chesed* (lovingkindness) to close the eyes of the deceased immediately following death. This action preserves the honor/dignity and modesty of the deceased. Since s/he cannot look upon others, those dealing with the body should not look directly at them.

47:27 "Israel thus settled in the land of Egypt, in the region of Goshen. They struck roots in it, were fruitful and multiplied greatly." What begins as an era of peace and prosperity becomes the antecedent to slavery (Exodus 1:13-14).

TALK ABOUT

1. What could be a more dramatic scene than creation (Genesis 1:1-31), or Abraham's arguing with God on behalf of the people of Sodom (Genesis 18:22-33), or the Ten Plagues (Exodus 7:19-11:7), or the Revelation at Sinai

(Exodus 20: 1-18), or ... ? But for me, the opening scene in *Vayigash* ranks among the most dramatic in the Torah because it is filled with stark human emotion and true *t'shuvah*. Which Torah scenes do you find most unforgettable?

2. Rabbi Shai Held names his *Devar Torah* on *Vayigash* "Humiliation: Judaism's Fourth Cardinal Sin?" Held explains: "In Jewish ethics humiliating another person is regarded as an extraordinarily grave offense ..."[37]

How is humiliation antithetical to Jewish ideas about the dignity of the individual?

3. Three times Joseph attributes the momentous events leading to his presence in Pharaoh's court to God: in this portion (45:5 and 45:8), and again in the closing portion of Genesis (50:20). Joseph shows tremendous compassion towards his brothers, telling them they are not to blame for disposing of him many years prior. Joseph acts with humility and exemplifies the Torah's command not to bear a grudge (Leviticus 19:18).

Have any disappointing or traumatic events in your life ultimately led to positive outcomes? Have you ever sensed that God played a role in the unfolding of important events in your life?

4. In Genesis 46:17, we meet an ancestral granddaughter. The only other biblical reference to Serah bat Asher is in Numbers 26:46, as part of the census at the end of the Israelites' desert wandering. It is notable that she lived so long, seemingly for generations.

There are many *midrashim* about Serah. One says she was a musician and a singer. Another claims she is granted immortality for her role in sensitively revealing to Jacob that the son he presumed was dead, Joseph, was in fact still alive and prospering in Egypt.

5. Like Abraham in 22:11, Jacob says to God "*Hineni*" (46:2). Abraham is alert to God's requests from the start, but Jacob is not focused exclusively on God's desires. Moses also responds "*Hineni*" when God calls to him at the burning bush (Exodus 3:4). But like Jacob, Moses is sometimes reluctant to do what God asks. The Torah thrives on people responding affirmatively to God, but not all characters in the Torah (or Bible) answer God's call expeditiously.

---

37 Shai Held, *The Heart of Torah: Essays on the Weekly Torah Portion: Genesis and Exodus,* Volume I. Philadelphia: The Jewish Publication Society, 2017, p.99.

THINK ABOUT

1. Joseph reveals himself to his brothers in 45:1. This is the pivotal moment of this Torah portion. It took great courage for Joseph to show his true self. Have you ever revealed a previously hidden aspect of your self, with racing heart, not knowing how your revelation would be received? It is not easy to do, but often it results in a deeper and more honest relationship.

2. Joseph and his brothers have changed places. In 37:23, Joseph is stripped of his clothes, and in 45:22, he provides clothing for his brothers. In 37:24-27, Joseph listens helplessly as his brothers decide his future. In 45:3-16, he speaks while his brothers listen in stunned silence. How else does the text indicate Joseph's and his brothers' role reversal?

3. Can you sense the book of Genesis is coming to an end? In chapter 46, Joseph invokes the memories of his father and grandfather.

   As you get older, do you think more about your parents and grand-parents? Do you desire to visit places they visited or lived in? Do some of their life lessons bubble up in you unexpectedly?

4. Pharaoh asks Jacob, "How many years have you lived?" Jacob responds, "The span of the years of my lifetime has been 130; few and miserable have been the days of the years of my life (47: 8-9). Jacob questions and regrets the trajectory of his life. This reminds me of his mother, Rebecca, grappling with the meaning of her life: "If this is so, why do I exist?" (25:22)

   Are any of your struggles reminiscent of your parents' challenges? Do you emulate your parents' values and personal qualities or have you tried to develop in opposition to them?

FOCUS PHRASE (45:24)

Al teer'g'zu ba'darech—Don't be anxious along the way.

Va-y'chi (Genesis 47:28-50:26) "Transmission"

OVERVIEW

This portion focuses on Jacob, the third and final patriarch of the Jewish people. In *Va-y'chi*, Jacob prepares for his death and imparts instructions for his burial. He adopts Ephraim and Manasseh, Joseph's sons. He blesses each son, bequeathing to each a plot of land. Jacob speaks words of rebuke as well. Jacob dies and is buried in the family plot. Joseph and his brothers return to Egypt, where he reassures them of his favorable intentions. Joseph dies, having asked his brothers to return his bones to his ancestral home, Canaan. This portion marks the end of the book of Genesis.

STANDOUT PHRASES

47:28 "Jacob lived in the land of Egypt for seventeen years." Where else was "seventeen years" noted in conjunction with Jacob? In 37:2, we read that Joseph was 17 when he left home in search of his brothers and ended up being sold into slavery. Joseph spent the first seventeen years of his life with his father, and Jacob spent the last seventeen years of his life with his son.

48:10 "Israel's eyes had grown clouded with age; he could no longer see." Years earlier, Jacob/Israel faced his visually impaired father, Isaac, pretending to be Esau (Genesis 27:1-33). Here, Joseph is not trying to fool his father, but Jacob likely recalled how he tried to fool his father on his deathbed.

48:20 "May God make you like Ephraim and Manasseh." Jacob delights in his grandchildren. These are the very words some people use to bless sons on Friday night. The equivalent blessing for daughters is, "May God make you like Sarah, Rebekah, Rachel, and Leah."

50:14 "Joseph then returned to Egypt—he, his brothers, and all who had gone with him to bury his father." How did the Israelites get to Egypt in the first place? Genesis 39:1 records that Joseph was sold into Egypt, and years later, his family followed in search of food. The closing chapters of Genesis indicate that Egypt had become a comfortable home. Having fulfilled their father's dying wish to be buried outside Egypt, Joseph and his brothers return there to live out their lives. And then, "A new king arose over Egypt who did not know Joseph ..." (Exodus 1:8).

TALK ABOUT

1. The text reports that Jacob asked Joseph to treat him with "faithful kindness" (47:29). In Hebrew this phrase is *chesed v'emet*. Over time, this phrase came to describe a good deed for which there is no expectation of reciprocity. In particular, *chesed v'emet* now refers to caring for the dead by being part of a *chevra kadisha*, a group who prepare bodies for burial in a Jewishly mandated way. If you know someone who is/ has been a member of a *chevra kadisha*, invite them to share this rare experience with your group.

2. In 48:5, Jacob adopts Joseph's sons. In Exodus 2:10, Pharaoh's daughter adopts Moses. Since ancient times, Judaism has valued and encouraged adoption. Which Jewish values are demonstrated by adoption? There is no ancient Hebrew word for adoption, but in modern Hebrew, adoption is called *immutz,* from the verb "to make strong." Why do you think this word was chosen for adoption?

3. Jacob singles out Joseph to discuss his dying wishes. Hadn't Jacob learned that showing favoritism for one child could have devastating consequences?

4. After Jacob's death, Joseph "observed a mourning ceremony of seven days for his father" (50:10). This is probably the origin of the seven-day mourning period known as "*shiva*" (from the Hebrew word for seven). There are many customs for mourners during *shiva*, including sitting on low chairs, not leaving the house, and receiving consolation visits from family and friends. Which *shiva* customs are you familiar with? Does a week (not including Shabbat) seem like the right amount of time for a person to separate from the responsibilities of daily life? If you have sat *shiva* for any amount of time, do you recommend this practice?

5. There are two more references to death and burial in this portion. Regarding Joseph, "They embalmed and he was put into a coffin in Egypt" (50:26). Embalming is not a Jewish practice because it requires unnecessary interference with the body. For the same reason, autopsies are not allowed unless required by law.

A traditional Jewish casket is simple in design and construction. It uses wooden pegs instead of nails and has unlined interiors. It is made from wood that naturally decomposes, as opposed to metal that prevents the natural process of the body's return to the earth.

THINK ABOUT

1. Rabbi David Novak cites Armistead Maupin's term "logical family" as "the people we choose to be with in life." In the 21st century, Novak says, we can enjoy the blessings of both "biological family" and "logical family." He continues, "Joseph, who has created a logical family in Egypt, finds himself reunited with the biological family, which has long been separated. Yet he does not fall back into the original family dynamic ... Joseph has grown beyond the dynamic of his biological family ... Our "logical family" gives us the opportunity to move forward in life, unshackled from past experiences that may have held us back."[38]

2. Jacob mentions twice that he doesn't want to be buried in Egypt (47:29 and 47:30). Why did he not want to be buried in Egypt? What would have to take place (what tasks would the brothers share) for Jacob to be buried in Canaan? Was Jacob thinking of himself or his children when he made the request to be buried in Canaan? What reasons do you have for choosing a particular burial place or requesting particular remembrance activities?

3. After Jacob dies, Joseph's brothers fear that he may indulge feelings of resentment kept hidden while their father was alive. They suspect that Joseph may now want revenge. They beg for mercy, unsure how their powerful brother may respond. In 50:19, Joseph says, "Have no fear, for am I in place of God?" Quite a contrast from the younger Joseph who arrogantly described dreams of his brothers bowing to him! (Gen. 37:5-10)

One reliable sign of *t'shuvah* (repentance and repair), is to find one's self in the same situation and choose a different response. That is what Joseph did after many years of growth and change. To act with restraint requires discipline. Joseph did not indulge feelings of resentment, and he was rewarded with healed relations with his brothers.

---

38 Rabbi David Novak in "Voices of Torah," *CCAR News*, November-December 2020, Volume 68 Issue 2, p. 4.

4. Jacob and Joseph die in this portion. A lot of attention is paid to their final words, deaths, and burials. The Torah recognizes value in facing death. When we recognize the brevity of our lives, each year and even each day becomes more significant, and each important relationship becomes more precious. Judaism encourages us to confront death without fear, and to use our awareness of it to add meaning to our lives.

5. Two pairs of estranged brothers reunite at their fathers' burials: Isaac and Ishmael (Genesis 25:9) and Jacob and Esau (Genesis 35:29). We don't know, though, what happened to these brotherly connections following the burial. With Joseph, we do know: The brothers continue to live in the same vicinity and presumably have ongoing contact (50:21). After a relationship resumes, having been severed earlier, how challenging is it to keep it on course, unhindered by prior accusations and earlier hostile acts? Can new relationships emerge strengthened having survived antagonism?

Focus Phrase (49:15)

Menucha ki tov—The resting place is good.

Exodus/Sh'mot

INTRODUCTION TO EXODUS/SH'MOT

Every Person Needs an Egypt by Amnon Ribak[39]

Everyone should have some kind of Egypt in their lives,

To find Moses within themselves,

To struggle out, and strive.

To have to fight

With a hand of might

Or with gritted teeth to seek the light,

To walk through darkness, and survive.

Everyone should have some kind of Egypt in their past:

The dream, the dread,

The bond, the hand that they can always trust.

---

39 Poem is used with the author's permission.

To learn to cast their sore eyes heavenward—

Every person needs a prayer, one, to know by heart.

Every person should, for once at least, be bowed,

Everyone should have a shoulder, to lean on in the crowd.

Everyone should have some kind of Egypt in their gears,

To go forth, at the mid of night, into the desert of their fears,

Redeem themselves from a house of bondage,

March straight into the sea,

And see the waters part before them, as if by decree.

Everyone should have a shoulder, calm, and firm, and strong,

On which to carry, through the desert, the remains of Joseph's bones.

Everyone once bowed should walk tall and free and proud.

Everyone should have some kind of Egypt cross their ways,

And Jerusalem in their prayers,

And a journey, long and hard

To remember in their heart

And with their feet until the end of days.

Sh'mot (Exodus 1:1-6:1) "Wise Women"

OVERVIEW

The growing Israelite population threatens the new pharaoh. He enslaves them and orders all male Israelite children drowned. A desperate woman places her infant son in a basket on the Nile. Pharaoh's daughter finds the baby and raises him as her child. She names him Moses. As a young man, Moses sees an Egyptian taskmaster abusing a Hebrew slave. Moses kills the man and flees to Midian. He marries Tzipporah, daughter of a Midiante priest. They give birth to two sons.

While tending sheep in the wilderness, Moses notices a burning bush that is not consumed. He recognizes this as a manifestation of God. God commissions Moses to free his enslaved people. Moses reluctantly agrees. God promises that Moses' brother, Aaron, will accompany him in pursuit of their people's freedom.

STANDOUT PHRASES

1:8 "A new king arose over Egypt who did not know Joseph." Over the centuries, this verse has often described the precarious situation of Jews following a leadership change in their host countries. For most of Jewish history, the ruler's desire to welcome or reject the Jewish community determined its security.

1:17 "The midwives, fearing God, did not do as the king of Egypt had told them; they let the boys live." Exodus preserves the names of these heroic midwives, Shiphrah and Puah. Their courage in upholding a moral standard is an example for the ages. In Tel Aviv, the cross streets of a maternity hospital are called Shiphrah and Puah! Al Axelrod, the Hillel rabbi at Brandeis University in the 1960s, established an annual award for nonviolent resistance to tyranny. He named it after the midwives who resisted and outsmarted Pharoah.

2:10 "When the child grew up, she brought him to Pharaoh's daughter, who made him her son. She named him Moses, explaining, "I drew him out of the water." Leading biblical scholar Robert Alter explains that Moses is an authentic Egyptian name meaning "son." The name also relates to the Hebrew word *mashah*, "to draw out from water." Alter posits that the name "Moshe" might have been chosen to foreshadow

Moses' leadership in taking his people successfully through the Sea of Reeds.[40]

3:4 "Moses answered, "Here I am." You may recognize this phrase, "*hineni*," from Genesis. Abraham says "*hineni*" to God in Genesis 22:1. Jacob says "*hineni*" to God in 46:2. What are the similarities and differences in these situations?

TALK ABOUT

1. Yoram Hazony notes that Exodus opens with three acts of resistance against the state: the midwives' refusal of Pharaoh's order to murder the male children born to slaves, a Hebrew woman hiding her infant son, and Pharaoh's daughter conspiring to save the boy. Later in the narrative, we meet this "child of disobedience" as a grown man. Moses sees an Egyptian beating a Hebrew slave and slays the Egyptian. Thus, like the women who saved his life years earlier, Moses violates the law of the state apparently because he determines it is the right thing to do.[41]

2. Five women play critical roles in the opening verses of Exodus: Shiphrah, Puah (midwives), Yocheved (Moses' birth mother), Moses' sister (not identified as Miriam here), Pharaoh's daughter (later named "Batya"). Each contributes to Moses' survival. Why do they take lifesaving actions? What woman in chapter 4 also saves Moses' life? Why are there multiple near-death experiences in Moses' early life and why are women of paramount importance in Moses' life?

3. Rabbi Gila Ruskin looks at *Sh'mot* to find the true origins of Judaism: "When did Judaism begin? Was it when God called to Abraham (Genesis 12:1-2) or when Israel celebrated the first communal *mitzvah* (Exodus 12:1) or the revelation at Mount Sinai (Exodus 20)? I nominate the cataclysmic moment described in Exodus 3 that heralded a deity of empathy and compassion ... a god declares: I see your suffering, I hear your outcry, I take note, and I will act to redeem you (Exodus 3:7, 9, 16). In the mythology of ancient gods, this, as far as I know, had never before been revealed by the self-serving deities."[42]

---

40 *The Hebrew Bible, Volume I*, New York: W.W. Norton & Company, 2019, p. 217, n. 10.

41 Hazony, Yoram, *The Philosophy of Hebrew Scripture*, New York, NY: Cambridge University Press, 2012, p. 143

42 *CCAR News*, November-December 2020, Volume 68, Issue 2, p. 4.

4. Moses intervenes in three encounters—2:11-12, 2:13 and 2:16-17. Why does Moses intervene? Why are these interactions placed in close proximity?

5. In 3:7, God sees and hears, and is moved by the plight of the people. Are these components of intense caring: seeing and noticing, hearing and becoming attuned, and acting?

6. Moses asks for God's name in 3:13. The response is: "*Ehyeh-Asher-Ehyeh*." This name of God doesn't appear anywhere else in the *Tanakh*. *Ehyeh-Asher-Ehyeh* is a declension of the Hebrew verb "to be." It translates to "I Am Who I Am," or "I Will Be That Which I Will Be."

Jewish theology primarily addresses what God does. What God *is* is not deemed fully comprehensible. This prioritizing of God's actions is revealed by the name *Ehyeh-Asher-Ehyeh*. *Ehyeh-Asher-Ehyeh* teaches that God exists and God becomes, but this name also subtly reminds us (through its awkward phrasing) that our understanding of God's essence will always remain incomplete and partial.

7. We are introduced to another enigmatic name for God in 3:15, "YHVH, the God of your ancestors—the God of Abraham, the God of Isaac, and the God of Jacob—has sent me to you: This shall be My name forever; This My appellation for all eternity." YHVH is also based on the verb "to be." YHVH consists of four Hebrew letters, which combined spell out "is," "was," and "will be," three tenses of the verb "to be."

Feminist theologian Mary Daly imagines God as a verb. She wrote, "Why indeed must 'god' be a noun? Why not a verb—the most active and dynamic of all? ... Isn't the Verb infinitely more personal than a mere static noun? The anthropomorphic symbols for God may be intended to convey personality, but they fail to convey that God is Be-ing."[43]

8. God reveals two existential names in this portion: *Ehyeh-Asher-Ehyeh* and YHVH. Moses poses two existential questions in this portion: "Why did You bring harm upon this people? Why did You send me?" (5:22)

I read these as Moses asking, why do (good) people suffer? And, how can I be of service in a world I can't fully comprehend?

How do you interpret Moses' questions? Is there a more important question than "why do good people suffer?"

---

43 *Beyond God the Father: Toward a Philosophy of Women's Liberation*, Boston: Beacon Press, 1973, pp. 33-34.

Think About

1. In 1:17, it says "the midwives feared God." The Hebrew word used here derives from the word for "awe," "*yirah*." I think a better translation would be "the midwives held God in awe." When have you experienced awe? The word "yarmulke," referring to a head covering for religious purposes, comes from the words "*yireh melech*," "awe of the King," (King = God). Someone donning a yarmulke is expressing their awareness of God's holiness (above them) and worldly matters (around and below them).

2. When Pharaoh's daughter opens a basket she retrieves from the Nile, "she saw that it was a child; a boy crying" (2:6). In Jonathan Safran Foer's novel *Here I Am*, a family gathers around the grandfather's grave, where the rabbi and mourners converse. They discuss how Pharaoh's daughter knew that the baby she found was a Hebrew. The text in Exodus says that she *saw* the baby cry, not that she *heard* him cry. The younger son, Benjy, suggests that the Egyptian princess knew he was a Hebrew because "only Jews cry silently."[44]

   Do you think Jews cry silently? What does this observation say about the Jewish people and Jewish history? How much do you think children should be made aware of the perils of Jewish history?

3. In 2:9, Pharaoh's daughter says to Yocheved, "Take the child and nurse it for me, and I will pay wages."

   This scene stands out because a (biblical) woman is paid for her work, and her work—"women's work"—is deemed valuable. Is it coincidental that in this situation, one woman values another woman's work? Even in our 21st century world, many jobs focused on children's needs are not appropriately valued in status or wages.

4. In 2:12, Moses turns to look at an Egyptian abusing an Israelite slave, and in 3:2 he turns to look at a burning bush that remains aflame. What is revealed about Moses by these incidents? Do you think a characteristic of leaders is that they notice things others might ignore, and respond quickly?

5. Moses says he is not good with words (4:10). He says, "I am slow of speech and slow of tongue." Some think this refers to stuttering. In "On

---

44 *Here I Am*, NY: Farrar, Straus and Giroux, LLC., 2016, p.475.

Stuttering and the Rabbinate," Rabbi Mark S. Glickman talks about stuttering in a profession highly dependent on public speaking:

"... stuttering can be an oratorical tool, and not merely an impediment. In word and in deed I can show that, although there is much that can handicap our bodies, the only things that can handicap the human spirit are those things we allow to do so. I was drawn to the rabbinate, in other words, because of the unique perspectives and skills I can bring to it as a stutterer."[45]

6. After Moses receives his mission from God, he returns to his father-in-law, Jethro (also called Jether and Reuel), and asks permission to leave. Jethro responds, "Go in peace" (4:18). Moses has antagonistic relationships with most people he encounters. Only with Jethro does he seem to experience trust and friendship (18:7). Moses is portrayed as a lonely figure. Although he has a family, they are not central to him.

As you proceed through Exodus and the rest of the Torah, look for Moses' connections to people. Are any of his relationships close and nurturing?

FOCUS PHRASE (5:9)

Al yish'u b'divrei sha'ker—Do not pay attention to false words.

45 *CCAR Journal:* A Reform Jewish Quarterly, Spring, 2000, pp. 25-29.

Va-eira (Exodus 6:2–9:35) "Habits of the Heart"

Overview

Moses is discouraged by Pharaoh's reluctance to free the Israelites, and by the people's ambivalence about leaving Egypt. God reassures Moses that he will succeed and creates a test for Moses and Aaron to demonstrate God's superiority. After Pharaoh's rejection of God's power vis-à-vis Pharaoh's magicians, God brings plagues (called "signs" or "wonders") to prove God's strength. After each plague, Pharaoh considers freeing the slaves, but always recants, and the Israelites remain in bondage.

Most scholars are doubtful that there is a historical basis to the Exodus story. Nevertheless, it has captured the imagination of countless individuals and numerous freedom movements. The Exodus story moves us because we recognize how unlikely it is for a small group of 'have-nots' to prevail over a powerful empire. The liberation of an enslaved people enables us to believe that redemption is possible and that good can prevail over evil.

Standout Phrases

6:6-7 "I will free you ... and deliver you ... I will redeem you ... I will take you ..." These expressions form the basis of the Four Cups of wine (grape juice) drunk at the Seder.

6:12 and 6:30 Moses: "I get tongue-tied!" "See, I get tongue-tied." Is Moses describing a speech impediment, fear of public speaking or lack of self-esteem?

7:16, 7:26, 8:16, 9:1, 9:13, "Let My people go." German feminist theologian Dorothee Soelle writes: "The Jewish tradition reveals to the human family that we are created for freedom and that freedom is our historical project. Judaism talks to us in the powerful language of the Exodus tradition about a God who wills freedom for the oppressed ... when there is no memory of liberation, there can be no hope ... to remember is a categorical imperative in Judaism."[46]

---

46 *To Work and To Love: A Theology of Creation*, Philadelphia: Fortress Press, 1984, pp. 9-11.

8:19 "And I will make a distinction between My people and your people." The importance of Israel being separate and distinctive is a recurring theme in the Torah.

TALK ABOUT

1. How are God's bona fides established in this portion? God establishes a family connection (6:3-4), demonstrates a particular interest in the people's well-being (6:5), indicates a willingness to act on the people's behalf (6:6), and promises continued allegiance to the people (6:7-8).

    Could God have mentioned other things to give Moses confidence in a shared, covenantal future?

2. In 7:3, God hardens (better translated as "strengthens") Pharaoh's heart. Nehama Leibowitz posits that initial choices are ours to make. But with each choice, some options are lost, and some opportunities fade. In the end, the choices available to us are impacted by events we were not able to anticipate and by outcomes we can't avoid.[47]

    Leibowitz points out that it becomes increasingly difficult to resist choices and patterns that become habitual. Do you agree?

3. In 7:8-13, Moses and Aaron (on behalf of God) vie with Egyptian sorcerers to prove who is more powerful. What is the difference between religion and magic? Magic is based on appearances. It can make one thing look like something else. The goal of magic is to fool or mislead. How does religion differ?

4. The first plague turns Egyptian bodies of water into blood (7:19). Commentators note that this plague connects to Pharaoh's decree to drown baby boys (thus, metaphorically, spilling their blood) in the Nile. Also, the first plague connects to the last plague, during which the Israelites identify their homes by smearing blood on their doorposts (12:13 and 12:23). Are there other reasons that the first plague turns the rivers, canals, and ponds into blood? Think about the importance of the Nile and other water sources to Egyptian civilization.

5. Torah commentator Avivah Gottlieb Zornberg calls Moses a "wounded healer." She says, "In order to achieve his pedagogical task— in his case, perhaps in all cases, also a therapeutic task—he must know

---

47 *New Studies in Shemot/Exodus*, Jerusalem, Israel: The World Zionist Organization, 1982, pp. 156-158.

the deepest loneliness and pain of his patients ... the life of healing—and teaching—involves fear and courage, loneliness, the disabling of the tongue, and an inner transformation ... It is such intimate interrogation of his whole being that initiates the healer, puts him in contact with powers of teaching, in the largest sense."[48]

Teachers and healers: Is Zornberg's description of your professions (callings) accurate? Does your work involve fear, courage, and loneliness?

Think About

1. No one knows how to pronounce God's revealed Name—*Yud-Hay-Vav-Hay* (6:3). People say "*Adonai*," or "*Yahweh*," or "Jehovah, or "*HaShem*." *HaShem* is nongendered, it is easy for non-Hebrew speakers to pronounce, and it is succinct.

Can you draw a teaching from being unable to pronounce God's Name?

To better grasp what is evoked by our inability to pronounce the Name of God, complete this sentence: "I'm unable to find words for _____."

YHVH consists of four Hebrew letters that are connected to breathing.

To better understand the sensation of YHVH as breath, begin this sentence: "_____ takes my breath away."

2. Moses is 80 years old when he first asks Pharaoh for his people's freedom. Abraham is 75 years old when he leaves Haran and sets out for an unknown destination (Genesis 12:4). It seems unlikely that biblical ages were determined as we do now, but consider 75 and 80 as mature ages. Do you know people who have embarked on stimulating, even courageous endeavors in their senior years? Can you imagine taking on new responsibilities or pursuing a dream in your retirement years?

3. In several places, Pharaoh has a "hardened heart." He is called "stubborn" in 7:14. The Torah uses the phrase *kaveide lev*, which literally means "heavy-hearted." Why does the Torah bring attention to this despot's heart?

To me, one of the most startling Torah verses is Deuteronomy 23:8, which instructs, "Do not hate an Egyptian." During the Seder, to recall

---

48 *The Particulars of Rapture: Reflections on Exodus,* New York, NY: Doubleday, 2001, pp. 127-128.

the death and destruction experienced by the Egyptians when the Israelites were freed, people take drops of wine out of their cups to diminish its sweetness.

I appreciate that the Torah challenges us to feel compassion for others, even those who once were our enemies.

4. Many are familiar with the phrase "Let My people go." Not everyone realizes that the sentence doesn't end there. It says in full, "Let My people go, that they may worship Me in the wilderness" (7:16). These words repeat (without mention of the wilderness) in 7:26, 8:16, 9:1, and 9:13.

Does "… that they may worship Me" enlarge your understanding of Moses' request for freedom? What does this added phrase tell you about (one of) the purposes of the Exodus and freedom?

5. Many assume that the plagues were brought to convince Pharaoh of God's power. It appears that the Israelites were also a perceived audience.

Rabbi Lucy H.F. Dinner suggests that the weakness Pharaoh displays in admitting his guilt to Moses (9:27) launches a necessary shift in balance between the Israelites and the Egyptians. Regardless of their material resources, the Israelites had to become psychologically and spiritually empowered to claim their freedom.[49]

6. Most children love listing and imagining the plagues. At your Seder (or now), list plagues that continue to damage the world, such as hunger, child/spousal abuse, pollution, etc. It is painful to realize how unredeemed our world is.

FOCUS PHRASE (8:1)

N'tei et yad'cha—Stretch out your hand.

49 The Women's Torah Commentary: New Insights from Women Rabbis on the 54 Weekly Torah Portions, Rabbi Elyse Goldstein, ed., Woodstock, Vermont: Jewish Lights Publishing, 2000, p. 134.

Bo (Exodus 10:1–13:16) "Questions"

OVERVIEW

The ferocity of the final three plagues results in Pharaoh's release of the Israelites. Their long journey from Egyptian slavery comes to an end, and their odyssey to becoming a free and covenantal people begins. As a sign of their newfound freedom, the people are instructed to acclaim the New Moon, thus laying the foundation for the calendar and festival cycle we follow to this day. Setting the calendar is a way of organizing time. Only free people can organize their time.

This portion includes the origin of telling the Passover story each year and several of the Seder's key elements.

STANDOUT PHRASES

12:40 "The length of time that the Israelites lived in Egypt was four hundred and thirty years." Most scholars doubt the accuracy of this number, but accept that four hundred and thirty years indicates a long time.

12:15, 13:6 "Seven days you shall eat unleavened bread ..." The celebration serves as a historical remembrance and as a source of community cohesion. What does the celebration of Passover mean to you?

12:38 "Moreover, a mixed multitude went up with them." Many scholars believe that other groups of slaves fled Egypt with the Israelites.

13:9, 13:16 "... a sign on your hand and a reminder/symbol on your forehead ..." This refers to t'fillin (phylacteries) that some men and women don during morning prayers. T'fillin consist of two small black boxes containing Torah passages. Leather bands attached to the boxes enable one box to be placed on the forehead while the other is wound around the arm.

If the purpose of t'fillin is to serve as a reminder of God, are the head and arm well-chosen places to experience this remembrance? After it is taken off, the t'fillin's imprint on the forehead and arm lasts for an hour or more. Does this imprint also play a role in remembrance?

TALK ABOUT

1. The Torah instructs teaching our children three times: 12:26-27, 13:8, and 13:14. What are the important lessons of Passover? Along with appreciation for freedom, consider social justice issues, promoting literacy, and valuing history. 10:9 adds to these ideas.

2. The questions and answers of The Four Children in the *Haggadah* are primarily found in this portion: The Wicked Child—12:26, The Child Who is Unable to Ask—13:8, The Simple Child—13:14. The Wise Child's Question originates in Deuteronomy 6:20.

    Many suggest this refers to four kinds of children. I think that these four types exist inside each of us. At different times, each of us is wise, wicked (alienated), naïve, and uninterested (distracted).

3. Three plagues are described in this portion: locusts (10:14), darkness (10:22-23), and the slaying of the first-born (12:29). What are contemporary societal parallels to these plagues? For example: locusts may represent failed crops due to climate change, and overuse of chemical sprays in farming. Darkness can represent prejudice and illiteracy. The killing of the firstborn could represent childhood disease and child labor.

4. In *The New American Haggadah*, the authors assert that there is no such thing as an immaculate liberation. The cost of freedom is high because of targeted and collateral damage. We want to believe that justice punishes the guilty and spares the innocent, but history rarely complies. The Hebrew slaves are liberated from Egyptian bondage, slavery officially ended with the Civil War, and fascism was vanquished in World War II. But no one could suggest that these outcomes were achieved without suffering on the part of the innocent and the guiltless.[50]

    Do you believe that in these historical examples, and in other cases you can cite, the ends justified the means?

5. Former UK Chief Rabbi Lord Jonathan Sacks reflects on the early stories of Exodus. They tell us "... who we are and who our ancestors hoped we would become ... it was the Torah's insight that a people who told their children the story of freedom and its responsibilities would

---

50 *New American Haggadah*, Jonathan Safran Foer and Nathan Englander, eds., New York, NY: Little, Brown and Company, 2012, p. 67.

stay free ..."[51] How do we teach each new generation to appreciate freedom?

It's well documented that Jewish people are great consumers of books. Do you agree with Rabbi Sacks' ideas on the importance of storytelling? What stories of the Jewish people are most compelling to you?

Think About

1. "Remember this day, on which you went free from Egypt, the house of bondage ..." (13:3) The Exodus story has universal appeal. Everyone, at some point, thinks there is a better place to live and dreams of a less-curtailed life. Most of us harbor a notion of a Promised Land.

What does your Promised Land look like?

2. The instruction for an annual Feast of Unleavened Bread to recall the Exodus appears in 12:14-20. The *Haggadah* teaches that liberation from slavery occurred not just for our ancestors but, for us.

Connecting the Hebrew word for Egypt, "*Mitzrayim,*" to the word for narrowness, "*metzarim,*" is instructive. We've all been impatient with our own narrowness, despising our pettiness, and withholding of love. Feeling trapped and constricted, enslaved to our desires and egos: This is what it feels like to live in Egypt.

Thinking of the Exodus not as something that happened *to* us but as something that continues to happen *within* us, is one way to make Passover personal, and use it as incentive for spiritual growth.

3. The *mitzvah* to mark each new month appears in 12:1. Emerging from slavery, the people begin a new relationship with time. Although the Torah sets aside the first day of the seventh month as the New Year for creation of the world (*Rosh HaShanah*), each spring, the month of *Nisan* begins the New Year for the creation of the Jewish people. *Nisan* is the first month of the Jewish calendar.

Each new month coincides with the new moon. This day (beginning in the evening as all Jewish holidays do) is called *Rosh Chodesh*. Each *Rosh Chodesh* appears on Jewish calendars and is announced the prior Shabbat at services. Women celebrate *Rosh Chodesh* by gathering for spiritual, intellectual, and social refreshment. There are *Rosh Chodesh* resources in the bibliography.

---

51 *Essays on Ethics: A Weekly Reading of the Jewish Bible,* Jerusalem, Israel: Maggid Books, 2016, p. 95.

4. Rabbi David J. Zucker writes about "Rhythms and Religious Rituals" in his Torah Reflection on *Parashat Bo*: "For the most part, we are creatures of habit ... it is easy to get into a pattern where all we think about is the physical realm: our bodies, our jobs, and real life practical responsibilities ..."

"We are however, more than just a physical being. We possess an eternal soul, a *neshama*. As our bodies require nourishment, so do our souls. In Exodus chapter 12, there is a conscious change in the subject ... The Bible is telling us, life should be more than our patterns of physical behavior. We also need to care for our souls."[52]

FOCUS PHRASE (10:17)

Sah nah cha'ta'tee—Please forgive my transgression.

---

52 Bay Area Jewish Healing Center, jewishhealingcenter.org, January 20, 2018.

B'shalach (Exodus 13:17-17:16) "Coming Out"

OVERVIEW

B'shalach chronicles a defining event in the Torah: crossing the Sea of Reeds. This event remains central to Israelite self-definition and it is referenced in daily and Shabbat prayers.

B'shalach shows the emerging character of the Israelites, recently freed from bondage. The people display qualities consistent with acquiring a new identity: confusion, insecurity, fear, and regression. Uncertain about this new life, the Israelites grumble and complain. They yearn for Egypt—a place they now associate with delicious and readily available food.

STANDOUT PHRASES

14:15 "Then YHVH said to Moses, "Why do you cry out to Me? Tell the Israelites to go forward." God chastises Moses for talking (praying?) when Moses needs to act.

16:31 "The house of Israel named it *manna*." In 16:31, *manna* is described as a "fine and flaky substance." In this verse, it is "coriander seed, white, and it tasted like wafers in honey."

17:14 "Then YHVH said to Moses, 'Inscribe this in a document as a reminder, and read it aloud ...'" Could Moses read and write? Perhaps he had these skills because of his upbringing in a royal household. It is unlikely these were skills taught to the slaves. Nevertheless, over time, literacy became a treasured and characteristic aspect of Jewish life.

17:16 "YHVH will be at war with Amalek throughout the ages." Compassion Activist Rabbi Amy Eilberg takes a nuanced look at the tradition of "hating Amalek." She writes, "... Rashi—perhaps the most revered of all medieval Jewish commentators—observes stunningly that Amalek attacked the Israelites at the rear of the camp at a time when the Israelites ... became physically and spiritually separated from the rest of the camp, and without the support of the community ..."

"... The imperative is *not* to rehearse the angry memory ... not to hate those who may seek to harm us, but ... to purify our inner lives; cleansing our hearts of needless enmity, small-mindedness, and self-importance, or anything that may obstruct our connection to God.[53]

TALK ABOUT

1. What is a miracle? 14:28-29 describes God splitting the sea. The result is the death of the pursuing Egyptian forces and the Israelites' march on dry land through the sea. Noam Zion and David Dishon say about miracles, "... the miracle is a symbol of spontaneity in history, a faith in the changeability of oppressive regimes ... God's miraculous intervention in Egypt presents history as an open text drama ... Belief in miracle is the basis of the hope model of Judaism. Exodus becomes a call to revolutionary hope regardless of the conditions of history."[54]

Do you believe that miracles are exceptions to the laws of nature? Or are miracles occurrences and events that inspire awe? Have you experienced what you consider miracles in your life?

2. Miriam is first named in 15:20. Prior to this, she is called Moses and Aaron's sister. Dr. Ellen Frankel notes that the name Miriam has both Hebrew and Egyptian origins: two linked Hebrew words—*mar*, meaning "bitter," and *yam*, meaning "sea," and (or) a derivation from the Egyptian word *mer*, meaning "beloved."[55]

See comments on Moses' name (2:10) in the "Standout Phrases" section on *Parashat Sh'mot*. Moses' name also draws on this dual identity as an Israelite and an Egyptian. As you read more about Miriam, notice ways in which her life was bitter, and ways in which she inspired devotion. Look at Numbers 12:1-15 and 20:1-5.

3. In 14:3 Pharaoh says of the Israelites, "They are astray in the land; the wilderness has closed in on them." To the Egyptian mind, the desert is a wasteland, a place devoid of civilization, a place to avoid. For Moses, the wilderness represents freedom, and a place to become stronger and more independent.

What does the wilderness represent to you?

---

53 "Religion and the Enemy (Parshat B'Shalach, Exodus 13:17-17)" www.huffpost.com. Jan. 28, 2015.

54 *A Different Night: A Family Participation Haggadah*, Jerusalem, Israel: The Shalom Hartman Institute, 1997, p.123; see also www.haggadahsrus.com.

55 *The Five Books of Miriam: A Woman's Commentary on the Torah*, Ellen Frankel, Ph.D. New York: HarperCollins, 1996, p. 113.

4. I love the question posed in 17:7, "Is the Eternal present among us or not?" The Torah explicitly answers this question twice, in Exodus 25:8 and in Numbers 14:14.

Does 17:7 ask the same question as, "Do you believe in God?" Does belief in God matter? Does faith require evidence? Is certainty the opposite of faith? What nurtures your faith?

THINK ABOUT

1. Moses tells the people, "Have no fear! Stand by, and witness the deliverance..." (14:13) "Zen" Rabbi Alan Lew writes, "The point of spiritual practice is simply to prepare us for the great moments of leave-taking ... to identify the moments of crisis as opportunities ... for seeing the world afresh, for encountering God."[56]

2. Rabbi Cantor Alison Wissot talks about the Mussar quality of *Bitachon* (trust) when she thinks of Miriam bringing musical instruments on the journey from slavery to freedom:

"... Miriam takes with her a timbrel (Exodus 15:20). She does not know what the events of life will bring. She only knows that there will come a time to rejoice. Life is full of tragedies, but the events of life do not make up the path of life. The power to rejoice, to celebrate the miracles that have already happened, and to trust that we have done all we can, these things change our experience of events, even if the events themselves do not change."[57]

3. "And Miriam chanted for them ..." (15:21). These words introduce the Song of the Sea, also called the Song of Miriam. The Shabbat when this portion is read is called "*Shabbat Shirah*," the "Shabbat of Song."

What role does music play in your life? Are you surprised that music is included in the Torah?

4. 15:20 describes women dancing. Music is an important part of many synagogue services, but dance rarely occurs as part of a praying experience. Why is there a discrepancy between using music versus dance in worship? Which biblical stories could be imaginatively depicted by dance?

---

56 *Be Still and Get Going: A Jewish Meditation Practice for Real Life*, New York, NY: Little, Brown and Company, 2005, p. 20.

57 *The Mussar Torah Commentary: A Spiritual Path to Living a Meaningful and Ethical Life*, Rabbi Barry H. Block, ed., NY: CCAR Press, 2020, p. 104.

FOCUS PHRASE (14:13)

Al tee'rah'ooh—Have no fear.

Yitro (Exodus 18:1–20:23) "Who Knows Ten?"

Overview

When Jethro, Moses' father-in-law, observes Moses' exhausting efforts to advise the people, he suggests Moses set up a judicial system to delegate responsibilities. YHVH instructs Moses to tell the people to prepare for Revelation. Moses and YHVH "meet" on Mt. Sinai and communicate the Ten Commandments to the people gathered below.

The Giving of the Ten Commandments (more aptly called "the Decalogue," or "the Ten Statements") constitutes a foundational moment in Jewish history, sealing the unique relationship between God and the Israelites. The Decalogue demands that the people act reverently towards God and honorably towards each other. By upholding these ethical and ritual responsibilities, the people will flourish in freedom.

Standout Phrases

18:21 "Capable individuals who fear God—trustworthy ones who spurn ill-gotten gain." Jethro describes ideal qualifications for judges, including social and moral characteristics. Do you agree with Jethro's criteria for choosing judges?

19:12 "You shall set bounds ..." This refers to regulating the Israelites' proximity to Mt. Sinai, but I see it is a key concept in the Ten Commandments: setting clear and respectful boundaries so that personal and communal relationships are most likely to succeed.

19:20 "YHVH came down upon Mount Sinai ... and Moses went up." A beautiful illustration of the interplay between God and Moses; they reach out to each other.

20:4 "You shall not make for yourself a sculptured image ... You shall not bow down to them or serve them." Rabbi Marcia Prager explains that the word "*pesel*," which we are accustomed to translating as "idol" or "statue," is something less than whole. A Torah scroll missing letters is called "*pasul*," less than whole. An idol is anything partial (anything but God) that we elevate to the status of wholeness.[58]

Does Prager's explanation increase your understanding of idols and idolatry? What is your definition of idolatry?

TALK ABOUT

1. Rabbi Sharon Sobel derives a "training manual for leadership development" from 18:1-27. She writes, "Jethro's behavior and actions show us that the following are crucial traits for a great leader:[59]

A. See your constituents where they are. (18:1-6)

B. Show care and concern for the well-being of others. (18:7)

C. Celebrate the accomplishments of others. (18:9-12)

D. Offer constructive criticism in a way that can be understood. (18:13-23)

E. In a nonjudgmental manner, give advice on how to improve things or help devise a plan for such action. (18:19-23)

F. Empower leadership (and encourage growth) in others by sharing responsibilities. (18:13-18, 21-23)

G. Remember to delegate responsibility and authority wisely. (18:21-22)

These traits share one common element: each helps to build supportive relationships. Do they share anything else?

2. Nahum Sarna explains that in the ethical literature of the ancient world, there are statements and laws similar to the Decalogue. What makes the Ten Commandments unique is "... the way in which these norms of conduct are regarded as being expressions of divine will, eternally binding on the individual and on society as a whole."[60]

What happens when individuals and society regard themselves as answerable to the deity?

---

58 *The Path of Blessing: Experiencing the Energy and Abundance of the Divine*, Woodstock, VT: Jewish Lights Publishing, 2003, p. 53.

59 "Moses and Jethro: Creating a Model of Leadership" in Living Torah: Torah Study from the Union of American Hebrew Congregations. Week of February 11-17, 2001.

60 Nahum M. Sarna, *The JPS Torah Commentary: Exodus*, Philadelphia: The Jewish Publication Society, 1991, pp. 102-103.

3. Anticipating the theophany (God's appearance), Moses says to the people, "Be ready for the third day; you should not go near a woman" (19:15).

About 19:15 theologian Judith Plaskow wrote, "There can be no verse in the Torah more disturbing to the feminist than Moses' warning to his people ... women have always known or assumed our presence at Sinai ... how is it then that the text could imply we were not there?"[61]

Plaskow's groundbreaking book challenged the Jewish community to transform the central categories of God, Torah, and Israel by adding women's voices and experiences to important Jewish conversations, written and oral. This book unleashed an outpouring of women's Torah scholarship, *midrashim*, *Haggadot*, rituals, and liturgy.

4. The Decalogue, 20:1-14, is usually called the "Ten Commandments." But there aren't ten and they aren't all commandments! Read this section and count the "you must" or "you must not" statements. It is possible to derive thirteen or more!

Many people are familiar with the term "*mitzvah*" meaning "commandment." Is 20:2 a *mitzvah*? Does 20:8 consist of two commandments? Is the 20:9 a positive commandment, and is 20:10 a separate *mitzvah*?

5. Which statements reflect the religious dimensions of life, and which statements reflect social concerns? Does any commandment straddle these two categories?

6. Which of the Decalogue statements include God's Name? Are you surprised that some of the statements don't reference God? Look at the first word of this section, "*Anochi*" (20:2), referring to God, and look at the last word, "*l'raeicha*" (20:14), "to your neighbor." Can you make a summarizing statement about the Ten Commandments by bridging these two words?

7. The commandments in 20:7 and the last part of 20:13 both deal with language and speech. Judaism is sensitive to the creative and destructive power of language. Creation in Genesis occurs through words. Animals communicate, but they don't use words. This is another distinguishing element between people and animals. The fifth book of the Torah is called "*D'varim*," "Words." We have all experienced how words can

---

61 *Standing Again at Sinai: Judaism from a Feminist Perspective*, New York, NY: HarperCollins, 1990, p. 27.

uplift and destroy; they can heal and inflame. It is significant that speech and language are the focus of two commandments.

THINK ABOUT

1. Giving the Ten Commandments is arguably the principal event in Jewish history, yet this event is shrouded in mystery. Think about the key events in your life. Is profound mystery part of what makes them central?

2. Author Cynthia Ozick values Judaism precisely because of its rejection of idols, of what is false. She said Judaism "trained her to be intellectually free," and it taught her to recognize distinctions "between reality and illusion, between the actual and the fraudulent."[62] What important ideas has Judaism taught you?

3. Author Thomas Cahill holds the Sabbath in high regard, noting that Israel was the first ancient society to institute a day of rest. He recognizes that just beneath the surface of the Fourth Commandment, lie connections to both freedom and creativity. Cahill writes that a day dedicated to God and spiritual refreshment allows people to "imitate the creativity of God."[63]

4. 20:14, "You shall not covet," is unique among the commandments. It is grouped with four other "you shall not" statements (20:13-14), but it is distinctive. How does the Tenth Commandment differ from the others, particularly from the four preceding "you shall not" commandments? Can people be commanded to feel or not to feel something?

5. To me, the Decalogue includes key elements to living "A Good Life," not "The Good Life." Does following the Ten Commandments lead to emotional, spiritual, and moral prosperity? Can you think of prosperity in terms other than financial? Does "A Good Life" differ from "The Good Life?"

Israel-based author and editor David Hazony summarizes the significance of the Decalogue: "... they embrace the nuance of humanity, the spectrum of real experience, the challenges of weakness and hope ..."

---

62 *The God I Believe In: Conversations about Judaism*, Joshua O. Haberman, ed. New York, NY: The Free Press, 1994, p. 153.

63 *The Gifts of the Jews: How a Tribe of Desert Nomads Changed the Way Everyone Thinks and Feels*, New York, NY: Anchor Books, 1998, p. 144.

Hazony describes the Ten Commandments as "a deeply optimistic text," sensitive to human imperfection.[64]

How do the Ten Commandments acknowledge our imperfections?

FOCUS PHRASE (18:15)

Lid'rosh Elohim—Seek God.

---

64 *The Ten Commandments: How Our Most Ancient Moral Text Can Renew Modern Life,* New York, NY: Scribner, 2010, pp. 260-261.

Mishpatim (Exodus 21:1-24:18) "Building a Life"

OVERVIEW

The Ten Commandments are straightforward and succinct. *Mishpatim*, which follows the Revelation of the Ten Commandments, contains diverse civil, criminal, cultic, and ethical laws.

Murder, abuse of parents, and kidnapping are capital crimes for which execution of the guilty is mandated. Monetary penalties for crimes involving livestock, crops, and other property are also established. Convictions of sorcery, bestiality, and apostasy incur the death penalty.

The Torah's attention moves from legal details to compassionate treatment of the disadvantaged: stranger, widow, orphan, and needy. The festival calendar (further developed in Leviticus chapter 23) is noted. *Mishpatim* ends with Moses' ascent of Mt. Sinai, where he remains for forty days and nights.

STANDOUT PHRASES

21:2 "When you acquire a Hebrew slave, that person shall serve six years—and shall go free in the seventh year, without payment." It is not surprising that the first laws (after the Decalogue) directed to a group of newly freed slaves deal with slavery. We shudder at reading about slavery as an accepted institution. Please refer to my comments in the Introduction about, "Why Study the Torah?" The discussion of slavery in *Mishpatim* refers to indentured servitude and not chattel slavery. The number seven here, as elsewhere in the Torah, signifies perfection. Freedom is granted in seven years.

22:17 "You shall not tolerate a sorceress." The explicit rejection of witchcraft suggests that sorcery was appealing to some people. This law made clear that there would be no tolerance of magic in the Israelite community. Monotheism required commitment to the one Israelite God, Who, the Torah asserts, has sole dominion over nature and cannot be manipulated. It is unfortunate but not unusual in ancient (and more modern) times that females are singled out for being dangerous, and in need of control.

23:19 "You shall not boil a kid in its mother's milk." This prohibition appears later in Exodus 34:26 and again in Deuteronomy 14:21. Talmudic Jewish law expands on this verse by prohibiting preparing, eating, or serving meat and dairy products together. I also address this law in my comments on Exodus 34:26 and Deuteronomy 14:21.

24:7 "All that YHVH has spoken, we will faithfully do." Referred to as "na'aseh v'nishma," this verse demonstrates the people's eagerness to follow God's laws. The wording indicates the people's readiness to acquiesce even before they fully understand what God expects.

TALK ABOUT

1. 21:10 is the only passage in the Torah that discusses a husband's obligations towards his wife: food, clothing, and conjugal rights. Scholars agree that a wife's legal entitlement to sexual gratification is a unique provision in ancient Near Eastern texts.

2. The only biblical reference to the "value" of a fetal life is found in this portion (21:22). When a miscarriage occurs as the result of an attack, the loss of the fetus is compensated monetarily. The destruction of the fetus is not a capital crime. If the mother is killed as a result of the attack, her death is a capital crime.

Although this verse says nothing explicitly about abortion, 21:22 becomes precedent for Jewish law regarding abortion. The distinction between the "value" of the mother's life and the "value" of the unborn baby indicates a variation in appraisal between a fetal life and a life outside the womb. In Judaism, acts that cause miscarriage or abortion are not considered murder. Judaism does not consider abortion to be murder, and, conditions applying, Judaism permits abortion.

3. 21:15 and 17 instruct that one who strikes or insults their father or mother shall be put to death. This is very disturbing! The related positive commandment for treating parents respectfully, "Honor your father and your mother" (20:12) is more familiar and palatable. Commentators agree that the regulation prescribing death for irresponsible children is addressed to adult children who are duty-bound for the survival and well-being of their parents. Nevertheless, it is a jarring proposition.

Can you understand or justify this legislation?

4. Twice in this portion we are told not to wrong or oppress a stranger, "for you were strangers in the land of Egypt (22:20 and 23:9). Pioneering biblical interpreter Nehama Leibowitz wonders if past memories and experiences of being strangers or slaves influence the newly liberated to "adopt an attitude of tolerance" to strangers or outsiders who later live among them. Or, she asks, "is the opposite what generally happens?"[65]

Does Leibowitz make a good point? The directive in 23:9 is elaborated with the addition, "... for you know the feelings of the stranger." Does this phrase deepen your understanding of the commandment not to wrong a stranger?

5. There are many ways to be a stranger. Reuben Zellman talks about being a stranger in the context of transgender identity. "Thirty-six times the Torah teaches us to treat the stranger with justice; even to love strangers as ourselves. But that is not enough. There is a very important distinction between the act of not oppressing someone and the act of truly including them ... We must welcome them to impact us, to better us, to change us ... We must not only make more room at the table; we have to change what's on the menu ... we must all be prepared to think differently, to do differently, to believe differently ... to be changed, institutionally and personally..."[66]

When we welcome strangers, do we welcome them to do things our way, or are we prepared to do things differently? What can strangers teach us about ourselves?

6. The reason for celebrating Shabbat in 23:12 is strikingly different from the intended purpose for Shabbat as described in the Ten Commandments (20:8-11). In *Mishpatim*, Shabbat observance is associated with ethical living. How do 23:6 and 23:9 inform 23:12?

Think About

1. In 22:20 and 23:9, the people are told not to wrong a stranger. The word for stranger is "*ger*." In Talmudic times, the word "*ger*" came to mean "a convert to Judaism." The command not to wrong a newcomer to the community remains relevant. Check in with family members or friends who became Jewish as adults. How do they feel treated?

---

65 *New Studies in Shemot/Exodus*, Jerusalem, Israel: The World Jewish Organization, 1981, p. 384.

66 transtorah.org/PDFs/No_Longer_Strangers.pdf, 2008.

What have they grown to love about Judaism? What parts of their prior religious life do they miss? How can we make the transition easier for those who choose to formally embrace Judaism?

2.   Misuse of speech is the topic of 23:1 and 23:7, "You must not carry false rumors," and "Keep far from a false charge." Careful use of language is a very serious issue in the Torah.

Jewish law prohibits three kinds of speech: *sheker*, "falsehoods" (Ex. 23:7); *l'shon ha-ra*, "slander"; and *r'khilut*, "gossip, rumors." The latter two categories recognize that there may be some truth being told about a person, but the information should not be communicated to those who have no need to know it.

Before speaking about someone, ask yourself if your comments fall under any of the above categories. In those brief moments of reflection, you may decide to keep your comments under wrap.

3.   Judges, litigants, and witnesses are directed not to show favoritism either to the poor or to the mighty (23:2-3). It seems obvious not to favor the powerful, but is it necessary to remind people not to bend the law for compassionate reasons?

4.   This portion shows concern for animals in 23:4, 5, 11,12. Animals also have a place in the Ten Commandments (20:10). There are numerous references to animal sacrifice in the Torah, yet compassionate treatment of animals is a recurring theme. Can you reconcile this disparity?

5.   In 24:12, God tells Moses to ascend the mountain and "be there." Why is "being there," (in some translations, "waiting") added to the instruction? It's obvious that Moses should remain atop the mountain until he receives the tablets he was promised. I think "be there" provides a spiritual message: Be present, be aware of yourself and your surroundings. Reread the section on Moses noticing the Burning Bush (Exodus 3:2-4). Was Moses "present"? Is being present necessary for spiritual encounters?

Our lives are filled with distractions. When you "solo-task" does it feel like you are wasting time?

FOCUS PHRASE (24:1)

Ah'lei el Adonai—Elevate yourself to God.

T'rumah (Exodus 25:1-27:19) "Building a Home"

Overview

"The Tabernacle texts in Exodus—much like the sacred building texts of other ancient peoples—begin with elaborate instructions for making the *Mishkan*, its furnishings, and the priestly vestments (Exodus 25-31) ... behind the mass of arcane details lies a yearning for God's presence and an attempt to establish a relationship between divine immanence and transcendence, in other words, between God's abilities to be "right here" and "everywhere at the same time."[67]

Standout Phrases

25:2 "... accept gifts for Me from every person whose heart is so moved." There are myriad obligations in the Torah, but here, the request is for what can be given with an open hand and an open heart.

25:8 "And let them make Me a sanctuary that I may dwell among them." We would expect this sentence to read, "And let them make Me a sanctuary that I may dwell IN IT." The verse suggests that God's true "home," or "sanctuary," is not a physical place (an "it"); God's dwelling place is wherever people gather. How people attend to themselves and others when they gather indicates God's Presence.

25:15 "The poles shall remain in the rings of the ark: they shall not be removed from it." The prohibition against removing the poles is indicative of the ark's purpose: to be readily available (mobile) to accompany the people wherever they go. The Torah's message is not tied to one location.

26:31 "You shall make a curtain ..." The word "*parochet*" used in this verse remains the designation of the curtain used in synagogues today. Some synagogues hang a curtain in front of the ark doors (the ark contains the Torah scrolls), and others hang the curtain behind the ark doors. Often the *parochet* is beautifully decorated.

---

67 Carol Meyers in *The Torah: A Women's Commentary*, Tamara Cohn Eskenazi and Andrea L. Weiss, eds., NY: URJ Press, 2008, p. 451.

TALK ABOUT

1. The building of the sanctuary and its appointments is the main topic in this portion and those that follow—*T'tzaveh, Ki Tisa, Vayak'heil* and *P'kudei*. About 300 verses are dedicated to these cultic matters. In contrast, the creation narrative in Genesis consists of 31 verses!

In *Accepting the Yoke of Heaven: Commentary on the Weekly Torah Portion*, Yeshayahu Leibowitz explains that the purpose of the Torah is not to provide information on the construction of the world, but to tell us something about our significance as human beings.[68]

Leibowitz argues that what we make ourselves (i.e., the Tabernacle) is paramount to what we are given (i.e., the works of creation). Do you agree with Leibowitz?

2. This portion describes men and women providing the labor and raw materials for building the *Mishkan*. The labor and materials are voluntary offerings of energy and expertise.

LGBTQ activist Rabbi Denise L. Eger suggests that we make free-will offerings to the institutions that serve the Jewish community: "Synagogue, Jewish centers, and Jewish communal agencies cannot survive on membership fees or dues alone ... these institutions require our heartfelt support ... Our *parshah* teaches that the *t'rumah*-gift is an offering that comes from the deep recesses of the heart. Then and now, it is a privilege to be involved in the sacred work of building community and constructing a dwelling place for the Divine."[69]

Do you agree with Eger that members of the Jewish community have a responsibility to support its institutions? Should we feel this responsibility if these organization don't directly serve us? Which Jewish communal agencies in your community do you particularly value?

3. The first time we find the Hebrew word for "dwelling" in relation to God is in 25:8 (*she'can'ti*). In the Bible and in Modern Hebrew, a "*sha'ken*" is a neighbor. "*Mishkan*" (same root letters) refers to God's dwelling place. You may find the word familiar from "*Shechinah*," the postbiblical term that refers to God's In-Dwelling Presence.

---

68 *Accepting the Yoke of Heaven: Commentary on the Weekly Torah Portion*, Jerusalem, Israel: Urim Publications, 2006, p. 80.

69 *The Torah: A Women's Commentary*, Tamara Cohn Eskenazi and Andrea L. Weiss, eds., NY: URJ Press, 2008, p. 470.

Jewish medieval mystics envisioned God as *Shechinah*, God's feminine presence who went into exile with the Jewish people, weeping with them and sheltering them in her wings. In recent decades, "*Shechinah*" has been a name of God used by those seeking balance in describing God. Rabbi Lynn Gottlieb envisions *Shechinah* as a Being who connects all life, expresses our longing for wholeness, and calls us to justice.[70]

What changes occur when female metaphors are added to male metaphors for God?

4. In Genesis, we find Abraham, Isaac, and Jacob (among others) engaging with God in multiple places, including hilltops, mountains, and streams. In *T'rumah*, the people are told to build a sanctuary as a "home" for God. Some think that synagogue sanctuaries are the places where God dwells. Others feel God's presence most strongly in nature.

Do you experience God or holiness differently in a sanctuary than in other locations? What is the purpose of a sanctuary? Synagogues are called houses of worship, houses of study and houses of gathering. Do these phrases describe synagogues you know?

5. Rabbi Helene Ferris writes about a place where she felt unparalleled holiness:

"Once a month I engage in an extraordinary Shabbat experience [at a group home for mentally challenged adults]. I look forward to being with the residents because I feel a sacredness that I feel in no other place ... I am awed by the joy in the room ... As I leave, I feel that I have experienced the blessing of the sacred ... Maybe it is because I marvel at the blessing of who they are. Maybe it is because they help me understand the blessing of who I am."[71]

In what unexpected places have you felt holiness and awe?

THINK ABOUT

1. The people donate gifts for the building of the *Mishkan*. The Hebrew word for dedicated gifts in this portion is "*t'rumah*," which comes from the root "to lift up." Although it may seem counterintuitive, giving can uplift people even more than receiving does.

---

70 *She Who Dwells Within: A Feminist Vision of a Renewed Judaism*, HarperCollins Publishers: New York, NY: 1995, pp. 25-48.

71 "Shabbat Knows No Disabilities" *CCAR Newsletter*, 2009/10

2. God asks for gifts from those "whose heart moves them" (25:2). We have all been on the giving and receiving end of perfunctory gifts. Taking time to choose a gift carefully and to offer it with joy is a remarkably different experience from giving something thoughtlessly.

3. The instructions concerning the ark include, "Overlay it with pure gold—overlay it inside and out..." (25:11). Why should gold be used (wasted?) on the inside? Read this in a *Mussar* context: Upright people live with integrity; what they display on the outside is expressive of who they are on the inside.

4. God says in 25:22, "There I will meet with you." Some find God's presence in the outdoors. Others are spiritually moved in prayer or study. Some find grand buildings—churches and synagogues—to be most conducive to awe. Others are moved by humble surroundings. When and where have you felt awe, or closeness to God?

5. 26:36 mentions embroidery as part of the Tabernacle's decoration. In 2013, Canadian textile and Judaica artist Temma Gentles began a project of stitching the entire Torah—that's 5,856 verses and 304,805 letters! About 2,000 people are participating, women and men from dozens of countries, and various ethnic and religious groups. This uniquely formatted Torah is being developed in dialogue with other Abrahamic faiths, and the piece includes cross-stitched extracts from the Gospels in Greek and the Koran in Arabic. You can learn more about this incredible and breathtaking piece of art at torahstitchbystitch.org.

FOCUS PHRASE (25:2)

Yeed'veh'nu li'bo—The heart motivates.

T'tzaveh (Exodus 27:20-30:10)
"Adoration and Adornment"

OVERVIEW

Atop Mt. Sinai, Moses receives God's detailed instructions for constructing a portable sanctuary, the Tabernacle, for worship. Its furnishings include an ark, altar, lampstand, and other accoutrements. This portion includes descriptions of the elaborate priestly clothing and ordination ceremony.

"The vestments here described are the direct antecedents of those now in use in the Roman Catholic and Greek Orthodox churches, whose priests—and especially whose bishops—wear similar robes while officiating. In the synagogue, it is the Torah scroll that is embellished: it is generally dressed in an embroidered mantle and sash and crowned by pomegranates and bells."[72]

STANDOUT PHRASES

27:20 "... kindling lamps regularly." This appears to be the origin of the *ner tamid*, the "eternal light" above the ark in every synagogue.

28:2 "... for dignity and adornment." The Torah scrolls and many furnishings in the synagogue are beautiful and embellished. Does this add to your appreciation of them? What is your reaction to kissing the scrolls with a *tallit* or prayer book, and bowing to the scrolls or the ark? Does this seem like a kind of idolatry?

28:30 "Inside the breastpiece of decision you shall place the *Urim* and *Thummim* ..." "*Urim* and *Thummim*" appear to provide oracular guidance, indicating God's desired outcomes for questions brought to priests.

29:35, 37 "You shall ordain them through seven days." "Seven days shall you perform purification." Aaron wears seven items. The number seven indicates that holiness is central to the priestly vocation. Seven symbolizes perfection and completion.

---

72 *The Torah: A Modern Commentary*, Revised Edition, W. Gunther Plaut, ed. David E. S. Stein, Revised Edition ed., New York: URJ Press, 2005, p. 561.

Talk About

1. Marla Brettschneider brings "queer perspective" to *Parashat Tetzaveh*. She expresses relief and validation that in the Tent of Meeting, excess is named not as an expression of depraved hedonism, but as the dwelling place of the Divine. In this place of "lavish beauty" God meets, speaks with, and abides among the Israelites.[73]

Do you think that the priestly clothing, rituals, and meals are exercises in extravagance?

2. Abi Weber looks at the visual extravagance in a different way: "In religious and spiritual communities, I am often asked to 'shed layers' ... discerning what truly matters and letting go of the rest. There is a sense that spiritual connection has to do with getting rid of the extra stuff that builds up ... this week's Torah portion, *Tetzaveh*, is all about putting layers on ... how strange it is that these Israelites are focusing on such things at this moment. They have just been liberated from four hundred years of slavery ... received the Torah at Sinai; they are now learning to survive in the wilderness. And what is it that they are to spend their time and energy thinking about? Fancy clothes! How odd."[74]

Do you find the lavish attention to clothing unexpected at this point in the wilderness journey? Do you agree with Weber's observation that "spiritual connection has to do with getting rid of the extra stuff that builds up, of drilling into the core of things?"

3. What does the *ner tamid* (27:20) symbolize to you? Does it symbolize the Jewish people, the light of Torah, the persistence of the Jewish spirit, God's light, the light that exists in each person's soul?

4. "Make sacral vestments for your brother, Aaron, for dignity and adornment" (28:2). Does beautification of items add to their holiness or to your experience of their preciousness?

5. This is the only Torah portion in Exodus where Moses' name doesn't appear. We don't know if this is arbitrary or purposeful. Can you suggest

---

73 *Torah Queeries: Weekly Commentaries on the Hebrew Bible*, Gregg Drinkwater, Joshua Lesser, and David Shneer, eds., New York: New York University Press, 2009, p. 108.

74 "The Finest That We Have To Offer" on https://www.truah.org/resources/the-finest-that-we-have-to-offer -parshat-tetzaveh/, 2019.

a reason why Moses is absent in *T'tzaveh*? There is no right answer; use this opportunity to think creatively about the text!

THINK ABOUT

1. 28:29 says that Aaron, the High Priest "... shall carry the names of the sons of Israel on the breastpiece of decision over his heart when he enters the Sanctuary, for remembrance before YHWH at all times." Aaron wore the breastpiece over his heart. Each stone symbolized a tribe. When Aaron entered the Sanctuary, he was reminded of his responsibility to work on behalf of the entire community.

2. What is the point of constructing this elaborate Tabernacle? Professor James Kugel suggests that if we open up a space in order to allow God to fill it, a space will similarly open up a welcoming space in our lives and in our hearts.[75]

Does Kugel's explanation resonate with you?

3. In Genesis, there are several episodes where clothing is used to deceive: Jacob dressing in Esau's garments to win his father's primary blessing, Tamar dressing as a prostitute to seduce Judah, Potiphar's wife using Joseph's abandoned robe to support her story that he tried to rape her. In the creation story, Adam and Eve, when innocent, are naked. In response to feeling moral qualms, they cover themselves with leaves, functioning as clothing.

In the first book of the Torah, clothes represent lack of transparency, even deception. In *T'tzaveh*, clothing represents something entirely different: holiness and authority.

Have you worn clothing to deceive someone? Have you worn clothing to establish authority?

4. Rabbi Shai Held notes the different emphases in the names of the prior portion (*T'rumah*) and this portion (*T'tzaveh*). *Terumah* (gift) connotes voluntary giving, *tetsavveh* (command) connotes obligation. Held observes that *Parashat Terumah* begins by appealing to the heart of the Israelites while *Parashat Tetsavveh* opens with a command.[76]

75 *On Being a Jew*, Baltimore, MD: The Johns Hopkins University Press, 1990, p.36.
76 *The Heart of Torah: Essays on the Weekly Torah Portion: Genesis and Exodus,* Philadelphia: The Jewish Publication Society, 2017, pp. 200-201.

Many relationships thrive on a combination of *T'rumah* moments of generosity and love, and *T'tzaveh* moments of commitment and obligation. Are both necessary for lasting, intimate connections?

Focus Phrase (27:20)

L'ha'ah'loat ner tamid—Kindle a light continually.

Ki Tisa (Exodus 30:11–34:35) "Pretending"

OVERVIEW

The episode with the golden calf occurs forty days after the Revelation at Sinai. At Sinai, the people said, "All that YHVH has spoken we will faithfully do" (24:7). Weeks later, in *Ki Tisa*, when the people see the idols made with jewels, they exclaim, "This is your god, O Israel" (32:4). The Israelites are often described as stiff-necked; here they seem impulsive and fickle.

When Moses descends the mountain and sees the people dancing around the golden calf, he shatters the tablets that contain God's laws. Moses approaches God to ask forgiveness for the people. God has a unique encounter with Moses in which Moses sees God's back.

Moses is instructed to carve two tablets like the first. God renews the covenant with the people. God repeats some central aspects of the covenant: not to make idols, not to boil a kid in its mother's milk, and to observe Shabbat and the festivals.

When Moses returns from the mountain, his face is radiant. Some Christian interpreters understood the Hebrew to mean he had grown "horns of light." Jewish commentators are mixed about whether Moses radiated light or was marked with horns as indicative of his close encounter with God.

STANDOUT PHRASES

30:13 "... a half shekel ..." A shekel is a specific weight of silver. Many commentators have cited this verse to support the idea that each of us is incomplete, "half" of what we could be, unless we join with others and share our resources, financial and otherwise.

31:16-17 "The Israelite people shall keep the Sabbath ..." Some people sing these verses, which begin with the Hebrew word "*V'shamru*" during Shabbat services and as part of the Shabbat *Kiddush* on Saturday afternoon.

32:24 "... out came this calf." Here is another biblical example of passing the buck. See my comments on the first portion in Genesis, *B'reishit*, "Think About" #6.

33:11, 33:20 "YHVH would speak to Moses face to face." "But you cannot see My face." These statements contradict one another. Is it possible to reconcile these different messages?

34:28 "... the Ten Commandments." The actual Hebrew says "the Ten Statements," or "the Ten Utterances." If you read the "Ten Commandments" (20:1-14), you will see there are not ten and they are not all commandments. The "commandments" are called *"d'varim"* in 20:1 and again here. *"D'varim"* does not mean "commandments." *"D'varim"* are words or statements.

If the "Ten Commandments" were called the "Ten Statements," would you have a different attachment to them?

Talk About

1. The Hebrew word *"vayak'heil"* (the people gathered) is used here (32:1) to describe the people's communal effort in demanding a false god. In 35:1, *"vayak'heil"* describes the people coming together to build the Tabernacle. Gathered/united people can be a source of constructive building or they can become a rowdy mob with destructive aims. What are your experiences with both kinds of groups?

2. Moses tries to reduce God's anger when the people build a golden calf: Moses describes the Israelites as Your (God's) people and praises God for freeing the people in dramatic fashion (32:11). In 32:12, Moses appeals to God's vanity, and in 32:13, Moses reminds God of better times with the people. Moses' efforts work: "And YHVH renounced the punishment ..." (32:14).

How have you talked someone down from an angry, vindictive mood? What tactics are effective in changing your mind when you are frustrated and disappointed?

3. Moses becomes enraged at seeing the people dancing around the calf (32:19) and he hurls the tablets to the ground, breaking them. Scholar Nahum Sarna notes that smashing the tablets signified the abrogation of the covenant. "In Akkadian legal terminology, to 'break the tablet' means to invalidate or repudiate a document or agreement."[77]

Do you understand Moses' anger?

---

77 Nahum M. Sarna, *The JPS Torah Commentary: Exodus,* Philadelphia: The Jewish Publication Society, 1991, p. 207, n. 19-20.

4. The set of commandments Moses destroys in 32:19 are the ones God inscribed. (24:12, 32:15-16) In 34:27-28, it says that Moses wrote a second set of commandments on tablets. These are the commandments that remain intact. What does it mean that the tablets God inscribed were destroyed but the commandments Moses inscribed were preserved?

D'var Acher (another thing): Tradition says that the first broken set of commandments were kept in the ark alongside the intact commandments. This is telling: We each carry the broken parts of ourselves with(in) us; they cannot be left behind or completely forgotten. On the contrary, our disappointments and failures continue to teach and impact us even as they recede further in the background. Has this been true for you?

5. 33:16 describes the Israelite people as being "distinguished from every people on the face of the earth." What makes the Jewish people distinctive?

THINK ABOUT

1. The word "*l'chaper*" and "*hakipurim*," referring to atonement, appear in 30:15 and 16. You may recognize these words from the holy day, "*Yom Kippur.*"

"Sin" is not a concept many of us understand. We think of "committing a sin" as having done something wrong or "bad." But there are more nuanced definitions of sin. Carol Ochs and Rabbi Kerry M. Olitzky offer these more subtle and apt definitions:

Sin as pride, as missing the mark, as alienation, as inauthenticity, as division, as impatience, as resistance to drawing closer, as refusal to grow, as cynicism.[78]

These expressions of sin refer not to acts but to attitudes and to a sense of feeling disconnected and inattentive. When we are not being true to ourselves, when we posture, deceive, falsify, and dismiss, when we refuse to show vulnerability, when we are unwilling to change or resent others' growth and accomplishments, when we are possessive, competitive, embittered, and ungrateful: these are all manifestations of experiencing sin. Although you may not think of these attitudes and behaviors as "sinful," would you like to distance yourself from any or all of these attitudes and behaviors?

78 *Jewish Spiritual Guidance: Finding Our Way to God,* San Francisco, CA: Josey-Bass, Inc., 1997, pp. 137-144.

2. Bernard M. Zlotowitz explains, "... Moses' encounter with the Divine resulted in a special radiance so intensely brilliant that the people begged him to cover his face because it was frightening for mortals to behold. But there is another interpretation ... In the ancient Near East ... the gods were depicted with horns to symbolize their divine state. And when men or women attained divinity, they were similarly portrayed with horns. What the halo represents to the modern mind, the horn signified to the ancient one ... These horns, with which Moses was now endowed, were the symbol of divinity ... The Israelites fully understood this."[79]

The editors of the Torah chose to omit Moses' burial place so that it would not become a shrine. In the *Haggadah*, Moses' name is absent except in one biblical quotation. There is a purpose in distinguishing between God and God's chosen prophet. Even Moses' colloquial name, "*Moshe Rabbenu*," "Moses our Teacher/Rabbi," avoids any indication of divinity.

Do you think of Moses as a (semi) divine figure? Had you noticed that his name doesn't appear in the *Haggadah*? Could that have been an oversight? If Moses had a known burial place, how would it have been treated over time?

3. God describes God's Self in 34:6-7: compassionate, gracious, slow to anger, abounding in kindness and faithfulness, extending kindness, forgiving iniquity, transgression, and sin, remitting punishment, etc. This list is known as the "Thirteen Attributes," and is part of the High Holy Day, festival, and fast day liturgy.

As you have "gotten to know" God in Genesis and Exodus, do these traits reflect how the Torah presents God? Slow to anger? Remitting punishment?

---

79 "Moses' Face Was Horned" in *CCAR Journal: A Reform Jewish Quarterly*, Fall 2003, pp. 53-38.

4. "I'm Weary of Mountains" by Rabbi Sandy Eisenberg Sasso[80]

Must we always go up to some

Mountain

With Abraham, with Isaac to Moriah?

The air is too thin up there, and it's hard to breathe.

Must we always go up to some mountain

With Moses to Sinai?

It's so far from the earth,

And what's below appears so small

You can forget it's real.

Must we always go up to some mountain

With Moses to Nebo?

Climbing—there's only one way

And loneliness.

Must we always go up to some

Mountain

With Elijah to Carmel?

The ascent is not hard,

It's the descending—

Too easy to slip

With no one to catch your fall.

I'm weary of mountains

Where we're always looking up

Or looking down and sacrificing

80 "Introduction: Unwrapping the Gift" in Women and Religious Ritual, Lesley A. Northup, ed., Washington: The Pastoral Press, 1993, p. 216.

So our neck hurts

And we need glasses.

Our feet upon the mountains

Are blistered,

And our shoes are always wrong

Not enough "sole."

Can we sit with Sarah in a tent,

Next to Deborah under a palm tree,

With Hannah in prayer

Alongside Miriam by the sea—

To wash our feet, and catch our breath and

Our soul?

Focus Phrase (31:3)

B'choch'mah u'veet'vu'nah uv'da'at—With skill, ability, and knowledge.

Vayak'heil (Exodus 35:1–38:20) "On Fire"

OVERVIEW

This is one of the seven designated portions that, depending on the number of *Shabbatot* (pl.) in a year, is either read on its own or is coupled with *P'kudei*. *Vayak'heil* repeats the commandment to observe Shabbat. Moses asks the Israelites to donate gifts for building the *Mishkan*. Under the direction of two skilled craftsmen, the people undertake and complete its construction and decoration. Much of this portion is a repetition of directives in *T'rumah*, *T'tzaveh*, and *Ki Tisa*.

STANDOUT PHRASES

35:1 "Moses then convoked ..." Then name of this portion, *Vayak'heil*, includes the root letters for the Hebrew word for "community," "*kehilla*." Some congregations use the words "*Kehilah K'dosha*," "holy community," in front of their synagogue name. What makes a community a "*Kehilah K'dosha*?"

35:1-2 "These are the things that YHVH has commanded you to do: On six days work may be done, but on the seventh day, you shall have a Sabbath of complete rest ..." Even when engaged in the holy work of building the *Mishkan*, the seventh day remains distinctive as a day of rest and refreshment.

35:10 "... skilled ..." The Hebrew is '*chacham lev*,' "wise-hearted." Do you think "skilled" is a good translation of "*chacham lev*?"

35:30-31 "YHVH has singled out by name Bezalel, endowing him with a divine spirit of skill, ability, and knowledge in every kind of craft." The name "Bezalel" brings to mind the expression in Genesis 1:26, when God says, "Let us make human beings in our image." The Hebrew word for "in our image" is "*b'zal'meinu*."

TALK ABOUT

1. A new dimension is added to the prohibition against working on the seventh day: "You shall kindle no fire throughout your settlements on the Sabbath day." (35:3). Why is this added? Translator and commentator

Richard Elliott Friedman notes, "Fire has not been associated with the Sabbath until now. What has happened between the instruction (31:15) and Moses' fulfillment of it ... The prohibition of fire on the Sabbath may be understood as a reminder of the golden calf rebellion ... it is a reminder that the Sabbath is not just about work and rest ...The Sabbath is about separation and sanctification of time."[81]

In *Friendly Fire*, the Israeli novelist A.B. Yehoshua describes fire as a living thing: it moves, changes shape and color, eats, makes noises, and provides heat. He notes that fire is the only thing in the world that man can kill and then bring back to life. Fire can help us create, but it can also be a source of destruction. Fire cleanses and purifies, and it can also kill. Yehoshua concludes that in contemplating fire, we learn something of death.[82]

Does Yehoshua's description of fire add to your understanding about why fire may have been prohibited on Shabbat?

Do you associate Shabbat more with what you add to or what you desist from the seventh day? What changes in your life occur if you don't use electricity (fire) for up to 25 hours on Shabbat?

2. The second part of 35:2 says, regarding the Sabbath, "Whoever does any work on it shall be put to death." This is certainly a troubling text.

The Conservative movement's Torah Commentary notes that commentator J. Eybeschutz does not take these words literally. He understands "be put to death" as becoming dead to the spiritual dimension of life. A *n'shamah y'terah* (often translated as an "additional soul," but I prefer "an expanded soul") comes to life at the outset of Shabbat, disappears at Shabbat's end, to be restored the following Shabbat. When the gift of Shabbat is ignored, the extra/expanded soul is forfeited.[83]

After many years appreciating the notion of receiving an extra soul on Shabbat, I now believe that the extra soul always resides in us, and is revealed on Shabbat when we celebrate the seventh day.

3. 35:31 describes Bezalel as being endowed with "skill, ability, and knowledge." According to trusted commentator Rashi, "skill" (*hokhmah*) is what a person learns from others, "ability" (*t'vunah*) results from

81 *Commentary on the Torah,* New York, NY: HarperCollins, 2001, p. 296, n. 35:3.

82 *Friendly Fire,* Translated by Stuart Schoffman New York, NY: Houghton Mifflin Harcourt, 2007, pp. 338-339.

83 *Etz Hayim,* David L. Lieber, ed., Philadelphia: The Jewish Publication Society, 2001, p. 552, n. 2.

insight and experience, and "knowledge" (*da'at*) is inspiration, an idea that comes from an unknown source.

How do you distinguish between skill, ability, and knowledge?

4. Theologian Rabbi Rachel Adler discusses the Menorah's symbolism (37:17-24): "The Menorah is a representation of a flowering almond tree ... Trees, as well as light are associated with consciousness for Jews. Our moral consciousness comes from having eaten the fruit of a tree (Genesis 3) ... But the Menorah is yet a different sort of tree, because its branches are crowned with bowls filled with oil that are lit regularly by the priests."

"Who ever heard of a tree perpetually on fire? ... We cannot relive the moment when a startled shepherd sees a terrible and wonderful sight: a tree on fire, unconsumed. We can only make a memory-tree to remind us of that moment ... reproducing the encounter with that fiery presence we seek and yet fear: the revealer of mysteries, the dweller in the bush."[84]

THINK ABOUT

1. The work involved in building the Tabernacle is called "*melachah*." This work is completed in 39:43. The slaves' efforts in Egypt are called "*avodah*." (e.g., 5:18, 6:6) This work for Pharaoh would never be completed. The work done for Pharaoh was somewhat constructive (the slaves made bricks), but mostly destructive (their bodies suffered and their spirits were broken (Exodus 1:9-10). In contrast, building the Tabernacle is entirely constructive—affirming and elevating—of an important project and of the community's cohesion.

2. "Their efforts had been more than enough for all the tasks to be done" (36:7). The Hebrew word for "more than enough" is "*dayam*," which shares a root with the familiar Seder song "*Dayeinu*," with the chorus, "it would have been enough."

3. "This is why the second time around the Torah was given quietly, without the thunder and lightning ... Moshe receives the second tablets and comes down from the mountain so quickly and so quietly that you would almost not realize that it had happened (it did, in last week's *parasha*—*Shemot* 34:28-29). The people had to reorient themselves to a

---

84 *The Torah: A Women's Commentary*, Tamara Cohn Eskenazi and Andrea L. Weiss, eds., New York: URJ Press, 2008, pp. 540-541.

new Torah, to the second tablets, to a Torah of God's presence in the quiet, not in the thunder and lightning:

"And, behold, the Lord passed by, and a great and strong wind tore the mountains, and broke in pieces the rocks before the Lord; but the Lord was not in the wind; and after the wind an earthquake; but the Lord was not in the earthquake; And after the earthquake a fire; but the Lord was not in the fire; and after the fire a still small voice" (Kings I 19:11-12).

It is the religion of the still small voice that is the message of *Parashat VaYakhel*.[85]

Does the description of God's presence in Kings I 19:11-12 speak to you?

4. This portion is called, "And they gathered," referring to the community. The commandment to observe the Sabbath is repeated in *Vayak'heil*. How important is community in celebrating Shabbat? While solitary time to rest, read, walk is welcome on Shabbat, it is difficult to imagine Shabbat meals or celebrations without family or friends.

What part of Shabbat practice is most appealing to you?

FOCUS PHRASE (35:2)

Ko'desh Shabbat Shaba'tone—The Sabbath day is holy.

---

85 library-yctorah.org "Blinded by the Light ," Rabbi Dov Linzer, March 12, 2010.

P'kudei (Exodus 38:21–40:38) "Getting it Right"

OVERVIEW

Moses keeps a detailed record of the metals used to fashion the *Mishkan* and its furnishings. The priestly clothing is also itemized. Everything is done "as YHVH commanded Moses." The various components of the Tabernacle are put in place; it is dedicated and the priests are installed. The Book of Exodus began with the Israelites in a desperate situation. Exodus ends with the people freed, confident in their future, and in God's presence in their midst.

STANDOUT PHRASES

39:1, 5, 7, 21, 26, 29, 31 "... as YHVH had commanded Moses." This summary phrase appears seven times in chapter 39. Our attention is drawn to Moses' obedience to God. Plus, as has been noted before, the number seven is connected to holiness and denotes totality or completeness.

39:14 "... the names of the sons of Israel ... the twelve tribes." The Tribes are the traditional divisions of the ancient Jewish people. They are descended from the sons and grandsons of Jacob, called "Israel" from Jacob's name given to him by God.

39:32, 42 "The Israelites did so; just as YHVH had commanded Moses, so they did." Earlier in chapter 39, Moses adhered to God's commands. Here, we see the Israelites doing what Moses asked. The line of authority is God, Moses, people.

40:38 "For over the Tabernacle a cloud of YHVH rested by day, and fire would appear in it by night ..." What a comforting scene! In the heat of the day, there would be a cloud covering. In the chill of the night, there would be a fire's warmth.

TALK ABOUT

1. Many commentators point out similar language in the creation story and in the *Mishkan*-building story. Close readers of the text notice the repetition of the words "saw," "finish," and "bless" in both stories. The

instructions for construction of the Tabernacle parallel the creation of the world in many ways.

Interpreter and exegete Rabbi Shai Held asks, "In a world so filled with callousness and inhumanity, where is there room for the God who shatters our indifference?" Held suggests we read about the *mishkan* (Exodus chapters 25-31 and 35-40), to remind us to make God's Presence manifest not just in the forms and rituals of religion, but in the ways we comport ourselves in the world. Do we make room for God in our private and public lives?[86]

2. God's Presence appears "in the view of all the house of Israel..." (40:38) It is uplifting to find this hint of unity among the people: they gather in one place and unite in their experience of the Eternal. Sadly, for most of Jewish history, there has been very little unity among Jews. What is the situation in your Jewish community? Does the community come together for any events or celebrations? Do synagogues share resources? Do you think a unified Jewish community is a realistic aspiration?

3. The last words of Exodus are "their journeys." (40:38) These words provide an excellent summation to the book as a whole. The people journeyed from Egypt to Sinai and beyond. Moses journeyed from confusion about his identity and purpose to visionary leadership and confidence. What other journeys have taken place in Exodus?

THINK ABOUT

1. Although the next (third) book of the Torah is Leviticus, the wilderness narrative that concludes at the end of Exodus picks up again with the Book of Numbers. The Torah is not chronological. It may be helpful to think about the Torah as the first two books and the last two books, with the middle book representing the "heart" of the matter. Leviticus mostly addresses cultic matters. The Book of Numbers finds the Israelites grappling with day-to-day concerns.

2. 40:2 announces that the Tabernacle will be erected on the first day of the month, the day of the New Moon. This is a time of near darkness in the sky and the expectation of growing light as the sliver of the moon expands with each passing day.

---

86 *The Heart of Torah: Essays on the Weekly Torah Portion: Genesis and Exodus, Volume I*, Philadelphia: Jewish Publication Society, 2017, p. 224.

The Exodus occurred on the fourteenth day of the month, when the moon is full and bright. (12:17-18) It makes sense for a night journey to begin under the brightest possible sky. But why was the dark night of the New Moon selected for erecting the *Mishkan*?

3. Rabbi Jonathan Sacks sees two different purposes in the Tabernacle: a visible symbol of God's presence among the people, and the communal effort required to construct the Sanctuary. Sacks notes that we are not changed by what is done for us, but by what we do for ourselves and each other.[87]

Do you agree with Rabbi Sacks' assertion that we are changed by what we do more so than what is done for us?

4. What journeys have been the most significant in your life? What are the differences between a trip, a journey, and a pilgrimage? Have you taken all three?

FOCUS PHRASE (40:36, 38)

Mas'ay'hem—Journeys.

---

87 *Covenant and Conversation: A Weekly Reading of the Jewish Bible*, New Milford, CT: Koren Publishers, 2010, p. 333.

Leviticus/Vayikra

INTRODUCTION TO LEVITICUS/VAYIKRA

Leviticus is focused on priestly behavior in two ways. First, Leviticus addresses designated priests who officiated at the Temple in Jerusalem (built by King Solomon in the 10th century B.C.E. and destroyed first by the Babylonians in 586 B.C.E., rebuilt, and subsequently destroyed by the Romans in 70 C.E.). Second, this book is concerned with the holiness (the "priestliness") of the Israelite people.

Most scholars believe Leviticus was written by and for priests who controlled rites at the Temple in Jerusalem and who also regulated matters of ritual purity in public and private domains. Here is one approach that endeavors to make sense of this book: "How do we make a home for God in our midst? What does it mean to be a *goy kadosh*, a holy community? Leviticus as the central book of the five books of the Torah is not some detour from our story. Just as the *Mishkan* sits at the center of the Israelite camp and houses the Divine Presence, Leviticus sits at the center of our Torah and houses the teachings and instructions to maintain that *Mishkan*."[88]

Leviticus addresses what it means to be set apart, and it is itself set apart from the other four books of the Torah. The entire book takes

---

88 Rabbi Jonathan Kligler, *Turn It and Turn It For Everything Is In It: Essays on the Weekly Torah Portion*, Eugene, Oregon: Wipf and Stock, 2020, p. 94.

place in one location, at the base of Mt. Sinai. Leviticus mostly consists of God's instructions to Moses, and contains very little narrative. It is the shortest book in the Torah and includes some of the most edifying verses in the Torah such as, "Love your neighbor as yourself" (19:18), and "When you reap the harvest of your land, you shall not reap all the way to the edges of your field, or gather the gleanings of your harvest; you shall leave them for the poor and the stranger" (23:22).

Vayikra (Leviticus 1:1-5:26) "Drawing Near"

OVERVIEW

The first portion in the third book of the Torah introduces themes of sacrifice, sin, ritual impurity, and reconciliation. Animal sacrifice was a well-accepted method of worship in the ancient Near East. We don't comprehend sacrificing animals or grains as a way of showing reverence for God, but these offerings demonstrate our biblical ancestors' desire to draw near to God. (The Hebrew word for "sacrifice," "*korban*," is based on the verb "to draw near.") Through a detailed and orderly process, sacrifice enables the penitent to achieve relief from an alienating experience, or to express thanks. Sacrifices gave our ancestors a tangible way to restore a sense of well-being and closeness to God. The closing verses of this *parsha* address social and economic justice.

STANDOUT VERSES

1:1-2 "YHVH called to Moses ..." At this point in the Torah, God "resides" in the Tabernacle, and invites Moses inside. But it is not a secret conversation that ensues. God says, "Speak to the Israelite people, and say to them ..." The priests have a distinctive role, but God wants the people to know the details and extent of their duties.

1:17 "... pleasing odor to YHVH." The text says that pleasing odors accompany offerings. Judaism rejects assigning human traits to God (anthropomorphism), but in the Torah there are several references to God's human qualities. Here, God appreciates appealing smells.

4:2 "When a person unwittingly incurs guilt ..." This phrasing indicates that people will sin, inadvertently if not willfully. The sacrificial system provides a way for the individual and community to deal with sin by tempering its ramifications and repercussions. In 4:20, 26, 31, 35, people are assured that if they offer a sacrifice, their good standing will be restored.

5:21 "When a person sins and commits a trespass against YHVH—by dealing deceitfully with another ..." The explicit inference here is that wronging a person equates to wronging God.

TALK ABOUT

1. In the Torah scroll (and some *chumashim*) you'll see the diminished size of the last letter (*aleph*) of the first word in Leviticus, "*Vayikra*." There are several explanations for this. One explanation is that this is a scribal error that continues to be replicated. A homiletic explanation that many rabbis use is that the small *aleph* demonstrates Moses' humility: He didn't want to draw attention to God's communicating with him (yet again) and the smaller *aleph* reflects his modesty. Similarly, the smaller *aleph* is a reminder not to overinflate one's self (n.b. the letter *aleph* is the first letter of the Hebrew word "*ani*," "I," the source of egotism).

2. In 1:1, God calls ("*Vayikra*") Moses. This word appears in Genesis 22:11 when angels (God's representatives) call Abraham to stay his hand from killing Isaac. And "*vayikra*" is used in Exodus 3:4 when God calls Moses from the Burning Bush. What do these three incidents—one in Genesis, one in Exodus, and one in Leviticus—have in common?

3. Chapters 1-7 delineate the major types of individual and communal sacrifices. Some *Yom Kippur* prayers refer to "my sin," some address "our sins." Consider how Judaism encourages us to honor the *yahrzeit* (anniversary) of a loved one when that specific anniversary occurs, and to join together to remember all our loved ones during the four annual communal *yizkor* (remembrance) services. Are there additional ways Judaism and other religions address both individual and communal needs?

4. There is no ritual remedy prescribed for intentional, premeditated offenses. Willful offenders were subject to punishment determined by law. But wouldn't people who commit intentional wrongdoings also benefit from a ritual that provides repatriation with the community or God? Today, what might that ritual look like?

5. Chapter 3 discusses offerings brought by someone feeling gratitude and well-being: These offerings are called *"shleimim,"* from the word *"shalom."* Many assume that all sacrifices atone for guilt and wrongdoing. The *"shleimim"* are motivated by appreciation.

How do you respond when feeling gratitude for good fortune, good health, and other blessings? Do you seek out tangible ways to show express thanks?

6. Sacrifice to secure atonement and forgiveness from God is the topic of chapter 4: "When a person unwittingly incurs guilt in regard to any of the Lord's commandments about things not to be done, and does one of them ..." (4:2). These sacrifices offer expiation when offenses are accidental. No ritual atones for intentional criminal behavior. Sacrifice was not a "get out of jail free" card.

7. In 5:5, the text instructs that when people realize their guilt, they "shall confess having sinned." The Hebrew word for "confess" occurs here in the reflexive form, suggesting that offenders admit to themselves that they have done wrong.

There are many reasons why we are reluctant to admit mistakes: It is tempting to find ways to justify our behavior and hold others to a higher standard. It's easy to ignore our complicity in our own dramas and in society's problems. Some feel that they lose face if they admit error, or that admitting mistakes is equivalent to capitulation. Others feel like their judgment in future situations will be called into question if they acknowledge error even once. Admitting error may feel like admission of having unworthy character.

THINK ABOUT

1. One way to understand biblical sacrifice is to see it as a way to rebalance and renew. Rabbi Janet Marder explains: "If we closely read the seemingly dry instructions and bloody details of *parashat Vayikra*, we learn that through the discipline of our faith, we can redeem what is broken and flawed within ourselves, transforming barbaric urges into opportunities for blessing."[89]

---

89 *The Torah: A Women's Commentary,* Tamara Cohn Eskenazi and Andrea L. Weiss, eds., New York, NY: URJ Press, 2008, p. 590.

2. Is it a primal human inclination to want to sacrifice? Rabbi Amy Scheinerman suggests that when we sacrifice something of value, "... we bind ourselves to the one who receives our sacrifice."[90]

What have been the major sacrifices in your life? Have outcomes in your life been worth the sacrifices made?

3. Judaism teaches people to take responsibility for their actions. In rejecting idolatry, the Israelite religion rejected the notion that we can sway capricious gods to do our bidding. This *parsha* repeats the phrase, "When you present an offering ..." The full weight of responsibility is on the individual who does wrong. The priest simply officiates, serving in a mechanical role. He doesn't stand in for the penitent. This is similar to a couple getting married. People say the official "marries" them, but the couple marries each other.

4. Some scholars have concluded that the *olah* (1:1-17), *chatat* (4:1-5:13), and *asham* (5:14-26) sacrifices were offerings to reduce guilty feelings. Nowadays, what have we substituted for sacrifice? Does *Yom Kippur* provide an effective means to reduce guilty feelings?

5. In 2:11 we read, "No meal offering ... shall be made with leaven, no leaven ..." You may recognize the Hebrew word for leaven, "*chametz*" from Passover grain restrictions. Why is there a restriction on *chametz* here? *Chametz* describes something fermented, decayed, or corrupted, something that "puffs up." Metaphorically, *chametz* refers to arrogance. We aim to distance ourselves from self-importance and pride during Passover, and to avoid those tendencies when reaching out to God.

FOCUS PHRASE (2:8)

V'hik'ri'vah—Bring it close.

---

90 *Voices of Torah: A Treasury of Rabbinic Gleanings on the Weekly Portions, Holidays and Special Shabbatot*, Hara E. Person, ed. New York, NY: CCAR Press, 2012, p. 277.

Tzav (Leviticus 6:1-8:36) "Open Hands"

OVERVIEW

Details of the sacrifices are further explicated here. Since the destruction of the Jerusalem Temple, almost 2,000 years ago, there have been no animal or other sacrifices, and therefore no apparent reason to study the laws governing sacrificial rituals. Scholars and teachers, in a desire to keep these instructions relevant, have creatively reinterpreted aspects of the sacrificial cult to provide ethical guidance. At the end of the portion, Moses ordains Aaron and his sons as priests.

STANDOUT PHRASES

6:1 "Command." A central concept throughout the Torah, God's authority is asserted through ritual and ethical commandments. For Jews whose lives are defined by Jewish law and tradition, a *mitzvah*, (meaning commandment) is binding and non-negotiable.

I understand *mitzvah*, which shares root letters with the word "*tsav*," as an act that builds or enhances my relationship to God, to a person, or to an experience. The word "*mitzvah*" is related to the Aramaic word meaning "connection." Aramaic is a cognate (related, connected) language to Hebrew. By performing a *mitzvah*, I am *connecting* to God, to a person, or to an experience.

7:26 "And you must not consume any blood." The Torah explains that the life of a living being, human or animal, is in its blood.

7:30 "One's own hands shall present ..." The donor/penitent participates in presenting the offering; the donor is not a bystander.

7:33 "... for seven days ..." The number "seven" recurs throughout the Torah. The seven-day week is part of the creation story and the seventh day is hallowed as Shabbat (Genesis 1:1-2:3). Leviticus 23:1-44 mandates seven festivals. Two of the festivals last seven days, and three of the festivals take place in the seventh month. What other Jewish customs are built around the number seven?

TALK ABOUT

1. In his Torah Commentary, distinguished Rabbi Harvey J. Fields poignantly observes, "... the duties of the priests are very ordinary and menial ... could it be that the most important religious deeds are found in the most ordinary and even menial tasks?"[91]

2. "YHVH spoke to Moses, saying: 'Take Aaron along with his sons ...'" (8:1). Only male descendants of Aaron supervised and officiated at the designated sanctuary.

    Why were women disqualified from the Israelite priesthood?

    Contemporary rabbis serve very different purposes from biblical priests, but until the late decades of the 20th century, women were not accepted in seminaries for ordination. How has the presence of women changed your perception of clergy? Has women's spiritual leadership impacted the atmosphere or focus of synagogues or churches you've attended or religious organizations you've supported? If your son or daughter expresses interest in religious/spiritual leadership, would you encourage them to pursue this path? Do you view the rabbinate, cantorate, chaplaincy, and ministry as professions or callings?

3. Aaron's and his sons' garments are described in this portion (6:3), and in greater detail in 8:7-9 and 8:13. Why do priests dress distinctively? In terms of clothing, no garb distinguishes a rabbi or cantor. Catholic priests and nuns often (not always) wear identifying collars or head coverings. Buddhist monks are also recognizable by their distinctively colored robes. Do you think it would be desirable to be able to identify Jewish clergy in public?

4. As part of the ordination ritual described in 8:22-23, Moses puts blood on Aaron's and his sons' right ear, right hand thumb, and right big toe. What do these body parts symbolize? Think of them as extremities, as the parts of the body that are closest to what is outside one's self.

5. Moses ordained Aaron and his sons as priests in a ceremony (8:22-30). What do you think constitutes a meaningful ordination ceremony?

---

91 *A Torah Commentary for Our Times: Volume Two*, New York, NY: UAHC Press, 1991, p. 109.

THINK ABOUT

1. In the first six Hebrew words of this portion (6:1), three verbs relate to speech: "spoke," "saying," and "command." The Torah uses words sparingly; why are three forms of speech employed here? What are the differences being "speaking," "saying," and "commanding?"

2. Regarding 6:2, Noach Dzmura has a fresh insight into the concept of "eternal." He thinks that "eternal" does not describe something "unchanging," but refers to an *endlessly renewable* relationship that "grows, changes, and appropriately adapts over time."[92]
    Do lasting relationships always require change and growth?

3. The thanksgiving offering is described in 7:12. The ancient Rabbis wrote that in the messianic era, of all the sacrifices, only the thanksgiving offering would remain. The Rabbis recognized the importance of gratitude. There is a rabbinic dictum that encourages (challenges?) us to offer one hundred blessings a day. Blessings express gratitude. Think of one hundred things for which you are grateful. When you sit with your (grand)children or students, help them reach one hundred in counting their blessings. Read my remarks on the name *"Yehudim,"* "those that are thankful," in *Vayeitzei,* "Talk About" #3.

4. There is very little narrative in Leviticus. One narrative includes the consecration of Aaron and his sons to the priesthood. Reading chapters 8-10, what stands out about the biblical consecration process? Can you imagine its power over the people who watched? What rituals have a powerful impact on you? What components of a *bris*, naming, *Bar/Bat Mitzvah*, wedding, and funeral touch you the most?

5. This portion is full of details. Did it really matter which parts of the sacrificial animals were offered and how they were eaten? Think of how you feel about a task you approach carefully, methodically, and what it feels like when you rush, just going through the motions.
    When I'm on the phone with someone and I'm doing something else simultaneously, I hear the distraction in my own voice. When I am on the receiving end of divided attention, I am annoyed. How do you feel when you have someone's undivided attention, and when you don't?

---

92 "Ner Tamid, dos Pintele Yid v'haZohar Muzar: The Eternal Flame, the Jewish Spark, and the Flaming Queer, Parashat Tsav" in *Torah Queeries: Weekly Commentaries on the Hebrew Bible,* Gregg Drinkwater, Joshua Lesser, David Shneer, eds., New York: New York University Press, 2009, p. 129.

6. *The Five Books of Miriam: A Woman's Commentary on the Torah* posits that the sacrificial system outlined in the Torah accomplished what psychotherapy aims to address today. Today when people feel guilt, shame, anxiety, and depression, many seek out trained healers "who for a sacrificial fee help us surrender these burdens."[93]

Do you recognize a kinship between sacrifice and psychotherapy?

FOCUS PHRASE (8:33)

Yim'ah'lei et yed'chem—Your hands will be lifted.

---

93 *The Five Books of Miriam: A Woman's Commentary on the Torah,* New York, NY: Putnam Books, 1996, p. 153.

Sh'mini (Leviticus 9:1-11:47) "Silence"

OVERVIEW

This portion includes the mysterious and shocking deaths of Aaron's two eldest sons, Nadav and Avihu. Their deaths have troubled many Torah commentators. Some have defended the young priests' deaths by suggesting they committed heinous sins and were appropriately punished.

Issues of ritual purity are center stage in this portion and the following two portions, *Tazria* and *Metzora*.

The book of Leviticus teaches us to sanctify what comes out of our mouths as well as what goes into them. *Kashrut* requires circumspection and discipline as does our use of language, especially vows and promises. What concerns you more—what you eat or how you speak?

STANDOUT PHRASES

9:1 "On the eighth day ..." In Judaism, the number eight represents a new beginning. The week is seven days long. On the eighth day, the cycle begins again. The primary Jewish association with eight is that a baby boy is circumcised on the eighth day. In this portion, Aaron and the priests begin their ritual duties on the eighth day.

10:3 "And Aaron was silent." Silence can be profoundly eloquent. Following the death of his sons, Aaron doesn't speak. Maybe he was in shock and his grief rendered him mute. The text doesn't explain Aaron's silence. But we all know the feeling of not finding adequate words to address a terrible loss.

10:10 "... for you must distinguish between the sacred and the profane ..." Separation and differentiation are prominent themes throughout Leviticus. These words form the core of the *Havdalah* ceremony. ("*Havdalah*" means "separation" and refers to the ceremony which separates Shabbat or holy days from the rest of the week.) What other separations do the *Havdalah* prayers highlight?

11:7 "... and the swine ... it is impure for you." Rabbi Israel Salantar (1810-1883), a leading figure of the *Mussar* movement is quoted as saying that all Jews are familiar with the Torah command not to eat pork, a prohibition appearing twice in the Torah. Far more frequent is the injunction to refrain from gossip and destructive speech, yet many do not recognize that this is a serious Torah violation.[94]

TALK ABOUT

1. Aaron's sons Nadav and Avihu are struck dead when they present "strange fire" to God (10:1-2). There is no explanation for this ultimate punishment. Some commentators suggest that the brothers were intoxicated, dressed unsuitably, or lacked decorum appropriate to their priestly roles. To me, the Torah text does not bear out these explanations. It is tempting to gloss over this section of Torah because of its harshness. Given the opportunity, would you omit this incident in public Torah readings?

2. Why does Moses speak to Aaron about God immediately following the death of Aaron's two sons (10:3)? Jewish tradition teaches that a visitor should not open the conversation with a mourner at a house of *shiva*. Rather than rush in with words of consolation, it is preferable to let the mourners speak first from their hearts. Do you find Moses' words consoling? Rather than platitudes, silence or an embrace might be most comforting at a time of loss.

3. Leviticus 11:2-23 delineates permitted and forbidden animals. Laws of *kashrut* offer a way to eat meat (which requires killing a living creature) while acknowledging that this is not the vegetarian diet God intended (Genesis 1:29).

Rabbi Arthur Green proposes vegetarianism as the fulfillment of *kashrut*:

> Cruelty to animals has long been forbidden by Jewish law
> and sensibilities. Our tradition tells us that we must shoo
> a mother bird away from the nest before we take her eggs
> so that she does not suffer as we break the bond between
> them. We are told that a mother and her calf may not be
> slaughtered on the same day. The very next step beyond
> these prohibitions is a commitment to a vegetarian way of
> living.

---

94 David L. Lieber, ed., *Etz Hayim: Torah and Commentary*, Philadelphia: The Jewish Publication Society, 2001 p. 638, n. 7.

We Jews in this century have been victims of destruction and mass slaughter on an unprecedented scale. We have seen every norm of humanity violated as we were treated like cattle rather than human beings. Our response to this memory is surely a complex and multitextured one. But as we overcome the understandable first reactions to the events, some of us feel our abhorrence of violence and bloodshed growing so strong that it reaches even beyond the borders of the human and into the animal kingdom.

If Jews have to be associated with killing at all in our time, let it be only for the defense of human life. Life has become too precious in this era for us to be involved in the shedding of blood, even that of animals, when we can survive without it. This is not an ascetic choice, we should note, but rather a life-affirming one. A vegetarian Judaism would be more whole it its ability to embrace the presence of God in all of Creation[95]

4. The dietary laws are not about hygiene or health. These laws reflect the Israelite preoccupation with separation and holiness. People who keep *kosher* make *kashrut*-based food decisions multiple times a day. Depending on their level of *kashrut* observance, they also make daily decisions about where to purchase food and where to eat it. Do you see benefits to keeping *kosher*?

5. The first list of permitted food sources concerns land animals (11:2-8) and then proceeds to water creatures (11:9-12). The next categories are flying and winged creatures (11:13-23).

A clear explanation for this complex system appears in *The JPS Torah Commentary* by Baruch Levine. He describes "a practical system of food selection ... permitted animals are herbivorous ruminants ..." and no creature of prey can be consumed.[96]

Read Levine's full analysis. What qualities do the dietary restrictions inculcate? Is this a new way for you to make sense of *kashrut*?

---

95 *This Sacred Earth: Religion, Nature, Environment*, Roger S. Gottlieb, ed., New York, NY: Routledge, 1996, pp. 301-02.

96 Baruch Levine, ed., *The JPS Torah Commentary: Leviticus*, Philadelphia: The Jewish Publication Society, 1989, pp. 247-248.

THINK ABOUT

1. The Hebrew word for a scribe is *"sofer."* *"Sofer"* refers to "someone who counts." To ensure nothing was left out, ancient *sofrim* (pl.) counted each word and letter of the Torah. About 2,000 years ago, the *sofrim* located the middle words of the Torah in Shemini. They are *"darosh, darash"* (10:16), meaning "inquires, asks." Is the heart of Torah Study "inquiring and asking"?

2. Regarding silence (10:3), Catholic theologian and humanitarian Henri J.M. Nouwen describes a caring friend as someone who can be silent with us in despair or confusion, grief and bereavement. Nouwen praises friends who can stand with us in the face of powerlessness, who can tolerate not knowing and not curing.[97]

Do you welcome silence or does it make you uncomfortable?

3. Some commentators suggest that because Nadav and Avihu had rarefied access to God's "space," they lost their sense of appropriate distance from God's holiness. They were (too) eager to experience spiritual ecstasy and, in their enthusiasm, they overstepped the bounds set by God.

Judaism does not promote the life of the spirit over physical (embodied) life. We are not encouraged to lose ourselves with God but to find ourselves with God through interactions in the world.

Do you see the real world and our daily lives as impediments to spiritual growth or as avenues to spiritual growth? Or both?

4. Moses is angry (10:16). Is his anger towards God who had killed Aaron's older sons? Is his anger meant for Nadav and Avihu because their cavalier actions led to their deaths? Or, is Moses indeed angry with Aaron's remaining sons, Eleazar and Ithamar, who did not follow the exact rules of sacrifice? Perhaps Moses is angry that the younger brothers appeared to have learned nothing from their older brothers' mistake.

Most of us have deflected anger by overreacting to a later event when we couldn't express frustration in an earlier situation. Maybe something we thought we could control went awry, and we felt responsible and lashed out.

Why do you think Moses was angry?

---

97 Henri J.M. Nouwen, *Out of Solitude: Three Meditations on the Christian Life*, Notre Dame, IN: Ave Maria Press, 1974.

5. This portion concludes with the admonition, "For I YHVH am the One who brought you up from the land of Egypt to be your God: you shall be holy, for I am holy" (11:45). Careful attention to food and other fundamental areas of life enable the Israelites to emulate God's holiness. To the Israelite mind, was any part of life secular? Do you think holiness can be an aspect of all parts of life?

Focus Phrase (10:10)

Ul'hav'deel bein ha'kodesh u'vein ha'chol—Distinguish between the sacred and the profane.

Tazria (Leviticus 12:1-13:59) "Contagion"

OVERVIEW

Tazria addresses purification for those afflicted with *tzara'at*. *Tzara'at* appears as a skin disease or scaly infection. Once translated as "leprosy," this biblical disease does not correspond to Hansen's disease (known as leprosy). *Tzara'at* in the Torah affects walls, furniture, and clothing, along with human bodies. No medical condition corresponding to *tzara'at* has ever been documented.

Rabbi Ruth Adar draws social comparisons to *tzara'at*: "Medicine addresses disease these days, but what if we used Torah's teaching to address modern plagues such as racism, sexism, enviousness, and unkindness?

"Perhaps a family member points out our unkind behavior or a friend identifies an opinion we have voiced as racist. Our first impulse ... may be denial. Torah offers us a different path: it directs us to go to a priest (in our day, a trusted counselor) and confess, 'My wife says I am unkind ... or, envious of accolades paid to others ... or ...' The priest-counselor would consider both evidence and context and explore with us whether things are other than they seem ... helping us change for the better.

"Beyond physical illnesses are moral plagues crying out for attention and progress. Perhaps the approach of *Tazria-M'tzora* can help us cure the plagues of the human spirit."[98]

STANDOUT PHRASES

12:2 "... impure ..." We think of "impurity," (in Hebrew, "*tamei*") as evidence of dirt, defilement, or sin. But in the Torah, impurity is not a matter of hygiene or morality. Impurity results from contact with death (a human corpse) or with loss of potential life (through menstruation or abnormal genital discharges).

13:3 "the priest shall examine ..." Throughout this section, the priest diagnoses *tzara'at*, even when it appears on garments. This shows that *tzara'at* is not a medical condition. The Israelite priest does not attend to medical concerns.

---

98 *CCAR News*, March 2020, "Voices of Torah", p. 4.

13:47 "... a cloth of wool or linen ..." These were common fabrics for garments in biblical times. The obscure prohibition against wearing wool and linen together, called *shatnez*, appears in Leviticus 19:19 and Deuteronomy 22:11.

13:59 "Such is the procedure ..." The Hebrew word translated as "procedure" is "Torah." We don't think of the Torah as a book of procedures, but the Torah does include standard ways to approach different situations. "Torah" means "Instruction" or "Guide." It shares root letters with the Hebrew words for "teacher" and "parent."

TALK ABOUT

1. What do you think about Rabbi Adar's interpretation of this portion?

2. Ritual impurity was a central feature of most, if not all, ancient religions. In contrast to neighboring ancient Near Eastern cultures, the Israelite system did not connect ritual impurity to sin or demons. Ritual impurity does not result from evil, but from contact with substances that render a person or place impure.

Rabbi Michael Hattin explains, "Significantly, the Torah is silent concerning the causes of *tzara'at* ..."[99]

"... There is, however, a single textual feature that unites all of the various forms of the disorder ... whosoever is stricken with tzara'at, be it person, garment or house, must be subjected to a period of isolation and confinement."[100]

"... when the ancients came to ponder these laws, they arrived at the inescapable conclusion that the condition of tzara'at ... is intrinsically connected to the spiritual state of the ailing victim's soul ... the Rabbis associated the ailment of tzara'at with the particular transgression of *lashon hara* or disparaging speech ..."[101]

3. One association of *tzara'at* with disparaging speech emerges from the episode of Miriam and Aaron discussing Moses (Numbers 12:1-15). Does that section give credence to the idea that *tzara'at* is connected to abuse of language?

---

99 *Passages: Text and Transformation in the Parasha*, Jerusalem, Israel: Urim Publications, 2012, p. 201.

100 Ibid., p. 202.

101 Ibid., p. 203.

4. Why do you think that Miriam, but not Aaron, was punished with *tzara'at*?

5. I am writing this book in 2020–2021, while COVID-19 rages through our communities, our country, and the world. The word "quarantine" has become very familiar. Separation from family, friends, and normal social discourse has afflicted everyone.

When you returned to an in-person social life, did you have a new sense of gratitude for your relationships? Were there aspects of quarantining that you enjoyed more than you expected?

THINK ABOUT

1. *Tazria* opens with a discussion of a mother's ritual impurity following childbirth. Ritual impurity does not result from sin, but from unsuitability to engage in certain activities. For most women, giving birth is awesome, but it may also be traumatic. Although some women reject the language of 12:1-5, many women can appreciate the value of sanctioned absence following childbirth. This time can provide healing of body, mind, and spirit.

2. Why are forty days required for a woman's purification after giving birth to a son? Reconstructionist Rabbi Jonathan Kligler suggests one possible explanation:

"A due date was and still is calculated as forty weeks from the first day of a woman's last menstrual period ... forty represents a time of conception, gestation, and maturation until a new being is ready to be born ...

"No wonder the Children of Israel must wander for forty years before they can pass through the Jordan River (birth canal?) into the Promised Land ...This would explain why a new mother is restricted (or perhaps protected) for forty days after the birth of a son: one day for each week of pregnancy, a symbolic correlation during which she becomes reintegrated into the life of the community."[102]

3. Even if Rabbi Kliger's explanation seems plausible, why is there a forty-day separation for a son, and an eighty-day separation for a daughter? Some explain this by noting that a daughter will someday menstruate and this justifies the doubling of separation time. This

---

102 *Turn It and Turn It For Everything is in It: Essays on the Weekly Torah Portion*, Eugene, OR: Wipf and Stock Publishers, 2020, pp. 109-110.

reasoning does not satisfy me. Can you think of other reasons why ritual impurity time is doubled when a daughter is born?

4. A woman who gives birth brings an offering after her period of purification (12:6). Rabbi Helaine Ettinger explains, "... the sin offering served as a vehicle for returning someone in a contaminated state to a pure state; it was not an indictment of that person. The required offerings provided a means of transition from the exceptional experience of giving life back to the everyday experience of living."[103]

5. Mayyim Hayyim ("Living Waters," the waters of creation in Genesis 1:9-10) is the flagship 21st century pluralistic *mikveh* in Newton, MA, where nearly 25,000 men, women, and children have immersed for celebrations, transitions, and healing. Reasons for immersions include engagement, marriage, divorce, menstruation, menopause, conversion, moving, gender transition, coming out, leaving home, starting or ending a medical treatment, or completing a project.

Look at the Mayyim Hayyim website (www.mayyimhayyim.org). Since Mayyim Hayyim's opening in 2004, more pluralistic *mikvaot* (plural of "*mikveh*") have been established. Mayyim Hayyim also has outstanding educational materials on *mikveh* and related topics.

FOCUS PHRASE (13:3)

Amok—Deeper.

103 *The Women's Torah Commentary: New Insights from Women Rabbis on the 54 Weekly Torah Portions*, Rabbi Elyse Goldstein, ed., Woodstock, VT: Jewish Lights Publishing, 2000, pp. 208-9.

M'tzora (Leviticus 14:1-15:33) "Speech"

OVERVIEW

Genesis is full of great stories and interesting characters. Exodus has unparalleled drama and aspirational laws. Many sections of Leviticus, and *M'tzora* in particular is full of ... blood! Recurring themes of Leviticus (and *M'tzora*) are separating the pure from the impure, and the permitted from the prohibited. This portion, like the two preceding *parshiyot*, focuses on bodies: what goes in, what comes out, what contaminates, and what purifies.

STANDOUT PHRASES

14:14 "... put it on the ridge of the right ear of the one who is being purified, and on the thumb of the right hand, and on the big toe of the right foot." This is also the procedure for the priests' ordination (8:22-23). This similarity is another reminder that the Israelites as a whole are a "priestly people."

14:21 "If, however, one is poor and without sufficient means ..." In 5:7, 5:11, 12:8, and 14:30-31, people with lesser means also have the opportunity to make offerings in a dignified manner.

14:34 "... an eruptive plague upon a house ..." Venerated Torah scholar Nehama Leibowitz explains how the early treatment of a plague teaches about noticing early incidents of misconduct in our communities and society as a whole. She notes that a disease with early symptoms can be stopped if detected quickly. Similarly, a moral disease can be prevented from spreading if effective steps to contain it are taken swiftly.[104]

15:31 "You shall put the Israelites on guard against their impurity ..." This section concludes with a summarizing admonition to protect the sanctity of the people and the Tabernacle. The priests carry out sacrificial offerings and rites of purification, and the people monitor their bodies, homes, and interactions.

---

104 *Studies in Vayikra*, Jerusalem: The World Zionist Organization, 1980, pp. 137-138.

TALK ABOUT

1. Author George Robinson views the purpose of the topics covered in *M'tzora* and in the prior two *parashiyot* as an attempt to confront "the often messy necessities of our biological nature."[105]

Do you think that one of the purposes of *mitzvot* is to impose some order on the messiness (chaos) of our lives? Can all aspects of life be imbued with spiritual meaning?

2. Water is splashed all over this portion: 14:5, 9, 47, 50, and 15:5-13. Water is essential for hygiene, and it also symbolizes birth and rebirth. Immersion in the *mikveh* mimics birth. Commentators point out that the Israelites were born as a nation when they came through the Sea of Reeds (Exodus 14:21-22). What other stories and customs in Jewish life draw heavily on water? There are many water references in the next book of the Torah, Numbers/*B'midbar*.

3. Rabbi Eryn London thinks about this portion in terms of lonely people: "It is very easy for us to be in our spaces that make us feel comfortable ... But we have to push ourselves to leave our comfort zones, to even peek outside our encampments ... It is in these laws of the *metzorah*, I believe, that we can learn that it is up to us to seek out those who feel alone or isolated and offer them comfort and community ... to 'go out of the camp,' to pick up a phone or send out an email so someone that is outside our camp will have a way in."[106]

THINK ABOUT

1. *M'tzora* contains elaborate details for purification following diagnosis of *tzara'at*. Underlying this is recognition that both the afflicted person and the community need reassurance that they can safely interact again. We send messages of support to ill friends, but often avoid in-person encounters with ailing friends even when contagion is not an issue. It can be embarrassing to see (or be seen by) loved ones in weakened, vulnerable states. To be given a clean bill of (spiritual) health by the priest and to make an offering of gratitude might serve to ease people into normal relations following illness or alienation.

105 *Essential Torah: A Complete Guide to the Five Books of Moses,* New York: Schocken Books, 2006, pp. 461-467.

106 "Isolated But Not Forgotten," Tazria-Metzora 2020/5780, yeshivatmaharat.org/divrei-torah

2. Leviticus 15:19-24 is a biblical text that influenced Jewish attitudes towards menstruation. "The original meaning of the key term for menstruation in the Bible, *niddah*, is unclear, but several Hebrew roots with the letter combination *n-d* have the general sense of "expel" or "throw." It is possible that the word was used for the expulsion or elimination of the menstrual blood (see also 12:2). In Leviticus 15, the term is neutral and without any stigma."[107]

3. The rabbis played with the text by altering the word *"m'tzora"* to *"motzi ra,"* referring to someone who lies or gossips. We have all been on the giving and receiving end of poisonous language. Recognizing that lies and gossip contaminate relationships do you understand how the condition came to be interpreted as abuse of language? How are lying and gossip "cured"?

The largest category of sins in the Yom Kippur list concerns speech—gossip, flattery, exaggeration, arguing, slander, shaming, etc. Which of these is most challenging to you? Some are accustomed to fasting from food on *Yom Kippur*. Try a fast from talking about other people. It's not so easy!

FOCUS PHRASE (14:3)

V'ra'ah ... v'hinei—Look and behold.

---

107 *The Torah: A Women's Commentary,* Tamara Cohn Eskenazi and Andrea L. Weiss, eds., New York: URJ Press, 2008, p. 668, n.15:19-24.

Acharei Mot (Leviticus 16:1-18:30) "Boundaries"

OVERVIEW

This portion describes the *Yom Kippur* duties of the High Priest and the scapegoat ceremony. Moses teaches the atonement laws to Aaron. The text moves from matters of ritual purity to the "Holiness Code" (chapters 17-26). This Code includes laws promoting respectful relationships among the people and between the people and God. The text enumerates forbidden sexual relationships.

STANDOUT PHRASES

16:16 "Thus he shall purge the Shrine of the impurity and transgression of the Israelites, whatever their sins ..." People move in and out of pure and impure states, and priests mediate between these states. Sin is not the cause of impurity.

16:29-31 "In the seventh month, on the tenth day of the month, you shall practice self-denial ... you shall practice self-denial; it is a law for all time." This references *Yom Kippur*.

17:11, 17:14 "For the life of the flesh is in the blood." "For the life of all flesh—its blood is its life." "The ancients were just as much aware as we are that blood is indispensable for physical life. They thought of blood as a powerful and dangerous agent, endowed with uncanny, supernatural potencies. Many peoples have had taboos against seeing and touching blood, as well as against shedding or consuming it. Yet the biblical laws on the subject have no real parallel in the records of the ancient Near East ... Nor is there any known rule that resembles the rigorous and consistent prohibition of tasting blood ..."[108]

18:22 "Do not lie with a male as one lies with a woman; it is an abhorrence." *The Torah: A Women's Commentary* offers this corrective: "In the early 21st century, this is one of the most misinterpreted, abused, and decontextualized verses in the Torah. This verse, ripped from its place in the system of levitical laws, is often mobilized to justify

---

108 W. Gunther Plaut, *The Torah: A Modern Commentary*, Revised Edition. New York: Union of Reform Judaism, 2005, p. 785.

discriminatory legislation and behavior against homosexuals and their families."

"In Leviticus, the priestly writers want to prevent the mixture of different types of fluid, as well as uphold distinctions. In terms of blending fluids, anal intercourse is problematic for the same reason as is intercourse with a menstruating woman: semen, an agent of life, potentially mixes with feces, a substance that symbolizes decay and death ... In addition, the priestly writers want to avoid the blending of gender categories, as evident in their choice of language. They do not command, "do not lie with a male," but rather "do not lie with a male as one lies with a woman."[109]

TALK ABOUT

1. In many synagogues, the *Yom Kippur* morning Torah reading is Leviticus 16, which establishes an annual day of atonement and the scapegoat ritual. However, some congregations elect to read from *Nitzavim* (Deuteronomy 29:9-14 and 30:11-20) on *Yom Kippur* morning.

How are these portions different? The long-established Torah reading for *Yom Kippur* afternoon is Leviticus 18:1-30. Some communities substitute Leviticus 19:1-4, 9-18, and 32-37. Do you support these changes?

2. Leviticus 16:7-10 describes the strange ceremony of the scapegoat. Aaron takes two goats into the wilderness. One goat is set free; the other goat is sacrificed. Some commentators suggest that this drama served to urge people to distance themselves from their sins—to send their sins "into the wilderness" on this spiritually charged day.

Rabbi Harvey J. Fields wonders if the ceremony of the two he-goats was conceived as a magical way of ridding the people of Israel of its sins. Was the scapegoat sent into the wilderness as a sacrifice? On *Yom Kippur*, does the scapegoat ceremony provide a symbolic release of our spiritual and ethical failings?[110]

3. The text says to "afflict ourselves" on *Yom Kippur* (16:29). This is understood as prohibiting eating and drinking, major body washing or

109 Rachel Havrelock in *The Torah: A Women's Commentary*, Tamara Cohn Eskenazi, Andrea L. Weiss, eds., New York: URJ Press, 2008, p. 692.
110 *A Torah Commentary for Our Times, Volume Two: Exodus and Leviticus*, New York, NY: UAHC Press, 1991, p. 131.

anointing, wearing leather (i.e. comfortable) shoes, and sexual relations. In the 21st century, are these meaningful restrictions?

4. *The Torah: A Women's Commentary* critiques 18:22 (above, in "Standout Phrases"), a verse that has served as justification for homophobia. Does this help you respond to those who cite 18:22 to justify intolerance of homosexuality?

Think About

1. Rabbi Steven Carr Reuben discusses *Aharei Mot* through the lens of his teacher, Rabbi Mordecai Kaplan. Kaplan recognized that when we wrong another human being, our natural reaction is to blame the other, to scapegoat them. This allows us to avoid accepting full responsibility for our actions. Unexpectedly, in many cases when we forgive someone, we are the ones who benefit the most. Kaplan taught that reconciliation is a powerful gift and a "sign of spiritual elevation."[III]

What have been your experiences with forgiveness, as the one who forgave and as the one who was forgiven? Which provided you with greater relief?

2. This portion begins (16:1) by recollecting the deaths of Aaron's sons (Leviticus 10:1-2). Why is this event mentioned now? This portion describes *Yom Kippur* as a time of complete rest. To this today, *Yom Kippur* stands out in the Jewish calendar as a time of reflection, a day dedicated to self-reckoning. Tragic losses, often incomprehensible and cruel, may particularly come to mind during the quiet soul-searching hours of the day.

Additionally, we recognize that memories of deceased loved ones sometimes appear without warning, leaving feelings of emptiness, longing, and perhaps guilt. The recollection of the priests' deaths appear unexpectedly early in chapter 16, reflecting the convergence of memory, loss and guilt at significant times.

3. You may recognize the word "*kipare*" (16:6) from the Day of Atonement, "*Yom Kippur*." Atonement is the process by which someone feeling distant returns. Atonement is the opposite of estrangement. Think of "atonement" as "at-one-ment." Is becoming more "at one" the purpose of *Yom Kippur*? "At one" with whom or what?

III *A Year with Mordecai Kaplan: Wisdom on the Weekly Torah Portion*, Philadelphia: The Jewish Publication Society, 2019, p. 115.

4. "You shall keep My laws and My rules, by the pursuit of which human beings shall live" (18:5). The promised reward for following the commandments is a long and fruitful life. What do you think contributes to a long and peaceful life? Does religion play a part?

Because of 18:5 (and similar verses elsewhere in the Torah), the ancient Rabbis decreed that, in order to save a life, any commandment of the Torah should be overridden with three exceptions: murder, idolatry, and sexual crime. Why were they selected? Are these three acts related?

FOCUS PHRASE (17:2)

Zeh ha'd'var—This is the word.

K'doshim (Leviticus 19:1-20:27) "Wholly Holy"

Overview

Judaism's basic goal is to show each person how to live so as to make his/her life holy. Relating to God and to other people are both arenas for cultivating a holy life. *K'doshim* emphasizes relations between people. The word *"kadosh"* (or its variants) appears in the book of Leviticus over 150 times!

The commandments in this portion do not appear to be ordered by importance or by any classification. This is an example of Deuteronomy 1:17, "As with the small, so with the large."

Standout Phrases

19:2 "You shall be holy." Under this heading, the Torah prohibits witchcraft, superstition, and related activities practiced by surrounding nations. A list of intermingled religious and ethical laws follow. These laws are practical, not esoteric. One way the people are instructed to distinguish themselves is by virtue of ... virtue!

19:3 "You shall each revere your mother and your father." This instruction is for adults, not children. When we mature, the obligation to show respect to parents remains. As parents age, the obligation intensifies.

19:9-10 "When you reap the harvest of your land, you shall not reap all the way to the edges of your field, or gather the gleanings of your harvest. You shall not pick your vineyard bare, or gather the fallen fruit of your vineyard; you shall leave them for the poor and the stranger."

This practice allowed indigents to enter the fields after harvesting was complete, and procure enough foodstuff to sustain themselves.[112]

19:18 "Love your fellow as yourself." Can love be commanded? German Jewish theologians Hermann Cohen and Martin Buber explain this passage as, "Be loving to your 'fellow man,' as to one who is just like you."[113]

---

112 *The Hebrew Bible, Vol. 1, The Five Books of Moses, A Translation with Commentary*, New York, NY: W.W. Norton & Company, 2019, p. 431, n. 9.

113 *The Torah: A Modern Commentary*, W. Gunther Plaut, ed., Revised Edition, David E.S. Stein, ed., New York: Union of Reform Judaism, 2005, p. 810.

German Jewish philosopher Franz Rosenzweig wrote about 19:18, "He is like you! 'Like you,' and thus not 'you.' You remain You ... But he is not to remain ... a mere It for your You. Rather, he is like You, ... a soul."[114]

TALK ABOUT

1. The "Holiness Code" includes laws given at Sinai: observing Shabbat, not worshipping idols, not swearing falsely, and not robbing. But laws are added: leaving parts of the field and vineyard for the poor, not spreading rumors, not delaying workers' wages, and not profiting from another's disadvantage.

Compare the Ten Commandments as a whole (Exodus 20:2-14) with chapter 19 of the Holiness Code, and discuss which laws on each list you would include in your Top Ten.

2. Why does the Torah link Shabbat observance and reverence for parents in 19:3?

3. In 19:13, three actions are grouped: defrauding someone, committing robbery, and withholding a laborer's wages until the next day. Do these sins/crimes seem comparable to you?

4. Chapter 19 intermingles ethical injunctions with ritual commandments. In the Torah's view, ethical and ritual laws have equal authority.

Do you value ritual commandments differently from ethical commandments? Do you have a favorite Jewish ritual? Is there a Torah-based ethical commandment that you find particularly inspiring?

5. Esteemed Rabbi Joseph Telushkin approaches the message of *K'doshim* in terms of the meaning of success. He invites us to ask this question to determine whether or not we are leading morally successful lives: "Are we growing in honesty, kindness, and compassion?" If we do not grow in these ways over time, we have "lived a failed life."[115]

Have you ever thought about what a morally successful life means? Would you add anything to Telushkin's definition?

6. In 19:19, three kinds of mixings are banned: hybrid animals, mixtures of seeds, and wool and linen in clothing (wool is from an animal and linen is from a plant).

---

114 Ibid., p. 813.

115 *A Code of Jewish Ethics: You Shall Be Holy, Vol. 1*, New York: Bell Tower, 2006, p. 37.

The well-being of animals might make the first prohibition plausible. But this justification would not apply to seeds or fabrics. The prohibition against all the mixtures reflects the Torah's commitment to keeping sharp, distinct categories.

The importance of separation is a recurring theme in Leviticus. Is this idea starting to feel more familiar?

THINK ABOUT

1. Dr. Wendy Mogel looks at 19:14 ("You shall not ... place a stumbling block before the blind,") as providing guidance for parents. She recommends noticing specific times of the day when a child has difficulty. By continuing to expect that child to respond in a specific way at times that have proved to be challenging, it may be that you (parent, caregiver, or teacher) are inadvertently "placing a stumbling block" before them. Mogel suggests restructuring situations that repeatedly cause frustration so that the child will have a greater opportunity to succeed.[116]

What are other ways to understand "not placing a stumbling block"?

2. The Holiness Code directs us not to hate, take vengeance, or bear a grudge (19:17-18). The Torah rarely tells us how to feel. Can emotions be prohibited? Why are hatred and resentment singled out as emotions to keep restrained?

3. "You shall not round off the side-growth on your head, or destroy the side-growth of your beard." The Hebrew word for "side-growth" is "*pei-ah*," the word used in 19:9 for "the edges of your field." This word connects the commandment to leave food for the hungry with the commandment to let hair grow on the sides of the head. "*Pei-ah*" is the singular form of "*pei-ot*" (sometimes pronounced *pei-is*), the long side curls worn by some Torah-observant men.

4. 19:28 says, "You shall not ... incise any marks on yourselves." This refers to tattoos. Currently, tattoos are popular. Would you mention this Torah prohibition to a friend or family member interested in getting a tattoo?

---

116 *The Blessing of a Skinned Knee*, New York, NY: Penguin Compass, 2001, p. 195.

5.   In contrast to fashion, character traits like honesty are timeless. 19:35 commands honesty (in the Hebrew text, "*tzedek*") in commerce. Did you expect the Torah to address business practices?

FOCUS PHRASE (20:7)

V'hit'kadeesh'tem—Make yourselves holy.

Emor (Leviticus 21:1-24:23) "Gatherings"

OVERVIEW

This portion begins with laws regulating the lives of priests who maintain purity in the sanctuary and among the people. *Emor* also summarizes the key Israelite festivals, many of which we recognize from our own observances today.

Chapter 24:17-22 decrees equal penalties for citizen and stranger for murder, destruction, and killing animals. This section insures a relational response to serious crime. "Lex taliones" is sometimes misunderstood as promoting physical retaliation. Almost without exception, commentators understand these verses as identifying financial payment as compensation.

STANDOUT PHRASES

22:32 "You shall not profane My holy name." Called *"chillul haShem,"* "desecration of God's holy Name," is not specifically named as one of the 613 commandments, but it is a significant Jewish value not to speak or act in any way that brings dishonor to God or the Jewish people.

23:4 "These are the set times of YHVH, which you shall celebrate each at its appointed time." Chapters 21-22 deal with sacred space; chapter 23 addresses sacred time.

23:15-16 "And from the day on which you bring the sheaf of elevation offering—the day after the Sabbath—you shall count off seven weeks ... you must count until the day after the seventh week—fifty days." This refers to the practice of "Counting the Omer." From the second night of Passover until Shavuot, we "count" each day, connecting the Festival of Freedom to its underlying purpose: to live a life of responsibility as set forth by Torah teachings pronounced at Mt. Sinai (and celebrated on the holiday of *Shavuot*).

23:22 "And when you reap the harvest of your land, you shall not reap all the way to the edges of your field, or gather the gleanings of your harvest; you shall leave them for the poor and the stranger: I am YHVH your God." Providing for marginalized people is not optional; it is an obligation to remember the poor and the outsider.

TALK ABOUT

1. Leviticus 21:16-23 stipulates that priests with physical impairments may not make offerings. They remain priests, but they may not oversee sacrifices. This is a discriminatory text. Today we are hard-pressed to justify this text, but why do you think this regulation was instituted?

2. Rabbi Abraham Joshua Heschel characterizes Judaism as a "religion of time." He notes that the Bible senses the diversified character of time. Heschel points that to the "space-oriented" person, time is unvaried. To the time-oriented person, time has meaning and purpose.[117]

How do the festivals listed in 23:1-43 (*Shabbat, Rosh HaShanah, Yom Kippur, Pesach, Shavuot,* and *Sukkot*) make us sensitive to and appreciative of time?

3. Harvey Cox comments that in an interfaith marriage, the first thing a Christian spouse notices about Judaism is that "it is about calendar." Cox observes that holy days and sacred seasons, more so than creed and catechism, is what gives significance to those who strongly identify with Judaism.[118]

Do you agree?

4. In 23:6, the Israelites eat *matzah* ("unleavened bread") in commemoration of the flat bread—bread without ample time to rise—that our ancestors ate when leaving Egypt. To think about *matzah* in spiritual terms is to concentrate on its plainness and lack of flavor. *Matzah* symbolizes humility.

"You are what you eat." Does eating *matzah*, or anything else about the Passover week, make you feel humble and unpretentious? Does understanding *matzah* in this spiritualized way affect how you feel about eating it?

5. "If anyone kills any human being, that person shall be put to death" (24:17). Capital punishment is sanctioned for intentional homicide. Unlike other crimes, loss of human life cannot be compensated through money.

Today, Jewish opinions vary on the complex issue of capital punishment.

117 *The Sabbath: Its Meaning for Modern Man,* New York: Farrar, Straus and Giroux, 1951, p. 8.

118 Harvey Cox. *Common Prayers: Faith, Family and a Christian's Journey Through the Jewish Year,* New York, NY: Houghton Mifflin Books, 2001, p. 7.

THINK ABOUT

1. The Torah's first reference to divorce is in 21:7. Regarding priests, "... nor shall they marry one divorced from her husband." The following verse explains that a divorced woman doesn't meet the holiness standard required to marry a priest. To many of us, this reads like a discriminatory text.

Divorce is acceptable in Jewish law, and a document, called a "*get*," "sanctifies" the divorce just as the *ketubah* (marriage contract) sanctifies the marriage. Look at how divorce is portrayed in Deuteronomy 24:1. Can divorce proceedings be "sanctified"?

Divorce is not a sin; it is a tragedy for everyone involved.

2. Many celebrate Shabbat by adding specific food or blessings to Friday night or Saturday meals. But another way to honor Shabbat is to abstain from daily tasks that are tedious or stultifying, and to engage in activities that refresh the soul. What are those activities for you?

3. In describing the celebration of Sukkot, the text says, "... and you shall rejoice ..." (23:40). Can rejoicing be commanded? The Hebrew word is "*semachtem*," which you may recognize from its variation, "*simcha*." Read my comments on "*simcha*" in the discussion of the *parashat Ki Tavo*, "Talk About" #1.

4. Rabbi Mark Katz writes about "*Sh'vil HaZahav*—Moderation: Affliction, Elevation and Celebration" in the context of *Emor*. He says, "Judaism lives on a continuum between hedonism and asceticism, and it fears both. This tension between self-indulgence and self-denial is seen, perhaps in its most salient form, in the way that we are commanded to celebrate our holidays."[119]

Rabbi Katz explains that Judaism's goal is for us to follow a "middle path," writing, "Both Yom Kippur and Sukkot are powerful lessons on the subject of the *sh'vil hazahav*, the golden path of moderation ... If we mark our holy days properly, our Jewish festival calendar grounds us, guiding us toward restraint and allowing us to control our impulses, rather than letting them rule us."[120]

119 Block, Rabbi Barry H., ed., *The Mussar Torah Commentary: A Spiritual Path to Living a Meaningful and Ethical Life,* New York, NY: Central Conference of American Rabbis, 2020, p. 193.

120 Ibid., p. 194.

FOCUS PHRASE (23:37)

D'var yom b'yomo—Each day for itself.

B'har (Leviticus 25:1-26:2) "Ethical R and R"

OVERVIEW

B'har explains the laws regulating the sabbatical and jubilee year. For six years, the people work their land, but the land rests during the seventh year; the land is treated to a sabbatical. Every fiftieth year is a jubilee year in which farmers don't cultivate their land and vineyards. Any Israelite enslaved during the prior forty-nine years is granted freedom. Properties return to the families who inherited them when the Israelites entered the Promised Land. Sound like a utopian vision? It is!

STANDOUT PHRASES

25:2 "The land shall observe a Sabbath ..." After six years of being worked, the land lies fallow. The ancients may have recognized that crops grew more vigorously following a year of resting. But there is an ethical component to this law as well: During the sabbatical year, landowners eat in the field alongside slaves, laborers, and sojourners— all sharing an equal claim to the land's ownerless produce.

25:8 "You shall count off seven weeks ..." The number seven repeatedly recurs in in Torah narratives and practices. It determines the weekly cycle, culminating in Shabbat, a day set apart to elevate humanity and honor God. The number seven also determines the cycle in which the land lies fallow in the seventh year. In *B'har*, the number seven draws our attention to the events that separated the departure from Egypt and the arrival at Sinai to receive the Torah. By "counting the *Omer*," for seven times seven weeks (49 days), increasing the number each day, we experience ourselves moving closer to spiritual fulfillment.

25:10 "You shall proclaim release throughout the land." This phrase from Leviticus is inscribed on the Liberty Bell in Philadelphia.

26:1 "You shall not make idols for yourselves ..." Why is the Torah obsessed with idols? An idol is a thing; it is static. God, in contrast, is living and dynamic.

TALK ABOUT

1. Rabbi Kenneth J. Weiss asks an excellent question, "Wouldn't *B'har*—"On the Mountain"—have been a more apt name for the *sidrah* in Exodus when God transmitted the Ten Commandments on Mount Sinai?"

He answers, "Perhaps not ... I suggest that this *parashah* called *B'har* comes here and now precisely to make a point: that the revelation on Sinai—far from being a single episode or experience—is perpetual and ever renewable."[121]

2. What ethical lessons can be drawn from the Torah's description of the sabbatical and jubilee years? Think in environmental, social, and economic terms. Scholars disagree whether or not the jubilee was actually implemented, but we can appreciate its vision: rich and poor living with greater equality, and freedom for slaves.

3. The Torah posits that the land of Canaan (Israel) belongs exclusively to God: "But the land must not be sold beyond reclaim, for the land is Mine" (25:23). Psalm 24:1 echoes this: "The earth is the Lord's and all that it holds."

Do people treat land differently if they believe they own it rather than lease it? On the one hand, people take extra care with things they own. On the other hand, if something is perpetually on loan for future generations, it may be treated as a precious inheritance.

What do you think?

THINK ABOUT

1. "The Torah highlights the need for regular breaks ... For instance, a day of rest and reflection and renewal is prescribed for us each week. This week's Torah portion presents a yearlong break!" (Leviticus 25:2-6)

"Think what the effects might be of this sabbatical practice; how important—and challenging—it would be in the lives of the ancient Israelite community! In the Torah, workers get breaks, new mothers get breaks, people who have come in contact with the dead get breaks—even the land itself, and livestock, require their "down time." And this

---

121 B'har/Bchukotai, 2005, in *Voices of Torah: A Treasury of Rabbinic Gleanings on the Weekly Portions, Holidays and Special Shabbatot*, Hara E. Person, ed., New York: Central Conference of American Rabbis, 2012, p. 349.

time off—whether connected to an illness or a festival, the seasonal agricultural cycle or the weekly Shabbat—is not seen as a drag on productivity, but rather as an integral and sacred part of the eternal fabric of life."[122]

Do you take a break when you need one? Many think of breaks in terms of vacations from work. Academics take intellectual breaks and clergy take spiritual breaks. What kind of break would you welcome in your life now?

2. What is the custom of counting of the *Omer*? The Torah records the agricultural completion of the grain harvest begun at *Pesach* with the bringing of the *Omer* as an offering. After the destruction of the Jerusalem Temple when offerings were no longer required, a historical connection was formulated between the journey begun in the Exodus and the journey's apex realized in the arrival at Mount Sinai at *Shavuot*. Jews began counting the days between Passover and Shavuot to display their enthusiasm for receiving the Torah.

We are accustomed to counting "down" towards an event. What is the significance of counting "up" from one to forty-nine as we get farther from slavery and confusion and closer to responsibility and maturity?

3. For forty-nine consecutive evenings, the day is "counted" with a blessing. In and of itself, this counting may not be spiritually edifying but undertaken as a *mitzvah* with inspiring readings and intentional behavior, it can be a beautiful practice to eagerly return to each spring. (See *Omer: A Counting* by Rabbi Karyn D. Kedar, and additional resources in the Bibliography and online.)

4. The phrase, "you shall not wrong one another" appears in 25:14 and 25:17. This admonition comes in the context of economic relationships. Do you think this verse should be read in a broader context, beyond financial matters? Some commentaries extend its meaning to include not deceiving with words.

Prior *parashiyot* addressed the corrupting influence of misused language. How important is this idea in building and sustaining a "holy" community?

122 Rabbi Natan Fenner in Bay Area Jewish Healing Center Torah Reflections: "Giving Each Other a Break; Torah Reflections on Behar-Bechukotai, May 16, 2020.

FOCUS PHRASE (25:3)

Teez'rah ... teez'more—Plan ... prune.

B'chukotai (Leviticus 26:3-27:34) "Consequences"

OVERVIEW

This is the last portion in Leviticus. Chapter 26:3-45 lists rewards and punishments, detailing the positive outcomes of upholding God's commandments and the negative consequences of ignoring them. When people follow the laws, rain will fall when expedient, and people will thrive in a peaceful land. When people disregard the commandments, a complete breakdown of society will ensue.

STANDOUT PHRASES

26:12 "I will be ever present in your midst." The Hebrew word describing God's presence in this verse is the same word used to describe God strolling in the Garden of Eden (Genesis 3:8). The phrasing is also reminiscent of God dwelling in the Tabernacle (25:8). In both instances, God is readily accessible to people.

Rabbi Dov Linzer explains, "If we see God's presence in our midst as static, then our religiosity will be static. If, however, we see God as moving in our midst, then we will seek out God. We will seek opportunities to grow, to reach God, to understand what it is that we must do in the world. The relationship will be dynamic; it will be alive."[123]

27:8 "But if one cannot afford the equivalent ..." In the same way that more modest sacrifices were available to people who needed concessions (e.g. 12:8, 14:21), here too flexibility enables people to make dedications appropriate to their means.

27:24 "In the jubilee year the land shall revert to the one from whom it was bought, whose holding the land is." Discussed at length in 25:10-24, the book of Leviticus concludes by repeating legislation that symbolizes the inalienable connection between the Land of Israel and its people.

27:34 "These are the commandments that YHVH gave Moses for the Israelite people on Mount Sinai." The commandments included in Leviticus were not given at the time of Revelation. They were given to

---

123 "Has Our Relationship with God Lost its Sizzle?" posted on May 16, 2014, library. yctorah.org/2014/05/relationship-sizzle/

Moses at the Tabernacle (Tent of Meeting). Nevertheless, the Torah views them as equally binding as the laws pronounced in Exodus.

TALK ABOUT

1. You've made it to the end of Leviticus!! Well done!! Of all the books of the Torah, *Vayikra* most directly addresses the challenge of how to maintain and restore spiritual equilibrium in our imperfect and conflicted world, and in our imperfect and conflicted selves.

Commentator Richard Elliott Friedman sums up Leviticus: "Leviticus thus is a design for an organized society of people who help one another, who do not intentionally injure one another, who respect one another's property and relationships, who regularly assemble to celebrate together, who acknowledge their errors and atone for them, who regard life—in humans and in animals—as sacred, who pursue purity in various forms, who respect law, and who are utterly loyal to one God."[124]

How would you summarize Leviticus?

2. There is a tradition that children begin learning Torah with *Vayikra*. A reason is that Leviticus deals with purity, and little children are pure. Now that you've had exposure to Leviticus, why do you think it is the first book taught in traditional Jewish schools? If you've read Genesis and Exodus, do you think one of them might be a better choice to introduce Torah Study?

3. 26:4-12 describes an ideal existence, imbued with peace, prosperity, fertility, abundance, and security. Closeness to God will be the capping joy.

What would your perfect life look like? Does it depend on having "enough" or does it require excess? Imagine your perfect life now. Can you do something today, this month, or this year to help realize the life you desire?

4. God's role in freeing the Israelites from Egyptian slavery is mentioned many times in the Torah. In 26:13, it is mentioned in a unique way: "I am YHVH your God ... who ... made you walk erect." The Hebrew word for "walk erect," suggests a confident, upright position. Moses is commended for being humble, but here, a strong, confident posture is praised.

124 *Commentary on the Torah*. New York, NY: HarperCollins, 2001, p. 418.

Can someone be humble and self-assured simultaneously? What is the opposite of humility, and what is the opposite of confidence?

5. "There is something profoundly unsettling about *B'chukotai* ... It claims that there is a direct correlation between our actions and the natural order of the universe ... The seeming system of reward and punishment ... appears to contradict the troubling reality that we witness ... good people suffer, and evil people often prosper."

"Perhaps this *parashah* is telling us, in its own theological language, that there is a moral order to the universe that is intrinsically connected to the natural order of the universe ... human action is ... essential to the proper functioning of the cosmos ... the physical and ethical dimensions of God's Creation are wholly dependent on each other, and we ignore that relationship at our peril.[125]

Is *B'chukotai* unsettling as Sager suggests? Does her understanding of the intertwining of the physical and ethical dimensions of the world make sense to you?

Think About

1. In 26:3, God asks the people to "follow and faithfully observe" the commandments. Is there a difference in those two verbs of acquiescence?

2. In 26:12, the text says that God will walk amongst the people. The same verb appears in Genesis 5:22, 6:9, 17:1, and 48:15. God is more available to people in Genesis than in the following biblical books. Here again in Leviticus, God is promising to stay close.

When you have felt God's Presence, what have you noticed about yourself when you experience being in God's Presence?

3. The consequences for failing to observe the laws are pain, exhaustion and war (26:14-38). In 26:16 and 26:20, the outcome for disregarding the laws is described as "*rik*"—the experience of emptiness and purposelessness. This description includes living and working in vain, feeling helpless, and despairing.

Have you ever felt "*rik*?" Some people suffering from depression describe feeling "*rik*." For brief, situational depression, what is useful to help someone move from feeling "*rik*" to being motivated?

---

125 Cantor Sarah Sager in *The Torah: A Women's Commentary*, Tamara Cohn Eskenazi and Andrea L. Weiss, eds., New York: URJ Press, 2008, pp. 782-783.

4. Much of this portion consists of reproofs. The Hebrew term for "reproof" is "*toche'chah*." There are many Jewish texts that address how to properly reprove someone. The desired result is not shame or guilt but *t'shuvah*, an acknowledgement of having done wrong coupled with actions that will foster return to honest, productive relationships.

It is a delicate undertaking to reprove someone. A reproof can end with the recipient feeling defensive, guilty, or ashamed. Jewish teaching promotes giving healthy criticism at the right time, in the right place. It is important not to embarrass someone receiving *toche'chah*, and to honestly assess one's motivation: Am I doing this to hurt or shame the person, or is my goal to give constructive help?

Have you received healthy criticism that you viewed as helpful? What elements distinguished it from *toche'chah* that you rejected?

FOCUS PHRASE (26:6)

Shalom—Peace, wholeness.

Numbers/B'midbar

INTRODUCTION TO NUMBERS/B'MIDBAR

B'midbar takes place in the wilderness, a place of beauty and stark-ness, a place where one can become easily disoriented in the external environment, and acutely oriented to one's inner landscape. The wil-derness can be dangerous and overwhelming. It tests a person at every turn. And for that very reason, it can also be a place of realization, resourcefulness, and resilience.

This fourth book of the Torah is multidimensional: it includes narrative, poetry, civil and cultic laws, family squabbles and military adventures, plans achieved, and plans thwarted. The events of *B'midbar* take place over thirty-nine years, during which time most of the slave generation dies, and a new generation's leaders emerge.

Leviticus is primarily concerned with God's rules for the people. In Numbers, we see how the people live when these rules are operational. Numbers is the story of a people in community, deciphering their rela-tionship to holiness and to God. Moses remains a singularly important figure in Numbers. We experience his efforts, his disappointments, and his weariness.

B'midbar (Numbers 1:1-4:20) "Transition"

OVERVIEW

A lengthy period of wandering begins. The early chapters include lists and demarcations for creating order in wilderness living.

Scholar Everett Fox concludes that the large number of Israelites mentioned in the opening census—totaling 603,550 (Numbers 1:3)—is extremely unlikely. Fox suggests that that number may have been exaggerated "as an attempt to impress the audience."[126]

STANDOUT PHRASES

1:47 "The Levites, however, were not recorded among them by their ancestral tribe." The Levites occupied a special position that included serving the priests (the *kohanim*). The Levites were exempt from military service and were not given tribal land.

2:34 "The Israelites did accordingly; just as YHVH had commanded Moses." This is more fantasy than reality. On numerous occasions, the Israelites balked at what Moses requested or ordered.

3:1 "This is the line of Aaron and Moses ... Aaron's sons ..." Moses' sons and Miriam are missing. Why aren't they included in this family genealogy?

4:19 "... each to his duties and each to his porterage." I prefer the translation: "... each to their work and to their burden." Sometimes work is a blessing and sometimes it is a burden. How we judge the work we do depends on the nature of the work and our own perspective on it at any given moment and over time.

TALK ABOUT

1. This portion is read just before the holiday of *Shavuot*. In the Torah, *Shavuot* commemorates the barley harvest. Later Jewish tradition associates *Shavuot* with the Giving of the Torah. Can you make a connection between the themes of *B'midbar* and the holiday of *Shavuot*? Why was the Torah given in the wilderness? What would have been

---

126 Everett Fox, *The Five Books of Moses*, New York: Schocken Books, 1990, p. 654.

different if the Torah had been given in Egypt at the start of the journey, or in the Promised Land at the end of the journey?

2. Why do so many key events in the Torah take place in the wilderness? Wilderness inspires awe and respect. People spend time in the wilderness to challenge themselves, to gain self-understanding, to clarify questions and concerns, and to spur spiritual growth.

How do you view the wilderness? Is it welcoming? Inspiring? Threatening? What kinds of wilderness, besides geographical, have you experienced?

3. Why is so much attention (so many verses) paid to the census? Why are the names of the tribes detailed again and again? It's possible the Torah wishes to draw attention to the importance of individuals, something absent from life in slavery. By mentioning dozens of individual names, the Torah repudiates the ideology that people are indistinguishable from one another.

Look at the Genesis creation story to see the first place the Torah demonstrates the singular importance and absolute uniqueness of the individual. Do other Genesis stories demonstrate this?

4. 3:15 and 3:39 both refer to the age of one month. Centuries ago, Jewish law specified that a baby who dies before the age of one month was not considered fully viable, and therefore, did not necessitate a funeral, mourning practices and recitation of the *Kaddish*. In the last few decades, some have pushed back against this exclusion and have asserted the necessity of treating a stillborn or early infant death as deserving full rites of loss. You can find heartfelt prayers and rituals for addressing the anguish of abortion, stillbirth, and infant death online in Ritualwell.org and in *LifeCycles: Jewish Women on Life Passages & Personal Milestones*.[127]

THINK ABOUT

1. The Hebrew name for this fourth book of the Torah is *B'midbar*, meaning, "in the wilderness." But the same root letters, *d-b-r*, translate to "speak." Is the wilderness a place for speaking or listening? Are there "voices" that can be uniquely heard in a place rarely associated with excess human speech?

---

127 Debra Ornstein, ed., Woodstock, VT: Jewish Lights Publishing, 1994.

2. Reading the lists of names in this portion is tiresome. One name is recognizable: Nachshon son of Amminadab (1:7). Nachshon is the nephew of Aaron's wife, Elisheba. He is well known from a *midrash* (Mechilta d'Rabbi Yishmael 14:22), which describes how the Israelites are trapped between the Sea of Reeds and Pharaoh's army on land. Moses prays for help. Nachshon becomes impatient, and jumps into the sea. God tells Moses to stop praying, and to observe how Nachshon takes action, demonstrating faith in a crisis moment. Only after seeing Nachshon's initiative does God part the waters for the Israelites' safe crossing.

Was Nachshon motivated by fear, impatience, or courage? Does it matter? Are you risk-tolerant or risk-averse? Would you prefer to be otherwise? If so, how can you move in the more-desired direction?

3. "The Israelites shall camp, each man with his standard" (2:2). "Standard" refers to an identifying banner or flag. If you were to make a banner or flag to symbolize your identity—your values and priorities— what images would you include?

4. Men who are 30 to 50 years old are singled out to perform certain tasks for the Tent of Meeting (4:3). This suggests that the tasks required physical, mental, or spiritual strength presumed most available during those years of life. What were or are your strengths from 30 to 50? If you are under 30 or over 50, what are your strengths now?

FOCUS PHRASE (4:19)

Chay'yu v'lo ya'mutu—Live and do not die.

Naso (Numbers 4:21-7:89) "Desire and Discipline"

OVERVIEW

This is the longest portion in the Torah. God speaks to Moses about ritual uncleanliness, repentant people, and jealous husbands. Nazirite vows are explained. Individuals who take such vows abstain from alcohol and do not cut their hair. Individuals can choose nazirite living for defined periods of time; the Torah does not condone longterm monastic behavior. The familiar and powerful Priestly Blessing is recorded in *Naso*.

STANDOUT PHRASES

5:6 "When men or women individually commit any wrong toward a fellow human being, thus breaking faith with YHVH ..." Note the intersection here between acts that wrong others and acts that wrong God. Do all transgressive acts against a person constitute transgressive acts against God? And vice versa?

5:18 "... water of bitterness ..." The potion prescribed here for a woman accused of sexual infidelity reminds us of the potion Moses forced the Israelites to drink after they worshipped the golden calf (Exodus 32:20). How would you describe the nature of the infidelity in the golden calf incident?

6:4, 6:5, 6:6, 6:8 "Throughout their term as a nazirite ..." This expression is repeated four times, indicating the importance of recognizing limits to the length of nazirite commitment.

7:89 "When Moses went into the Tent of Meeting to speak with [God], he would hear the Voice addressing him ..." Even Moses, while standing in God's abode, does not see God—Moses hears God's voice. Numerous biblical figures hear God's voice. In the Hebrew Bible, God's incorporeality negates the possibility of seeing God.

TALK ABOUT

1. "When men or women individually commit any wrong ... they shall confess the wrong ... they shall make restitution ..." (5:5-7). There are

three parts to this description of *t'shuvah*: recognition of wrongdoing, confession, and restitution. Are these equally important components of *t'shuvah*? Is there added value in confessing directly to the wronged person?

2. Regarding 5:27-28, there is no consensus about what is meant by a sagging thigh and distended belly. The expectation is that, if pregnant, the woman will have a severe reaction in her pelvic area after swallowing the potion—perhaps a miscarriage. If she is not pregnant, regardless of whether or not she has engaged in adultery, the woman will appear innocent and return to her family as a loyal wife. Her husband may not trust a court to determine the truth, but this ritual gives judgment to God. There is no similar ritual for a husband accused of adultery.

3. Nazirite vows and behavior are the topics in 6:1-21. The word *"nazir"* (as in "nazirite") may be derived from the same root as *"zerizut,"* meaning enthusiasm. It also may be related to the verb *"l'hazir,"* "to set apart." Both connections increase our understanding of the Nazir.

   What is the difference between a vow, a promise, and an oath?

4. How do you think the Torah regards Nazirite vows? 6:13-21 describes a *Nazir* presenting a sin offering following completion of his or her vow. Does this give some insight into how the Torah views ascetic behavior?

   D'var Acher (another thing): The Talmud (Yerushalmi Kiddushin 4:9) says that at the end of life when God questions people about their behavior, they will be asked if they enjoyed all permitted pleasures. In *The Seven Questions You're Asked in Heaven*, Rabbi Ron Wolfson explains that Judaism encourages us to feel joy, value our relationships, and experience pleasure. He says that we are invited to " ... evaluate our time on earth not by how much we learned, not by how badly we messed up, not by how often we prayed," but by the depth of our love and our enjoyment of the world.[128]

THINK ABOUT

1. The early verses in this portion describe how to respond when people recognize they have been wayward, and want to address their regret. *Naso* requires that people confess—not an easy task. Rabbi Shai Held explains that saying sorry is often much harder than merely

---

128 *The Seven Questions You're Asked in Heaven: Reviewing & Renewing Your Life on Earth*, Woodstock, VT: Jewish Lights Publishing, 2009, p.98.

feeling sorry. Owning up to mistakes requires us "to recognize our shortcomings and resist the temptation to make excuses."[129]

When have you found the courage to ask for forgiveness? Was it accepted or were you rebuffed?

2. 5:12-31 describes the *Sotah* ritual (named for the expression in v. 12), a procedure undertaken by a wife accused of adultery. The main issue here is not the wife's suspected sexual impropriety, but the husband's consuming jealousy (5:14). The ritual's purpose is to allay the husband's jealousy and allow the marriage to continue harmoniously.

3. 6:21 says, "Such is the obligation of a nazirite ..." In Hebrew, the phrase is, "*Torat haNazir.*" We don't usually translate "Torah" as "obligation." Is "obligation" an apt definition of "Torah"?

4. Many people are familiar with the Priestly Blessing (6:22-27). Torah scholar Jacob Milgrom describes this blessing as "a rising crescendo of increasing intensity:" three, five, and then seven words in the third line; fifteen, twenty, and finally twenty-five consonants in the third line.[130]

FOCUS PHRASE (6:26)

V'ya'sem l'cha shalom—May God grant you peace.

129 *The Heart of Torah, Vol. 2*, Philadelphia: The Jewish Publication Society, 2017, p. III.

130 *The JPS Torah Commentary: Numbers*, Philadelphia: Jewish Publication Society, 1990, p. 51.

B'haalot'cha
(Numbers 8:1-12:16)
"The Shortest Prayer"

OVERVIEW

The people dedicate the Tabernacle, and the Levites receive instructions about their particular duties. A dispensation is granted for Israelites unable to participate in the Passover offering at its designated time; this "second Passover" allows for those who are ritually impure to take part a month later.

After many detailed preparations, the Israelites leave Sinai for the first time. They complain about their simple diet; they crave meat.

This portion includes the longest Torah narrative involving Miriam. She complains about Moses' new marriage, and, along with Aaron, challenges Moses' solo leadership. God punishes Miriam with a skin disease, and she recovers with Moses' intercession.

STANDOUT PHRASES

11:1-6 "The people took to complaining bitterly ..." This is the third time the issue of food or water and leadership are combined. See also Exodus 15:24 and Exodus 17:2-3. There will be more such episodes as Numbers continues.

11:4 "If only we had meat to eat!" The Hebrew text actually says, "Who will give us meat to eat?" The Israelites retain the childlike dependency of their slave years.

11:23 "Is there a limit to YHVH's power?" The Hebrew words are, "Is YHVH's hand too short?" Look at Exodus 6:6 where God frees the Israelites with an outstretched arm. Here in Numbers, the people doubt the span of God's reach.

12:15 "So Miriam was shut out of camp seven days; and the people did not march on until Miriam was readmitted." The people show solidarity with Miriam. Did Moses anticipate this?

TALK ABOUT

1. Much of chapter 8 is devoted to establishing the unique role of the Levites. In some congregations, there is an order for calling up people to read from the Torah: "*Kohein*" (descended from the priests), "*Levi*" (connected to the tribe of Levi), and finally "*Yisrael*" (any Jewish person 13 and older). This can be meaningful for people whose family line is traced through the *Kohein* or *Levi* category, and/or for those who grew up with this practice.

It's interesting that these categories have no bearing on becoming a rabbi, cantor, or holding any other station in the Jewish world. There is a humorous saying, "Nine rabbis can't make a *minyan*, but ten shoemakers can," drawing attention to the irrelevance of someone's knowledge or lineage to recite certain prayers.

What is your reaction to classifying Jews as *Kohein, Levi*, or *Yisrael*? These affiliations do not render any favors or privileges (except in some congregations where a *Kohein* and *Levi* are called in the first and second position to recite the Torah blessing, and *Kohanim* are invited to offer the Priestly Blessing). *Kohanim* (pl.) who choose to honor this aspect of their identity follow a few restrictions, including not coming in contact with a dead body (except for a close family member). Many *kohanim* feel honored to be descended from the priestly line.

2. Israelites unable to participate in the Passover sacrifice have an additional opportunity to celebrate this ritual one month later (9:9-11). This became known as *Pesach Sheini*, "Second Pesach." Why is there a second chance available for the Passover ritual and not for other holidays? What was unique about Passover in the Torah and what is unique about it now?

3. The people complain to Moses in 11:1-9. Moses complains to YHVH in 11:11-15. How could the people have responded more constructively? How could Moses have responded more constructively?

4. Rabbi Ruth Sohn considers Miriam's treatment in Numbers 12 as symbolic of her treatment in the Torah as a whole. Miriam is called a prophet (Exodus 15:20), but there is no Torah record of her prophecy. She is afflicted with disease and banished for her comments to Moses, but Aaron is spared.[131]

131 Rabbi Ruth H. Sohn, "The Silencing of Miriam" in *The Women's Torah Commentary: New Insights from Women Rabbis on the 54 Weekly Torah Portions*, Rabbi Elyse Goldstein, ed., Woodstock, VT: Jewish Lights Publishing, 2000, pp. 274-278

5. *Midrashim* are stories about biblical characters that imagine thoughts or events in their lives. In the past 50 years, there have been many *midrashim* written about women in the Torah. If you were to write a *midrash* about Miriam, what aspect of her life would you focus on?

THINK ABOUT

1. The quality of Moses' leadership changes from Exodus to now. Look particularly at how he handles the people's complaints in Exodus 16:3-20 and how he handles them in our portion, 11:4-15. Is there a difference? What events may have contributed to Moses having less patience with the people?

2. In 11:12, Moses asks God if he, Moses, conceived and gave birth to the people. The questions are rhetorical, but they use motherhood as the optimal example of a relationship based on patience and devotion. An example of female imagery for God is in Deuteronomy 32:13. Do female images of God enrich your experience of God?

3. The word *ta'a'vah* appears twice in *B'haalot'cha* (11:4 and 11:34). "*T'a'vah*" means "craving." The word also appears in Genesis 3:6 where the fruit of the Tree of All Knowledge is called "*ta'a'vah*," translated as "alluring." In verb form, this word appears in the Deuteronomic version of the Ten Commandments: Deuteronomy 5:18 records that a person should not "*teet'a'veh*" his neighbor's house, field, etc. In Deuteronomy, the word is translated as "covet."

Do people exclusively crave things we "shouldn't" want? Are our cravings doomed to get us in trouble, as in the Genesis story? Are most cravings based more on fantasy than on reality, as in Numbers 11:5?

4. This portion identifies food recalled by the Israelites from their years of enslavement in Egypt. It seems unlikely that slaves ate fish, cucumbers, melons, leeks, onions, and garlic (11:5). In recognition of this portion, prepare one or more dishes using these ingredients during the week of *B'haalot'cha*.

5. "O God, pray heal her!" Moses responds to the appearance of white scales on Miriam. Rabbi Patricia Karlin-Neumann describes this as a "stark, parsimonious prayer." She embellishes: "Five words—eleven Hebrew letters—are all that Moses speaks (12:13) ... it is a primal cry, capturing fear, powerlessness, and incomprehensibility in the face

of sudden illness, accident, or injury ... Our contemporary prayers of healing may have become longer and more specific ... but Moses' wisdom abides. The essence of what we seek is still found in his direct and eternal prayer. God! Please! Heal! Please! Her!"[132]

6. What words have you spoken, silently or aloud, when praying for healing for yourself or someone else?

FOCUS PHRASE (11:6)

Naf'shei'nu y'vei'sha—Our souls are parched.

---

132 *The Torah: A Woman's Commentary*, Tamara Cohn Eskenazi and Andrea L. Weiss, eds., New York: URJ Press, 2008, pp. 864-65.

Sh'lach L'cha (Numbers 13:1-15:41) "On the Fringe"

OVERVIEW

The Israelites approach the end of their wilderness sojourn. Moses sends twelve men to report on the conditions of Canaan's people and land. Ten of the men express dismay at the toughness of the land's inhabitants, but Joshua and Caleb deliver a positive report. Once again in *Sh'lach L'cha*, there are challenges to Moses' leadership and widespread complaining.

STANDOUT PHRASES

13:25 "At the end of forty days they returned from scouting the land." Forty days is a familiar amount of time: the duration of the Flood (Gen. 7:17) and the number of days Moses spent on Mt. Sinai (Exodus 24:18).

14:3-4 "It would be better for us to go back to Egypt!" "Let us head back for Egypt." As they did previously in Exodus 14:11-12, the people yearn for a fantasized past. They fear the future and the unknown.

14:20 "And YHVH said, "I pardon, as you have asked." This phrase is sung at the beginning of the *Kol Nidrei* (Yom Kippur Eve) service. Why is the notion of God's forgiveness affirmed in the *opening* moments of Yom Kippur?

15:38 "... make for themselves fringes on the corners of their garments throughout the ages; let them attach a cord of blue to the fringe at each corner." In the ancient Near East both men and women wore fringed garments. The law of *tzitzit* was likely designated for Israelite women and men.

TALK ABOUT

1. The portion opens with Moses sending men to assess the land the Israelites are about to overtake. Many translations use the word "spies" to identify those sent on this mission, but the text indicates that Moses sends tribal leaders; they are not identified as spies. Because they are leaders, their opinions carry weight. That is why their negative comments have such an impact.

Is the role of a leader to encourage at all costs or to be realistic about planned undertakings? Does this story read differently if you think of the people who brought negative reports as leaders instead of spies?

2. Many commentators conclude that the sin of the ten tribal representatives and the sin of the golden calf are the two most serious breaches in the relationship between God and the people. After both offenses, God threatens to destroy the people and relents only after Moses intervenes. The incident with the golden calf is about idolatry, and therefore, the nature and seriousness of the transgression is self-evident. But why do the actions of the ten returning men warrant such recrimination? Has a sin been committed?

3. You will find different version of this story (13:17-33) in Deuteronomy 1:19-33. Why are there differences in these accounts?

4. Haviva Ner-David was the first Orthodox woman to claim the title "rabbi." She charts her courageous journey in the book *Life on the Fringes: A Feminist Journey Toward Traditional Rabbinic Ordination*.[133] As of 2021, there are about fifty women who have attained Orthodox ordination. Their titles are: Rabbi, *Rabba*, *Rabbanit*, and *Maharat*, a Hebrew acronym for the words Leadership, Jewish Law, Spirituality, and Jewish Text.

In 2009, an Orthodox women's rabbinic seminary called Maharat opened. It offers serious Jewish study for various professional goals. Maharat's flagship program confers rabbinic ordination. Maharat offers online *divrei Torah* from students and graduates. You may want to check this resource for your own Torah Study.

For centuries, until a few decades ago, wearing *tzitzit* (either daily as a *tallit katan* or as a prayer shawl during services) was a man's prerogative. Do you wear *tzitzit*? What do they signify to you?

THINK ABOUT

1. This *parsha* is called "*Sh'lach*," ("Send") or "*Sh'lach L'cha*" (Send to/for yourself). "*Sh'lach L'cha*" is reminiscent of the phrase "*Lech L'cha* (Genesis 12:1). If we understand *Sh'lach L'cha* to mean, "Send to or for yourself," the entire verse would read, "Send to/for yourself people to assess and evaluate ..."

Right now, when you look into yourself, what do you see, assess, and evaluate? Where do you see strength and where do you see weakness?

133 Teaneck, NJ: Ben Yehuda Press, 2014.

About what are you open and about what are you guarded? Do you see yourself (as the Israelites described the inhabitants of the land and themselves) as a "giant" or a "grasshopper"?

2. In 13:30, Caleb encourages the people to take on the challenge of confronting a daunting foe. In 13:33, the people despair of succeeding in their efforts.

Are there times you have been daunted by your goals? Do you think that some of our goals should exceed our reach? I came across this sign: "If your dreams don't scare you, they're not big enough." Do you agree?

3. 13:28 begins with an unusual word—*efes*. In modern Hebrew, *efes* translates to "zero." In this portion, it is translated as "however," a word with a hint of negativity. "*Efes*" changes the tone of the prior sentence, which is factual—the land flows with milk and honey (13:27)—to something far more subjective. With "*efes*," the report disintegrates to words of fear and doubt.

A single word can mislead, demoralize, and dispirit. Which words have that impact on you?

4. *Tzitzit* can be worn on a "*tallit katan*"—an undershirt with fringes that hang outside one's clothes. Some believe that *tzitzit* function as a kind of talisman or charm to protect the person wearing them from danger. But in most cases, people wear *tzitzit* as a sign or reminder of what Judaism requires.

Look at 15:39. What does this verse say is the purpose of looking at the *tzitzit*?

FOCUS PHRASE (14:25)

P'nu—Start out (Turn).

Korach (Numbers 16:1-18:32)
"Questioning Authority"

OVERVIEW

With Dathan, Abiram, On and an additional 250 community leaders, Korach organizes a rebellion against Moses and Aaron. Moses questions why Korach is not satisfied with his Levite role. The rebels challenge Moses' and Aaron's authority. God's response is to kill the insurrectionists. An absence of facts leaves us uncertain as to why such a severe punishment was warranted. In fact, we wonder: Can this extreme punishment be justified at all?

STANDOUT PHRASES

16:2 "... with fine reputations." Other translations are "people of repute," and "men of renown." The Hebrew words are "*anshei shem*," which mean: "people of name." Many Jewish texts laud earning "a good name." Ecclesiastes 7:1, Proverbs 22:1, and *Pirkei Avot* 4:13—each mentions the significance of a good reputation.

16:11 "For who is Aaron that you should rail against him?" Indeed, who is Aaron? Here are some places we learn about him: Exodus 4:14, Leviticus 10:13 and 10:19, Numbers 18:8 and 18:20.

16:13 "... you have brought us from a land flowing with milk and honey to have us die in the wilderness ..." Excuse me? The rebels, presumably sarcastically, describe Egypt as a land flowing with milk and honey. This is precisely the expression used by Moses to describe the Promised Land in Exodus 13:5 and by Joshua in 14:8.

16:22 "God, Source of the breath of all flesh." This name of God hearkens back to God's creation of Adam in Genesis 2:7, "... and breathed into his nostrils the breath of life, so that the man became a living being."

TALK ABOUT

1. Nehama Leibowitz notes that the holiness mentioned in relation to the *tzitzit* is a goal, not a fact (15:39-40), whereas the holiness Korach

speaks about is something already achieved: "You are holy."[134] How do you define holiness? Is it achievable or is it always at least slightly out of reach?

2. In 16:22, Moses and Aaron ask regarding the Israelites, "When one member sins, will You be wrathful with the whole community?" This is reminiscent of Abraham's questioning Sodom's destruction (Genesis 18:23-33). What do you think about collective punishment? See comments in *Parashat Bo*, Question #4.

3. Korach and his allies accuse Moses and Aaron of having "gone too far" in 16:3. Moses then replies to Korach and his crowd, "You have gone too far" (16:7). What are appropriate limits in life? How do we know when enough is enough?

"Abundance poses very different psychospiritual questions than scarcity ... The question of abundance is, how do I really know what I need? ... the question is not, how can I feel grateful for a small amount of food but how can I feel satisfied when I can have as much food as I want?"[135]

4. 16:25-27 depicts Moses' anger when Dathan and Abiram question his authority. Earlier in 11:26-30, Moses reacts in a completely different manner when Eldad and Medad threaten his leadership. Joshua implores Moses to stop them, but Moses rejects the idea that Eldad and Medad have hostile intent. Moses calms Joshua by suggesting it would be advantageous if all the people experienced God in an enthusiastic manner.

Why did Moses react differently to the two challenges? Why are Korach's and his fellow insurrectionists' actions considered threatening, but not Eldad's and Medad's actions? Some commentators explain that Eldad and Medad did not seek power, whereas Korach did. Reading the accounts in Numbers 11 and 16, do you think these individuals had different purposes? Do you think Moses was circumspect in seeking

---

134 *Studies in Bamidbar/Numbers*. Jerusalem: The World Zionist Organization, 1982, p.142.

135 Irwin Kula with Linda Loewenthal, *Yearnings: Embracing the Sacred Messiness of Life*. New York, NY: Hachette Books, 2006, p. 256.

punishment for Korach and his allies, but wise in not pursuing recrimination against Eldad and Medad?

Think About

1.   Korach asserts that the entire community is holy, not just Moses and Aaron (16:3). Perhaps it's not possible to "be holy" (that is reserved for God), but it is possible to engage in holy acts. Have you ever witnessed or heard about an act you consider holy? In Exodus 25:8 and 29:46, God states God's desire to live with and share holiness with all the people.

2.   Korach asks Moses and Aaron in 16:3: "Why then do you raise yourselves above YHVH's congregation?" This provocation is reminiscent of the Hebrew slave's response to Moses when he saw the one slave attacking another. Responding to Moses' intervention, the aggressor asks, "Who made you chief and ruler over us?" (Exodus 2:13-14) The Torah describes Moses as exceedingly humble, but there are hints that he felt empowered to act in keeping with his own convictions, not subject to other people's norms.

Erica Brown notes that Moses exhibits doubts and anxieties in nearly every narrative in Numbers.[136] Do you think he did (or should have) shared his doubts with the people? When you have been a leader, how did (do) you cope with self-doubt? How did (do) you address challenge or disillusionment from those you lead?

3.   The Israelites continue to complain throughout Numbers (e.g., 17:6). A Yiddish word that has taken hold in English is "*kvetch*." Do you find that complaining or "*kvetch*ing" is a recurring aspect of conversations among Jews? What do you tend to complain about most? What do people around you complain about? Can complaining be productive?

4.   "Yet, the Torah teaches, even though Korach dies, his descendants live on (Numbers 26:11) ... it is not only public leaders who play Korach's role today. We, too, live with an ongoing conflict between an 'inner Moses' and an 'inner Korach'—between humility and arrogance, between selflessness and selfishness. And until we can hear the difference between those two voices, our actions will not be effective in countering the power of the Korachs at large in the world. We need to be clear when it is the voice of our needy, small-minded self that advises us to

---

136 *Leadership in the Wilderness: Authority and Anarchy in the Book of Numbers.* Jerusalem: Maggid Books, 2013, pp. 98-99.

act, or when it is the wise voice that speaks from our deepest and best values and truth."[137]

5. Do you see value in Korach's position? Does Moses also display arrogance in rejecting Korach's bid to share power?

FOCUS PHRASE (18:31)

B'chol makom—In every place.

137 Rachel Cowan in *The Torah: A Women's Commentary*, Tamara Cohn Eskenazi and Andrea L. Weiss, eds., New York: URJ Press, 2008, p. 911.

Chukat (Numbers 19:1-22:1) "Water"

OVERVIEW

The word "water" appears over twenty times in *Chukat*: in relation to bathing bodies and garments, as a demand from the Israelites who are thirsty, when Moses strikes a rock, as part of a song/poem sung by the Israelites, and as part of the deal made by the Israelites as they traverse Sihon's territory.

This portion also includes three very significant events: the deaths of Miriam and Aaron, and the fateful incident when Moses strikes a rock to yield water. God tells Moses that he will be denied entry into the Promised Land because of how he spoke to the people.

STANDOUT PHRASES

19:2 "... a red cow without blemish ..." The ritual of the red cow is strange and seemingly impossible to decipher. It is possible that there is a psychological purpose in this biblical ritual: by sacrificing an unblemished (perfect) animal, the penitent acknowledges that "perfection does not belong in this world" which is dangerous, tarnished, and corrupt.[138]

20:5 "Why did you make us leave Egypt to bring us to this wretched place, a place with no grain or figs or vines or pomegranates?" This isn't the first time the Israelites remember Egypt as a place where they ate plentiful food. Seems unlikely that they were well fed as slaves!

20:11 "And Moses raised his hand and struck the rock twice with his rod." In Exodus 17:5-6, God instructs Moses to procure water by striking the rock with his rod. Here, God tells Moses to *speak* to the rock. Do you think God is being arbitrary by punishing Moses for striking the rock when the direction was to speak to the rock?

20:29 "All the house of Israel bewailed Aaron thirty days." This verse and Deuteronomy 34:8, recording the mourning period for Moses, are the sources of the thirty-day mourning period called "*sh'loshim.*"

---

138 *Etz Hayim: Torah and Commentary*, David L. Lieber, ed., Philadelphia: The Jewish Publication Society, 2001, p. 880.

TALK ABOUT

1. The text records thirty-day mourning for Aaron (20:29). Aaron's death is also recounted as a major event during the people's wandering (33:38-39). About Miriam's death, the Torah simply says, "Miriam died there and was buried there" (20:1).

Immediately following Miriam's death, however, the people quarrel with Moses (20:2-5), and Moses' angry and impatient response gets him into serious trouble (20:12). Perhaps the people grumbled and groused at least in part because of their anxiety at Miriam's death. Perhaps Moses' short temper was at least partially because of his grief at his sister's death.

If the Israelites, including Moses, had set aside time to mourn Miriam, would they have handled their agitation better? Addressing a loss or trauma as fully as possible when it happens usually results in less post-trauma over time.

2. 19:14 states, "This is the ritual ..." The Hebrew words are, "*Zot ha Torah.*"

In 6:21, "Torah" is translated as "obligation." In this verse, it is translated as "ritual." Is "ritual" a useful definition of "Torah"?

3. Persons who are exposed to a corpse, human bones, or a grave become ritually impure for seven days. A ritual enables them to reintegrate into communal life. When a close family member dies, Jewish tradition offers a week of *shivah* to intensely mourn, while being exempt from normal activities. If the deceased is not a close family member, we may "pay our respects" by visiting the family, but our routines are unchanged.

Does it seem reasonable to offer time and place to reflect on life and death following contact with a body, at a funeral or under other circumstances? What is the North American way of dealing with death?

4. Regarding 20:2, "Is the timing of the present complaint for water significant? Miriam is closely associated with water: She observes the deliverance of Moses from drowning in the Nile (Exodus 2:1-9), and she celebrates with him at the sea (Exodus 15:20-21). Right before she dies, new ritual instructions require "water of lustration" (19:9). Now, immediately after Miriam's death, the people desperately cry for water. Because the two episodes with water follow each other sequentially, the Rabbis explicitly connect Miriam's death to the lack of water."[139]

139 *The Torah: A Women's Commentary*, Tamara Cohn Eskenazi and Andrea L. Weiss, eds., NY: URJ Press, 2008, p. 923, n. 2.

THINK ABOUT

1. When a loved one dies, how have you coped with raging emotions? Does anything other than time help to integrate the loss?

Many people say that after the death of a close family member (not a child or young person, God forbid), or following a funeral, their appreciation of the simpler aspects of life dramatically increases. They feel a new sense of gratitude. How long do these feelings last? Are they sustainable?

2. "Moses and Aaron assembled the congregation in front of the rock, and he said to them, "Listen, you rebels, shall we get water for you out of this rock?" (20:10) Some commentators suggest that Moses' mistake was taking credit for providing the water, as in, "shall *we* get water for you ..."

All of us have misspoken and have needed to apologize or explain words spoken in haste. Most of us are familiar with feeling regret when we speak carelessly or press the "send" button prematurely. How do you handle those lapses?

3. Some commentators ascribe God's upset with Moses (20:12) to his inability to control his temper. This is strange because God's short temper has been problematic since the early chapters of Genesis! Nevertheless, many Jewish texts warn against anger. Rabbi Jonathan Sacks explains that angry people tend to be unforgiving, insensitive, and lacking in compassion and empathy. He concludes, "... irascible people end up lonely, shunned, and disappointed."[140]

Do you agree with Rabbi Sacks?

4. Numbers 20 includes death, disillusionment, and despair. How would you describe the mood and themes of Numbers 21?

FOCUS PHRASE (19:2)

T'mee'mah—Without blemish (complete, whole).

---

140 *Essays on Ethics: A Weekly Reading of the Jewish Bible,* Jerusalem: Maggid Books, 2016, p. 248.

Balak (Numbers 22:2-25:9) "Commission"

OVERVIEW

Balak, the Moabite king, wants to hire Balaam, a praised and prized seer, to curse the Israelites. Balaam initially refuses but, on receiving permission from God, he agrees to prophesy God's message. He refuses, however, to curse the Israelites.

The most well-known feature of this story is a talking jenny (a she-donkey). Balaam rides the jenny but beats her when she swerves from the road and lies down beneath him. When the jenny explains that an angel is standing in the way, Balaam apologizes. He returns to Balak explaining that he can only speak the words God puts into his mouth. Balaam then blesses the Israelites.

The portion closes violently: Israelite men engage in sexual acts and idolatrous worship with Moabites. God sends a plague to punish those who participate. Pinchas, a grandson of Aaron, kills a couple he sees engaging in the prohibited behavior. The following Torah portion bears the name "Pinchas."

STANDOUT PHRASES

22:5-6 "There is a people ... they are too numerous ..." Balak's words are very similar to the Pharaoh's words before he enslaves the Israelites, "... a people ... too numerous" (Exodus 1:9). In both cases, the individuals who speak these words decide to destroy the people.

22:34 "I erred ... I will turn back." Balaam's words in Hebrew are "cha'ta'ti, ashuva." These words are familiar from High Holy Day prayers. We own up to our errors and engage in t'shuvah, repentance and return. Balaam is another example of a non-Israelite being singled out for laudable, model behavior.

23:23 "There is no augury in Jacob, no divining in Israel." The Torah frowns on divination and sorcery as noted in Leviticus 19:26, 19:31, 20:27, and Deuteronomy 18:10-11.

24:5 "How fair are your tents, O Jacob, Your dwellings, O Israel!" Balaam's blessing of Israel, is sung in Hebrew at the beginning of each morning service, "Ma tovu oha'lecha Ya'akov ..."

TALK ABOUT

1. There are about a dozen references to seeing and to visions in the Balaam story (22:2-24:25), even though the story hinges on what *isn't* seen. What is the role of sight in the Balaam narrative?

2. "There is a people that dwells apart" (23:9). Is this the Torah's vision of the Israelite/Jewish people—Aloof? Different? Separate? Alone? The second part of the verse says, "Not reckoned among the nations." What does this mean? What are the advantages and disadvantages of a people "dwelling apart"?

3. God tells Balaam that Israel is a blessed people (22:12). Balaam later announces that those who bless Israel will be blessed and those who curse Israel will be cursed (24:9). God spoke these very words to Abraham in Genesis 12:3. Has history borne this out?

4. The account of Pinchas' vengeance (25:6-9) disturbs and horrifies. Rabbi Sue Levi Elwell attempts to make sense of it: "… [it] illustrates the tragedy of seeing the world dichotomized. Exhausted from a journey that seems to have no end, the Israelite men forget who they are. They forget their privileged relationship with the One who brought them out of slavery."[141]

Does Elwell's explanation satisfy you? Did the public nature of what Pinchas saw contribute to his outrage (25:6)?

THINK ABOUT

1. In this portion, Moabite and Midianite women are suspect and dangerous. Balak is read within a few weeks of *Shavuot*. On the holiday of *Shavuot*, we read the Scroll of Ruth, which records the extreme loyalty of Ruth, a Moabite. She joins the family of Israel and becomes the ancestor of King David.

In Exodus, Moses marries Zipporah, a Midianite. She saves Moses' (or their son's) life in a strange incident in Exodus 4:24-26. Regardless of whose life she saves, Zipporah is Moses' ally.

There are mixed messages about the Moabite and Midianite people. This may be an example of an intermingling of different traditions in the Torah text.

---

141 *The Torah: A Women's Commentary*, Tamara Cohn Eskenazi and Andrea L. Weiss, eds., New York: URJ Press, 2008, p. 956.

2.   Many commentators describe Pinchas as "zealous," a word that can mean anything from dedicated to fanatical. Is "zealous" the word you would choose to describe Pinchas?

3.   Balak tells Balaam he will reward him richly if he does what Balak asks (22:17). How easy or difficult is it for you to remain principled when financial (or other) gain is offered? It is not easy to resist enticing offers.

4.   Why was a donkey chosen as the main animal character in this story? Donkeys are usually portrayed as dull beasts of burden whose main purpose is to provide transportation. But in the Hebrew Bible, donkeys are spoken of with appreciation: Issachar is compared to a strong donkey in Jacob's blessing final blessing of his sons (Genesis 49:14). The messiah described in the prophetic book of Zechariah (9:9) will enter Jerusalem on a donkey. Perhaps in our text, the donkey represents the desirable qualities of simplicity, humility, loyalty, and hard work.

It is also possible that the donkey was chosen because it makes Balaam seem all the more ridiculous to be outdone by a simple beast.

FOCUS PHRASE (24:9)

M'var'che'cha va'ruch—Blessed are they who bless you.

Pinchas (Numbers 25:10-30:1)
"Five Sisters, One Voice"

OVERVIEW

Pinchas is rewarded for his zealotry, but he isn't chosen to lead the Israelites into the Promised Land. Is it possible that God didn't consider him as Moses' successor because of Pinchas' rash and ruthless behavior?

The tribes assemble on the eastern side of the Jordan, within sight of the land they are seeking. Moses gives final instructions for cultivating communal stability.

Unexpectedly, five sisters challenge the inheritance system in order to retain a share of land that had been given their deceased father. They succeed in procuring family property that would otherwise go to more distant male relatives.

STANDOUT PHRASES

26:46 "The name of Asher's daughter was Serah." The only other mention of Serah is in Genesis 46:17. She may have played an important role in biblical history, but we have only these two brief mentions by which to remember her.

27:1 "The daughters of Zelophehad ... Mahlah, Noah, Hoglah, Milcah, and Tirzah." In contrast to the lack of information about Serah, 27:1-11 records a rich account of an important incident in these women's lives and in the legacy of the Israelite people.

27:18 "Single out Joshua son of Nun, an inspired leader, and lay your hand upon him." Joshua shows leadership and loyalty to God in Numbers 14:6-9. Senior rabbis lay their hands upon the shoulders of newly ordained rabbis. Many Christian clergy also use this practice to transfer spiritual leadership.

29:39 "All these shall you offer to YHVH at the stated times." This verse concludes the list of daily and holy day offerings. The holy days are: *Shabbat, Rosh Chodesh, Pesach, Shavuot, Rosh HaShanah, Yom Kippur, Sukkot,*and *Sh'mini Atzeret.* Do you find it astonishing that after 3,000 years, these festival days continue to punctuate our lives with living traditions, beauty, and meaning?

TALK ABOUT

1. Six *parashiyot* carry people's names: Noah, Sarah, Yitro, Korach, Balak, and Pinchas. How many of these individuals are not Israelites? Do these people have anything in common? Are you surprised that there isn't a *parsha* called "Avraham" or "Moshe"?

2. It is tedious to read through the lists of descendants in 26:2-62. Why are such lists included? Do you think there is value in giving lists like these to Bar/Bat Mitzvah students to learn as their portion?

3. Moses requests a leader "who shall go out before them and come in before them, and who shall take them out and bring them in..." (27:17). How do you interpret these words? Do they apply exclusively to a military leader? When Moses asks for a leader who will guide the people like a shepherd guides sheep, what aspects of leadership is he describing?

4. Sadly, the story of the five sisters doesn't end in chapter 27. There is an addendum in Numbers 36:1-12. Read the addendum. What do you think?

5. Which of the holy days listed in 28:9-29:38 particularly appeals to you?

It is easy to feel uncomfortable with or alienated by all the sacrifices listed in this section: "... most Jews would consider the sacrificial cult described in these chapters and elsewhere in the Bible as a 'primitive' means of approaching the Creator ... While a simple dismissal of animal sacrifice as 'primitive' may satisfy our sense of modern superiority, it does not give consideration to the underlying purposes of the old practices.

"Private sacrifice was meant to place the offerer into a meaningful and direct relationship with God ... Public offerings like those prescribed for holy days were to reflect the awareness of the whole community that God dwelt in its midst."[142]

Think About

1. In this portion, five sisters succeed in achieving their goal. Here are two things that may have contributed to their successful petition: They spoke as a unit (27:1), and they spoke on behalf of another person (their father), and not just on their own accounts. How else did they make a compelling case? For example, at what location do they state their claim and who is listening? Do they propose a solution?

How do you ask for things you want? What is an effective way to make a request?

2. "Moses brought their case before YHVH" (27:5). "Let YHVH ... appoint a leader for the community ..." (27:16). In Deuteronomy, conversations are recounted, and God addresses Moses, but the topics in chapter 27 are the final matters that Moses brings to God's attention. The first matter is one of justice and women's rights. The second matter is about leadership. In both cases, Moses' concern is with the people, not with himself.

3. Rabbi Pamela Wax recognizes that inheritance is not merely a legal matter, but an emotional matter raising deep and complex feelings. Wax writes that inheritance, following the death of a loved one, "has the potential to serve as a source of comfort for the mourners."[143]

Rabbi Wax's words promote careful thinking about inheritance plans. Many of us are familiar with situations in which inheritance issues caused fissures in a family. How can this be avoided?

4. "Ascend these heights ... and view the land ... When you have seen it, you too shall be gathered to your kin ..." (27:12-13). We have seen Moses at various high and low points in his life, but in his response to God's directive, Moses is at his most magnanimous: He asks God to choose a wise and caring leader to accompany the Israelites on the next stage of their journey (27:15-17).

---

142 *The Torah: A Modern Commentary*, W. Gunther Plaut, ed., David E.S. Stern, Revised Edition, ed., New York: URJ Press, 2005, p. 1090.

143 *The Women's Torah Commentary: New Insights from Women Rabbis on the 54 Weekly Torah Portions*, Rabbi Elyse Goldstein, ed., Woodstock, VT: Jewish Lights Publishing, 2000, pp. 313-314.

We'd all like to think that our words and acts will be gracious when we are told that death is near. But we can't predict our response. Most of us have probably seen various reactions to, for example, a terminal diagnosis: anger, bitterness, gratitude (for life up until now, for the presence of loved ones to ease the current burden), humility, acceptance, urgency, forgiveness, despair. Is there any way to prepare for a diagnosis that indicates end of life is near?

Focus Phrase (27:18)

Ish asher ruach bo—An inspired leader (a person in whom spirit dwells).

Matot (Numbers 30:2-32:42) "Frustration"

Overview

This portion begins with laws regulating vows. Two tribes, the Reubenites and Gadites, ask Moses to settle lands on the east side of the Jordan River, claiming that these lands are better suited for their cattle than the land inside the borders. Moses is angry (yet again), questioning their loyalty. The Reubenites and Gadites maintain their position and agree to serve in the vanguard of the Israelites' battle for the land. They promise to remain until all the tribes are peacefully settled.

Standout Phrases

30:3 "... he shall not break his pledge; he must carry out all that has crossed his lips." The Torah and Judaism affirm the authority of words: It is a serious matter to break a pledge or vow.

31:2 "... then you shall be gathered to you kin." The same idiom is used for Abraham (Genesis 25:8), Isaac (Genesis 35:29), and Jacob (Genesis 49:33). The biblical notion of death is that one is reunited with ancestors.

31:14 "Moses became angry ..." As time passes and tension builds, Moses becomes increasingly impatient and suspicious.

32:6 "Are your brothers to go to war while you stay here?" Moses' priority is the unity of the Israelites.

Talk About

1. Shortly after Moses' acquiescence to the five sisters' request for inherited land (27:7), it is disconcerting to read about men's authority over most women in the matter of vows and oaths (30:4-17). Married women are subject to their husbands' authority, although a widow or divorced woman is responsible for her own vows and oaths (30:10).

"While we think we are free from these kinds of constraints, this is often not quite true. As mothers, when we choose to take emotional and physical care of our children, we voluntarily relinquish the freedom we might have enjoyed ... we may accept professional positions that do not sufficiently reflect our capabilities, in order to be available to support a beloved spouse, partner, or aging parent. We may not explicitly associate such situations with vow-making or breaking, but in a certain important way, the relationship to vows exists. Like vow-making in the Bible, women's aspirations, spoken or not, are promises we make ..."[144]

2.   Regarding 31:13-18, Robert Alter notes in his commentary that it is Moses, not God who perpetrates this general massacre. The practice of massacring a conquered population was widespread in the ancient Near East, but these verses offend us nevertheless. Attempts to "explain" this section (and similar ones), invariably leads to awkward and unconvincing apologetics. For Alter and for us, this is an instance in which "the biblical outlook sadly failed to transcend its historical contexts."[145]

3.   Compare the Reubenites' and Gadites' request from Moses for a separate land allotment (32:1-32) with the five sisters' request from Moses for their own land (27:1-4). How are the requests similar and how are they different? How are the outcomes similar and different?

4.   Rabbi Jonathan Kligler suggests that the message of this portion, based on 32:2-5, is "Do not separate from the community." He says: "This story is, of course, emblematic of one of the unwavering principles of Judaism: the primacy of community. The "Wicked Child" in the Passover *Haggadah* is labeled as such because he does not think of himself as part of the community ... One does not get to enjoy the blessings of being a Jew without also partaking in the difficulties ... that is what Judaism asks of us: to be committed to one another and to our collective project of bringing holiness into the world."[146]

Do you feel part of the Jewish people? Do you feel part of your city's Jewish community, your synagogue or *chavura*, and your extended Jewish family?

THINK ABOUT

1.   The Hebrew word for vow is *neder*. You may recognize it from the haunting *Kol Nidrei* melody sung at the outset of *Erev Yom Kippur* (often

---

144 Jacqueline Koch Ellenson in *The Torah: A Women's Commentary*, Tamara Cohn Eskenazi and Andrea L. Weiss, eds., NY: URJ Press, 2008, p. 1008.

145 *The Hebrew Bible, Volume I*, New York: W.W. Norton & Company, 2019, pp. 588-89, n. 17.

146 *Turn It and Turn It For Everything Is in It: Essays on the Weekly Torah Portion*, Eugene, OR: Wipf and Stock Publishers, 2020, pp. 163-4.

called "*Kol Nidrei*") services. The words of *Kol Nidrei* release us from any vows (promises) we have been unable to keep in the year past, and grants similar release from vows we might make in the year ahead. Do you think it is a valuable practice to provide absolution for future vows that are unfulfilled?

What are your associations with *Kol Nidrei*? For many, the music and the moment are extremely powerful.

2. Erica Brown notes that promises constitute "a language of commitment."[147] Do you take your promises, and other words you use, seriously? What is your experience with making promises? The older I get, the less willing I am to make promises. Is that true for you?

3. The Gadites and Reubenites say, "We will build here sheepfolds for our flocks and towns for our children" (32:16). Moses replies, "Build towns for your children and sheepfolds for your flocks" (32:24). The Gadites and Reubenites then confirm, "Our children, our wives, our flock, and all our other livestock ..." (32:26).

Notice how Moses changes the order of the Gadites' and Reubenites' concerns, and in their next remarks, they follow Moses' order of priorities. This is reminiscent of a passage from the Noah story. God says to Noah: "Go out of the ark with your wife, your sons, and their wives (Genesis 8:16). The text continues: "So Noah went out, together with his sons, his wife, and his sons' wives" (Genesis 8:18).

To what is the text drawing our attention when it changes the word order in Noah's and the Gadites' and Reubenites' stories?

4. In 32:23, it says, "... your sin will overtake you." This can also be translated: "... your sin will find you." Most of us have done things we regret, and dread being found out. If you are worried about a mistake you've made—large or small—is there a way to address the situation so you don't live with debilitating anxiety?

FOCUS PHRASE (30:9)

Va'do'nai yishlach—God will forgive.

---

147 Erica Brown, *Leadership in the Wilderness: Authority and Anarchy in the Book of Numbers.* Jerusalem: Maggid Books, 2013, p. 195.

Mas'ei (Numbers 33:1-36:13) "Are We There Yet?"

OVERVIEW

Mas'ei begins with a summary of the Israelites' wilderness travels: forty years of geographical and spiritual highlights and lowlights. Boundaries for the Promised Land—what we now call *Eretz Yisrael*—are defined, as are the boundaries for the cities of refuge. God declares the difference between murder and manslaughter. The changes in inheritance laws resulting from the five sisters' request (27:6-7) are modified: Tribes retain the right to receive ancestral territories inherited by women.

STANDOUT PHRASES

33:3 "... the Israelites started out defiantly, in plain view of all the Egyptians." There's a bit of spin in this verse. The Torah reports earlier "... they had been driven out of Egypt and could not delay; not had they prepared any provisions for themselves" (Exodus 12:39). That doesn't sound "defiant." It sounds frenzied.

33:52-53 "... you shall dispossess all the inhabitants ... you shall destroy all their figured objects; you shall destroy all their molten images, and you shall demolish all their cult places. And you shall take possession of the land and settle in it ..." It is very disturbing to read this account of destruction and displacement.

35:12 "The cities shall serve you as a refuge from the avenger, so that the killer may not die unless he has stood trial before the assembly." With this accommodation, "... the Torah offers those who kill accidentally a safe haven ... discouraging both those who may wish to take the law into their own hands and those who may otherwise feel obliged to avenge out of a sense of duty ... this institution protects the killer by making the victim's relatives liable for bloodguilt if they choose to disregard the law."[148]

35:33 "... for blood pollutes the land ..." Blood can render a person impure, and it can also make the land impure. "Your brother's blood is

---

148 *The Torah: A Women's Commentary*, Tamara Cohn Eskenazi and Andrea L. Weiss, eds., NY: URJ Press, 2008, pp. 1022-23, n. 12.

shrieking to Me from the ground," God says to Cain after he murders Abel (Genesis 4:10).

TALK ABOUT

1. "Upon arrival at the city gate, unintentional murderers presented themselves to elders who offered hospitality. Once rested, they were taken to a court where it was determined whether they were guilty. If judged guilty of premeditated murder, they were put to death; if guilty of unintentional homicide, they were allowed to live rent- and tax-free in the refuge city during the lifetime of the incumbent High Priest. After the death of the High Priest, they could return to their home cities, without fearing harm from avengers."[149]

See Deuteronomy 19:3-7 for elaboration on the cities of refuge. Is anything unexpected about this description?

2. Rabbi Shai Held describes homicide as a "theologically unimaginable crime."[150] What does he mean? Look at Genesis 1:26-27 to understand how he comes to this stark assessment.

3. In 34:2, 34:13, 35:2, and 36:5 the Hebrew says *Tsav*, meaning, "command." Some English translations say, "instruct." Surely there is a difference in tone and content between "instructing" and "commanding." In the Torah, God frequently commands, but Moses mostly instructs. Do you think these passages should use the word "command" instead of "instruct"? What about these passages would lead a translator to use "instruct"?

4. The testimony of two or more witnesses is required to assign the death penalty (35:30). Deuteronomy 17:6 and 19:15 also stipulate at least two witnesses in determining capital crimes. Bearing false witness is prohibited in the Ten Commandments (Exodus 20:13 and Deuteronomy 5:17). The Torah is careful to uphold the integrity of the legal system. This is another example of the Torah's preoccupation with truthful speech.

___

149 *A Torah Commentary for Our Times, Volume 3*, Harvey J. Fields, New York, NY: UAHC Press, 1993, p. 90.
150 *The Heart of Torah, Volume 2*, Philadelphia: The Jewish Publication Society, 2017, pp. 193-94.

THINK ABOUT

1. Beginning in 33:3, Moses recounts the marches, rest stops, and significant events of the wilderness years. It may not be an interesting read to us, but it likely was captivating to the people who shared those experiences, and to their immediate descendants who probably heard these stories from childhood. Consider Moses' recap to be an oral diary.

When you review significant events and "resting spots" from your past, which ones stand out? If you want to be sure that you remember an event from this year, what event would it be? Have you made a written record of it?

2. "Moses recorded ... their various marches as directed by YHVH" (33:2). Do you believe God directs your life events? What does the phrase, "meant to be" mean?

3. It is disconcerting to read Moses' instructions to pursue death and destruction in Canaan. But looking at this section in a broader sense, I recognize a truism: that some aspects of our lives are broken or even destroyed when we pursue new possibilities. Some things we are happy to leave behind; other things we dread losing and decry the pain we cause in letting them go.

4. You have come to the end of the book of Numbers! Are you sad, glad, or relieved to leave the wilderness? This fourth book of the Torah has addressed family, communal, and societal issues. What parts of *B'midbar* stand out to you?

FOCUS PHRASE (35:34)

YHVH sho'chein—YHVH abides.

Deuteronomy/D'varim

INTRODUCTION TO D'VARIM

The fifth and final book of the Torah is filled with ideas, laws, and traditions that remain integral to Jewish practice today. These includes monotheism, observance of *Shabbat* and the Pilgrimage Festivals, giving *tzedakah*, affixing *mezuzot*, wearing *tefillin* and *tzitzit*, engaging in prayer as a religious obligation, giving thanks for food and teaching children what being part of the Israelite (Jewish) people entails.

Deuteronomy consists of Moses' farewell speeches. As he prepares to die, he speaks with a growing sense of urgency. He wants his community to succeed by remaining united and committed to God's teachings. Deuteronomy highlights Moses' unique role as prophet, teacher, leader, and interpreter.

Most scholars agree that Deuteronomy's origin can be found in II Kings 22-23. This section describes how King Josiah entered into a covenant with God based on rules found in a "Book of Teaching," discovered while the First Temple was being repaired. It is widely thought that this "Book" refers to Deuteronomy.

As Deuteronomy opens, the Israelites stand on the precipice of a new stage of life. They are camped on the east side of the Jordan River, soon to enter the Promised Land. Will they retain their commitment to God and each other? Can Joshua ably lead them to their destination/

destiny? Deuteronomy is full of words, "*d'varim*," but also many actions that lead the Israelites to their long awaited home.

Each year, the latter portions in Deuteronomy are read in the weeks leading up to the High Holy Days. With this in mind, I've highlighted some High Holy Day themes in several of these *parashiyot*.

D'varim (Deuteronomy 1:1–3:22)
"Words that Matter"

OVERVIEW

The Israelites are poised to enter the Land of Israel. Moses begins to prepare the people for their future by reminding them of their past. He recounts the forty years of desert wandering and the people's continuous complaining. He recalls the mission to investigate the conditions of the land. The portion ends with Moses commanding Joshua to proceed with confidence toward Israel. God tells Moses he will not be able to enter the Promised Land.

STANDOUT VERSES

1:1 "These are the words ..." Having described himself as "not a man of words" in Exodus 4:10, Moses speaks expansively in the fifth book of the Torah.

1:8 "See, I place the land at your disposal. Go, take possession of the land the YHVH swore to your fathers Abraham, Isaac, and Jacob, to assign to them and to their heirs after them." Moses reminds the people that the Land of Israel was promised to their ancestors and that this legacy remains intact.

1:31 "... and in the wilderness, where you saw how your God YHVH carried you, as a man carries his son ..." The Hebrew Bible offers various descriptions of God's relationship to the Israelites. In Deuteronomy 32:13 (and also in Isaiah 46:3-4), God appears as a nursing mother. Here, God functions as a protective father.

2:7 "Indeed, your God YHVH has blessed you in all your undertakings. [God] has watched over your wanderings through this great wilderness; your God YHVH has been with you these past forty years: you have lacked nothing." God secured the people's well-being even in hostile environments.

TALK ABOUT

1.   Moses' reproof of the Israelites focuses on the incident with the land surveyors (Numbers 13:17-33). Why didn't Moses refer to the people's whining (e.g., Exodus 16:3 and Numbers 11:1), their challenges to his leadership (e.g., Numbers 16:1-3), and most objectionable, their building of the golden calf (Exodus 32:1-4)?

2.   How is the account in Deuteronomy 1:22-45 different from the one in Numbers 13:1-3 and 25-33? Review what has transpired in Moses' life between the Numbers and Deuteronomy renditions. Why do the stories differ?

3.   Deuteronomy 1:17 says, "You shall not be partial in judgment: hear out low and high alike." Compare this with three similar admonitions in the Torah: Exodus 23:6, Leviticus 19:15, and Deuteronomy 16:19.

4.   God's anger is repeatedly displayed in the Torah (e.g., Genesis 6:11-13, Exodus 32:10, and Numbers 22:22), and here in Deuteronomy 1:34. Many Jewish texts discourage displays of anger. Is this one way we are not supposed to emulate God?

THINK ABOUT

1.   Several times in Deuteronomy, Moses reviews the Israelites' departure from Egypt and their years of desert wandering. What is the value of reflecting on early, formative experiences, both positive and negative?

2.   Deuteronomy 1:6 says, "Our God YHVH spoke to us at Horeb, saying: You have stayed long enough at this mountain." God urges the Israelites to continue their journey. In Exodus 14:15, God says something similar to Moses: "Why do you cry out to Me? Tell the Israelites to go forward." Have there been times in your life when rumination was no longer productive and you realized that action and change was necessary to advance toward your goal?

3.   Moses' account of the report of the land differs in Numbers 13:1-33 and Deuteronomy 1:22-45. Has your perspective on life events

changed over time? Do you and your siblings have differing childhood memories? When two or more people experience a conversation or event in divergent ways, (how) is it possible to determine the truth? Is there one objective truth?

There is a Talmudic maxim that a person can be known by their "*koso, keeso,* and *kaaso:*" their cup (how they handle alcohol), their wallet (how they handle money), and their anger (how they handle frustration). Are these reliable and comprehensive indications of a person's character?

4. *D'varim* is always read on the *Shabbat* prior to *Tisha B'Av*, the Ninth of Av. This is the day dedicated to remembering the destruction of the First and Second Temples in Jerusalem along with other tragic events in Jewish history. The first word in Deuteronomy 1:12, "*Eicha,*" meaning "how," connects this Torah reading to the book of Lamentations, read on *Tisha B'Av*. That book also begins with the word "*Eicha.*"

The Torah rarely provides answers to the question why something happens. "How" is the word the Bible uses to confront catastrophe and evil. Can there ever be a satisfying answer to the question "Why did this happen to me?" or "Why does this happen at all? It is unlikely that any answer will provide comfort or resolve. What is more useful is to ask, "How can I respond most productively in this devastating circumstance?" or "How do I best cope with this difficult situation?"

Do you agree that asking "how" instead of "why" leads to a more constructive exploration when confronting tragedy and tribulation?

FOCUS PHRASE (1:17)

Kah'katan kah'gadol—Low and high alike (as with the small, so with the large).

Va-et'chanan
(Deuteronomy 3:23–7:11) "What's Worth Desiring"

Overview

Moses continues speaking to the Israelites, warning against idolatry and reminding them to observe the commandments received at Mount Horeb (Sinai). He describes the unique relationship between God and the people, calling them a "chosen and treasured people." To attain the land God promised, the Israelites must dislodge the inhabitants. Moses cautions against intermarriage with the surrounding Canaanite nations.

Standout Verses

4:12 "You heard the sound of words but perceived no shape—nothing but a voice." A key point in Jewish theology is that God is incorporeal—God has no body and cannot be seen. An identifying aspect of God's uniqueness is non-material existence.

4:27 "YHVH will scatter you among the peoples ..." The first expulsion of Jewish people from Israel was the Babylonian Exile, 586 B.C.E.. From then until now, Jews have been uprooted from numerous countries and have lived outside Israel, on all the inhabited continents. The narrative of the Jewish people includes dozens of accounts of dispersion, always resulting from persecution.

6:18 "Do what is right and good in the sight of YHVH ..." Details of how to behave are listed before and after this verse. This general injunction adds that justice and decency are the central goals of the Israelites' behavior. Even when a particular situation is not addressed legally, God desires righteousness.

7:6 "For you are a people consecrated to your God YHVH; of all the peoples on earth your God YHVH chose you to be God's treasured people." The Hebrew word used here, "kadosh," means "holy." The first time "kadosh" appears in the Torah is in reference to Shabbat (Genesis 2:3). Kadosh is a central concept in Leviticus, and it is also found in Exodus and Numbers.

Holiness is difficult to define. In Judaism, what is holy is dedicated (set apart) and elevated.

TALK ABOUT

1. God frequently denies Moses' request to enter the Promised Land. In Deuteronomy 3:25, Moses specifically asks to "SEE the good land." That request is granted in 3:27, "Go up to the summit ... Look at it well ..." Why was Moses not allowed to enter the Promised Land? Why was he permitted to see the land?

2. In Deuteronomy 4:1, Israel is told to "*shema,*" which is generally translated as "listen." But Moses does not ask that people simply listen to the laws and rules he pronounces; he asks them to obey. In other translations, *shema* is translated as "heed," which suggests, "abide by," "follow," or even "obey." In the prayer called "The *Shema,*" found in 6:4, is the intention that we LISTEN to the idea that God is one or that we "obey" that notion? What does it mean to obey the idea that God is one?

3. The laws and rules referred to in Deuteronomy 4:1 are called "*chukim*" and "*mishpatim.*" In traditional Jewish exegesis, these terms refer to two distinctive types of laws/commandments. *Mishpatim* are laws whose purpose are self-evident, such as the prohibition against theft and murder. *Chukim* are laws whose reasons are not obvious, such as not cooking or consuming milk and meat products together.

Here is a sampling of biblical rules. Which is a *mishpat,* a law whose purpose is clear, and which is a *chok,* a law whose purpose is not obvious?

You shall not ill-treat any widow or orphan. (Exodus 22:21)

When you encounter your enemy's ox or ass wandering, you must take it back. (Exodus 23:4)

Six years you shall sow your land and gather in its yield; but in the seventh you shall let it rest and lie fallow. (Exodus 23:10-11)

You shall not let your cattle mate with a different kind; you shall not sow your field with two kinds of seed; you shall not put on cloth from a mixture of two kinds of material. (Leviticus 19:19)

They shall not shave smooth any part of their heads, or cut the side-growth of their beards, or make gashes in their flesh. (Leviticus 21:5)

4. The phrase "with all your heart and soul" appears in 4:29. In 6:5, it says, "with all your heart, with all your soul, and with all your might." Traditional commentators recognize the heart as the locus of craving and aspiration. They suggest that a person should try to channel even

their less elevated desires ("*yetzer hara*") to building a relationship with God. According to Maimonides, the soul is the locus of the intellect. Therefore, loving God with one's heart means applying one's capacity for reason and understanding to building a relationship with God.

Perhaps the most interesting phrase here is "with all your might," "*m'odecha.*" The most literal translation is "with your very-ness." Some say this means "with all your resources," with material wealth, or with your intangible resources, i.e., your time, talent, and energy. I read "*m'odecha*" as loving God "down to your core," with internal resources. What does it mean to love God with material wealth? What does it mean to love God with internal resources?

5. The Ten Commandments are in Exodus 20:2-14. They are reiterated in Deuteronomy 5:6-18. See the pages dedicated to those verses (in *Parashat Yitro*, in Exodus) for related comments and questions. Here I will refer to a few ways the Deuteronomy and Exodus texts differ.

A. The Exodus version of the *Shabbat* Commandment (20:8) says, "Remember the Sabbath day and keep it holy." Deuteronomy (5:12) says, "Observe the Sabbath day and keep it holy as your God YHWH has commanded you." The Exodus version notes God resting on the seventh day as the reason for honoring (remembering) *Shabbat*. Deuteronomy connects celebration of *Shabbat* to God's freeing the Israelites from slavery. Do you think these reasons are complementary?

B. Commandment Five also differs in the Exodus and Deuteronomy versions.

Exodus 20:12 "Honor your father and your mother, that you may long endure on the land that your God YHVH is assigning you."

Deuteronomy 5:16 "Honor your father and your mother, as your God YHVH has commanded you, that you may long endure, and that you may fare well, in the land that your God YHVH is assigning you."

Why is the command to "honor" our parents and not to "love" them? Is it significant that father and mother are identified separately?

C. The last commandment is also stated differently in Exodus and Deuteronomy.

Exodus 20:14 "You shall not covet (*tach'mod*) your neighbor's house; you shall not covet (*tach'mod*) your neighbor's wife, nor male nor female slave, nor ox nor ass, nor anything that is your neighbor's."

Deuteronomy 5:18 "You shall not covet (*tach'mod*) your neighbor's wife. Likewise, none of you shall crave (*teet'a'veh*) your neighbor's house, or field, or male or female slave, or ox, or ass, or anything that is your neighbor's."

The Exodus version begins its list with a neighbor's house; in Deuteronomy, the wife is mentioned first. In Exodus, the wife is counted as an element of the household. The Deuteronomy version substitutes the word "crave" for "covet." How do these expressions of excessive desire differ?

6. The term "heaven and earth" invokes creation (Genesis 1:1, 2:1 and 2:4). In this portion, this pairing appears five times (3:24, 4:26, 4:32, 4:36, and 5:8). Why is it so frequent? The language of creation is also used in 4:16-18. The Torah regularly identifies God as the Redeemer from bondage, and only rarely as the Creator God of Genesis 1 and 2. Why is creation imagery employed here?

7. Consider the word "*yirah*," often translated as "fear" with the nuance of "reverence." "*Yirah*" appears in *Va-et'chanan* four times: 5:26, 6:2, 6:13, and 6:24. It shares root letters with the word "*Nora*" as in "*Yamim Nora'im*," the Days of Awe. To better understand "*yirah*," look at its usage in Exodus 1:17: "The midwives, *fearing* God, did not do as the king of Egypt told them; they let the boys live." The courageous midwives had every reason to fear for their safety by disobeying Pharaoh, but they believed God's desires carried greater weight. They didn't fear God. They *revered* God.

THINK ABOUT

1. In Deuteronomy 3:26, Moses blames the Israelites for God's decision to deny him entry into the Promised Land, "But YHVH was wrathful with me on your account and would not listen to me." The most memorable instance of blaming in the Torah follows quickly after the creation of humanity in Genesis 3:11-13. God asks Adam, "Did you eat the fruit of the tree that I forbade you to eat?" The man said, "The woman whom You gave me, she gave me the fruit of the tree, so I ate." God YHVH then said to the woman, "What is this that you have done?" And the woman said, "The serpent tricked me into eating it."

Since humanity's inception, blaming has been a problem! When you are blamed (wrongly or appropriately), how do you respond? How quickly do you blame others when something goes awry?

2. In 4:6, Moses intimates that the opinions of others should matter to the Israelites: "Observe them faithfully, for that will be proof of your wisdom and discernment to other peoples, who on hearing all the laws will say, 'Surely, that great nation is a wise and discerning people.'" Does Moses' interest in winning the respect of others surprise you? How do you feel when people say admiring things about the Jewish people? How do you react when a recognizably Jewish person is convicted of a heinous crime? Do you believe that something about "the Jewish way of life" fosters wisdom and discernment? What are the qualities of someone who is wise?

3. The word "*shema*" occurs multiple times in this portion: 4:1, 4:6, 4:12, 4:30, 4:32, 4:33, 4:36, 5:20, 5:21, 5:22, 5:23, 5:24, 5:25, 6:3, and 6:4. How do you most effectively get someone to listen? What quickly and fully grabs your attention?

4. In Deuteronomy 4:29, Moses says, "But if you search there, you will find your God YHVH, if only you seek with all your heart and soul." Some think that belief in God is something in-born or that it follows a miraculous event (e.g., a life being unexpectedly saved). This verse suggests that belief is attained through active searching and consistent effort.

Have you sought God's presence in your life? Some Jewish avenues for seeking God are engaging in *tzedakah*, prayer, study, acts of loving-kindness, and fulfilling *mitzvot*. Do any of these make you feel close to God?

5. Deuteronomy 4:39 expresses the most explicit statement of monotheism in the Torah: "Know therefore this day and keep in mind that YHVH alone is God in heaven above and on earth below; there is no other." The Hebrew word that is translated as "in mind," "*l'va'vecha*," actually means "in your heart." Most translations of this verse use "keep in mind" to describe how to understand God's Oneness. The older I get, the more my heart and mind work in consort and I can rarely separate a thought or feeling as being mind-based or heart-based. Is this true for you?

6. The phrase "that it may go well with you" appears several times in this portion: 5:16, 5:26, 5:30, 6:3, and 6:18. Moses is trying to show the people that God wants the Israelites to thrive. What is a "thriving" life? How do we raise children to thrive?

7. Many Jews today are uncomfortable with the notion of the "Chosen People." Others ask: Why did God choose the Jews? In this portion, one reason is given for why the Israelites were *not* chosen: "It is not because you are the most numerous of people that YHVH grew attached to you and chose you; indeed, you are the smallest of people" (7:7). Do you think our small numbers have been advantageous? Many who believe that Jews are the Chosen People explain that this does not attest to Jewish superiority, but to being beholden to live by numerous commandments. The emphasis in Judaism has always been on doing more so than believing. This is described as the primacy of "deed over creed."

FOCUS PHRASE (4:1, 4:5)

She'mah ... Re'eh—Listen. See.

Eikev (Deuteronomy 7:12–11:25) "What Fills Us"

Overview

Moses explains that the Israelites will be fruitful and victorious over their enemies if they maintain their covenant with God. Moses reminds the people that God provided for them, despite their complaining, during their years of wandering. God freed them from Egyptian slavery, Moses asserts, in fulfillment of the covenant made with Abraham, Isaac, and Jacob. If the people remember their redemption and observe the commandments, they will be blessed with security and well-being.

Standout Verses

7:18 "You have but to bear in mind what your God YHVH did to Pharaoh and all the Egyptians: the wondrous acts that you saw with your own eyes, the signs and the portents, the mighty hand, and the outstretched arm by which your God YHVH liberated you." Each festival celebration and every worship service reinforces the Israelite story of becoming a nation through liberation from slavery. This seems to be God's "calling card" to the Israelites and to future generations of the Jewish people. During the Passover Seder, we think of ourselves as if we were freed from Egyptian bondage.

8:10 "When you have eaten your fill, give thanks to your God YHVH for the good land given to you." This verse provides the inspiration for the Grace after Meals (*Birkat haMazon*), in its admonition: eat, be satisfied, and give thanks. Note that being "satisfied" is specified. Judaism does not encourage asceticism.

10:12 "And now, O Israel, what does your God YHVH demand of you? Only this: to revere your God YHVH, to walk only in divine paths, to love and to serve your God YHVH with all your heart and soul." The prophet Micah speaks similar words: "It was told you what is good and what the Lord demands of you—doing justice and loving kindness and walking humbly with your God" (Micah 6:8). Are 613 individual *mitzvot* necessary to express reverence and love of God?

10:19 "You too must befriend the stranger, for you were strangers in the land of Egypt." Legal pronouncements in the Torah consistently include statements for treating strangers favorably. Other examples appear in Exodus 22:20 and 23:9. The Torah consistently expresses concern for the most vulnerable in society. The Israelites are commanded to redress exploitation.

TALK ABOUT

1. In 7:13 and 7:14, the Israelites are told God favors them. Being distinguished as God's "very own people" (9:26) is a recurring theme in Deuteronomy. Yet no explanation is given for why God chose the Israelites. 9:5 says explicitly: "It is not because of your virtues and your rectitude ..." and in 9:6, "It is not for any virtue of yours ..."

The Torah doesn't give an explanation for why Abraham (Genesis 12:1-3), or Moses (Exodus 3:1-10) was chosen. In contrast, this is why Noah was spared from the Great Flood: "Noah was a righteous man; in his generation, he was above reproach; Noah walked with God" (Genesis 6:9). Why was Noah's selection explained but not the choice of Abraham, Moses, and the Israelite people as a whole?

Maimonides suggested that God recognized Israel's spiritual potential and that is why they became God's treasured people. What do you think?

2. The word "*mussar*" appears in 11:2 in the phrase, "the lesson of YHVH your God." Another translation is "discipline." In recent years, people have become familiar with the term as referring to principles of character development. *Mussar* study and practice helps people achieve and maintain equilibrium in pride, honesty, humility, patience, orderliness, and appropriate speech.

3. Moses warns that abundance may result in the Israelites' forgetting their covenant with God and their history as slaves (8:11-17). Moses urges the Israelites to practice gratitude and humility. Is it counterintuitive to expect people living in scarcity or fearing deprivation to be more grateful than those who live with security and abundance? Can the qualities of humility and gratefulness be taught?

4. Compare chapter 9:8-21 with the same story told in Exodus 32:7-35. One difference is Moses telling the Israelites he interceded on behalf of Aaron (Deuteronomy 9:20). Another disparity is when Moses neglects to include his instruction to drink a potion made from the ground up golden calf (Exodus 32:30). Do you think Moses did not accurately

remember the events or did he have other motives for telling the story differently the second time?

5. In 10:6, Moses recounts Aaron's death (Numbers 33:38-39). Miriam dies in Numbers 20:1. Greater attention is paid to Aaron's death, and Moses mentions it as he recalls significant events of the desert years. Aaron was the High Priest; Miriam was a prophet (Exodus 15:20). She played a key role in sustaining Moses in his infancy (Exodus 2:4 and 2:7-8) and played a vital role during the desert years. A great deal of women's scholarship, ritual creation and *midrash* focuses on Miriam. Why has she captured Jewish women's imagination more so than the Matriarchs about whom the Torah gives more detail?

6. Consider the themes of Rabbi Arthur Waskow's interpretive translation of 11:1-21:

> If you listen, if you REALLY listen, to the teachings of YHWH, the Breath of life, especially to the teaching that there is Unity in the world and interconnection among all its parts, then the rains will fall as they should, the rivers will run, the heavens will smile, and the good earth and all its creatures will feed you and feed each other.

> BUT if you shatter the harmony of life, if you chop the world up into parts, and choose one or more of these parts to idolize, such as the god of wealth or the god of greed, or the addition to Make and Produce without pausing to Be and to Rest, then the Breath of Life will come as a hurricane to shatter your harmony.

> For if you pour poison into the earth and air and water, then it will be poison that you eat, and drink and breathe. The rain won't fall–or, it will turn into acid when it does. The rivers won't run—or they will overflow, because you have no earth where the rain can soak in, and the heavens themselves will become your enemy.

> The ozone layer will no longer shield you, the Carbon Dioxide you pour into the air will scorch your planet, and you will perish from off the good earth that the Breath of Life gives you.

Therefore, set these words in your heart and in every breath. Carry them in every act towards which you put your hands, and make them the pattern through which you see the world. Teach them to your children, to repeat to their children. Stay aware of them when you are at home, and when you travel;

When you lie down to dream and when you rise up to act. Write them on the thresholds. Write them on the doorposts of your houses and of your city gates.

So that your days and the days of your children grow more, grow deeper, grow higher, grow better upon the earth that the Breath of Life swore to your ancestors to give them. So that, as *Shamayim*—which is Heaven—is where *Esh* and *Mayim*—fire and water—meet together and live in peace. So you can make of earth a place where all creatures live together in harmony. The days on earth will be as peaceful as the days of the heavens are.[151]

THINK ABOUT

1. In 7:14 the text says that the Israelites will "be more blessed" than other peoples. Here it implies fertility and good health. What are the blessings in your life?

2. In 8:5 we read "Bear in mind that your God YHVH disciplines you like a parent disciplines a child." In 11:19 it says, "... and teach them to your children ..." Some of the examples of parenting in Genesis leave many disappointed or outraged. Here, the parental role involves teaching and gentle discipline.

3. In this portion, we find the injunction to "be satisfied" (Deuteronomy 8:10). Perhaps feeling satisfied is more difficult to uphold than any other commandment! For some, being satisfied is challenging with food or drink. For others, the relentless desire for more is felt with possessions or experiences.

---

151 Eco-Torah: "The Wind & Rain, The Sun and Soil, are One." Theshalomcenter.org/node/219 9/8/2001

It's not easy to say, "I have enough. I don't need more." Can people train themselves to be satisfied? Daily practice/prayer in the morning begins with "*Modeh/Modah ani*," meaning, "I am grateful." For some, starting the day with gratitude results in less grasping during the ensuing hours.

4. Moses mentions fasting in 9:9 and 9:18. Fasting either contributed to or was Moses' response to his intense spiritual experience on Mt. Sinai. Have you found that fasting heightens spiritual awareness?

5. Moses refers to the Ten Commandments in 10:4. They are spelled out in detail in Deuteronomy 5:6-18. What kind of person and what kind of society do these commandments foster? The two commandments that seem to challenge people most frequently are honoring parents and not coveting/craving. Are these challenging to you?

6. Deuteronomy 10:16 says, "Cut away, therefore, the thickening about your hearts and stiffen your necks no more." Literally the words are, "circumcise the foreskin of your heart," suggesting the removal of emotional and spiritual barriers to loving God. What impediments interfere with strengthening the spiritual dimension of your life?

FOCUS PHRASE (8:2)

L'da'at et asher bel'va'vecha—Learn what is in your heart.

R'eih (Deuteronomy 11:26–16:17) "Look Around"

OVERVIEW

Moses urges the Israelites to choose life and blessing by following God's commandments. Moses forbids idol worship in the Promised Land. There will be a dedicated place for sacrifices, tithes, and gifts. Regarding eating meat, Moses reiterates the ban against ingesting blood. He adds restrictions as to which kinds of meat, fish, birds, and insects can be consumed. Moses expresses concern for the poor, the Levite, the stranger, the fatherless, and the widow. Finally, there are descriptions of Passover, Shavuot, and Sukkot.

STANDOUT VERSES

11:26 "See, this day I set before you blessing and curse." The punishments for not obeying God are severe, but the rewards of compliance are great. People can choose; people have free will.

15:1 "Every seventh year you shall practice remission of debts." Leviticus 25:5-7 declares that seventh year crops are free for the taking. This verse ordains that loans are canceled every seven years.

15:7 "If, however, there is a needy person among you, one of your kin in any of your settlements, in the Land that YHVH your God is giving you, do not harden your heart or shut your hand against your needy kin." Once again, the Torah demands sensitivity and material support for those in need.

16:3, 16:12 "... you may remember the day of your departure from the land of Egypt as long as you live" and "Bear in mind that you were slaves in Egypt ..." The Exodus is central to Israelite identity. God acted in their history by liberating them from slavery. The Torah is preoccupied with taking the Israelites out of Egypt and with taking Egyptian values and norms out of the people. But, the people are also instructed to keep the experience of slavery and dislocation at the forefront of their communal awareness.

TALK ABOUT

1. The word "rejoice" appears in this portion in 12:7, 12:12, 16:11, and 16:14. In each case, God commands the people to rejoice with others. Can rejoicing be commanded? Does rejoicing require the presence of other people?

2. The Garden of Eden was a vegetarian environment (Genesis 1:29 and 2:16). Later, God reconsidered and eating meat was allowed (Genesis 9:3). But this compromise included delineation of acceptable and unacceptable animals for consumption. Because blood symbolizes life, eating blood was prohibited (Genesis 9:4, Leviticus 17:11; and Deuteronomy 12:16, 12:23, and 15:23). Do you have any qualms about eating meat? If you are a vegetarian, what contributed to your decision not to eat meat?

3. The Israelites are a "consecrated and treasured people" (14:2). The text continues with a detailed list of dietary laws. Most scholars agree that one of the purposes of the dietary laws was to distinguish Israel from other nations. What are other reasons for prescribing a particular diet? What are possible outcomes from communally observing specific dietary practices?

4. Why are mourning and dietary laws paired in chapter 14? What stands out to me is what they *don't* have in common: dietary laws affect people multiple times a day. Laws and practices surrounding mourning are relevant much less frequently in a person's life.

5. The command not to "boil a kid in its mother's milk," appears in 14:20 for the third time (prior references are Exodus 23:19 and 34:26). This prohibition is consistent with other biblical laws stipulating humane treatment of animals. There is a prohibition against sacrificing an ox or sheep on the same day as their offspring (Leviticus 22:28) or taking a mother bird with her eggs (Deuteronomy 22:6-7). The Ten Commandments include a day of rest for working animals. Animals of unequal strengths may not be yoked together. Compassion for animals is frequently authorized in the Torah.

6. Three verbs used in 13:15 assure meticulous care in determining capital cases. The verbs are: "investigate, inquire, and interrogate." This indicates a high level of due diligence when considering the most serious cases.

7. Chapter 16:1-17 describes the three Pilgrimage Festivals: Passover, Shavuot, and Sukkot. These were the central holy days of biblical times. For the majority of Jews today, it is the High Holy Days and Passover that dominate the holiday calendar. Why has this changed over time? What do the Three Pilgrimage Festivals have in common? Why do the High Holy Days in particular call to us so strongly?

"Nowhere is the difference between the spiritual life and its material counterpart more clearly seen than in the possibility of turning. In the world of nature, the principle of irreversibility obtains: Events move in one direction only and once they have happened, they cannot be undone. Not so with repentance: it provides for turning back the clock through a joining of human will and divine acceptance. This is why *Yom Kippur* became Jewry's most important holy day."[152]

THINK ABOUT

1. 13:7 includes the Hebrew phrase *"rei'echa asher c'nafshecha,"* which is translated as "your closest friend," but actually means "your friend who is (like) your own soul." Are you surprised to find a description of friendship in the Torah? Do you have friends who are "like your own soul"?

2. Frequently in the book of Deuteronomy, and in this portion, God *chooses* the people of Israel (14:2). In the prior four books of the Torah, Moses declares the Israelites separate and holy, but the word "chosen" isn't used. How do you understand "chosenness"? The concept makes many Jews uncomfortable, even embarrassed. In the blessing chanted before the Torah reading, the Reconstructionist movement offers an alternative to the words "Who has chosen us from all the peoples." They propose, "Who has drawn us to Your service." What do you think of this change?[153]

3. "You are what you eat." It appears that the laws of kashrut took this notion into account. Maimonides reflected that non-kosher food engenders spiritual insensitivity. Other sages described the forbidden foods as destructive to the soul. Animals of prey may not be consumed.

152 *The Torah: A Modern Commentary*, Revised Edition. W. Gunther Plaut, ed., David E.S. Stern, Revised Edition ed., New York: URJ Press, 2006, p. 1380.

153 *Kol Haneshama: Shabbat Vehagim*, Teutsch, David A., ed., Elkins Park, PA: The Reconstructionist Press, 2004, p. 399.

Animal blood cannot be ingested. Milk products (representing life) and meat products (resulting from the death of animals) require separation.

4. In this portion, the people of Israel are called "*am segulah*," a "treasured people." This relates to being "chosen." If you accept the notion of being part of the Chosen People, do you think it requires anything of you?

Focus Phrase (11:27)

Hab'rachah—The blessing.

Shof'tim
(Deuteronomy 16:18–21:9) "Pursuing Justice"

OVERVIEW

This portion focuses on justice, administered by impartial, non-religiously sanctioned citizens. Judges must be objective and impervious to bribes. *Shof'tim* discusses witnesses, refuge cities, and rules of war. "Justice, justice shall you pursue" (Deut. 16:20), one of the most touted verses of the Torah, appears in this section. Without the pursuit of justice, the people will not flourish.

Shof'tim also includes the law prohibiting destruction of fruit-bearing trees in a besieged city (Deut. 20:19-20). This prohibition became part of *"bal tash'chit,"* the practice that forbids reckless destruction. Maimonides states that this also applies to breaking vessels, tearing garments, wasting food and water. In several places, the Torah enacts environmental responsibility.

STANDOUT VERSES

16:20 "Justice, justice shall you pursue." Repeating the word "justice" indicates how important it is. That this verse is so well known reflects its centrality as a fundamental tenet of Judaism.

17:15-17 "You shall be free to set a king over yourself, one chosen by your God YHVH, one of your own people ... he shall not keep many horses ... he shall not have many wives, lest his heart go astray: nor shall he amass silver and gold to excess." The Torah recognizes that power can lead to decadence. These verses mandate moderation for the ruler.

18:9-12 "When you enter the land ... you shall not learn to imitate the abhorrent practices of those nations ... consign a son or daughter to the fire ... soothsayer, diviner or sorcerer, who casts spells or consults ghosts or inquires of the dead. Anyone who does such things is abhorrent to YHVH."

The Torah reviles magic and divination. However, Joseph is praised for interpreting dreams (e.g., Genesis 41:12) and Moses displayed supernatural signs to convince Pharaoh of God's power (e.g., Exodus 4:6-7). The difference in the examples with Joseph and Moses is that

God precipitated the displays of extraordinary manifestations, as noted in Genesis 40:8: "Surely interpretations are in God's domain"; and in Genesis 41:16: "Not I—it is God who will account for Pharaoh's well-being."

19:21 "Life for life, eye for eye, tooth for tooth, hand for hand, foot for foot." You may recognize this principle as *lex talionis*, physical retribution in which the punishment is equitable to the injury (also in Exodus 21:24 and Leviticus 24:17-20).

This is one of the most thoroughly misunderstood passages in the Torah. There is no physical retribution of this sort in the entire Hebrew Bible. Critical scholarship supports the idea that compensation scaled to the degree of the injury was the intention: an eye's value for the loss of an eye, and so on. The point of the law was to restrict violence, not sanction it. Only intentional homicide was not included in this paradigm. Money could not compensate for a lost life.

TALK ABOUT

1. Why is the word "*tzedek*," "justice," repeated in 16:20? Commentators have suggested that the repetition is designed as a reminder to first carefully consider, and then, carefully review a conclusion before making a final decision. Others explain that the repetition suggests consultation before deciding even an initial determination of a sentence. Some understand the repetition as conveying the idea that justice be the concern of the courts as well as the concern of individuals in private matters. One commentator explained the verse as communicating that justice is required in word and in deed, in business and in personal relationships, with all people. Can you think of other explanations for using the word "*tzedek*" twice?

2. *Parashat Shof'tim* includes many verses about judging. Some wonder: How will God judge me? For others, the pertinent question is: How do we judge ourselves? How easily and how frequently do you judge others? Being judgmental is problematic for many. For those who have found ways to be less judgmental, how have they achieved it?

3. 17:20 says that observing the Torah will generate humility. Here are some insightful reflections on humility:

A. Humility is not a feeling per se; it is less a state of mind than a trait of character. Humility is an abiding awareness that arises within you when you discover the interconnectedness of all things. Humility is the key to wonder. As humility grows, wonder deepens. Aware of your impermanence, you become brother and sister to all life. You realize the common fate of all beings and find in that realization a compassion that embraces all beings.[154]

B. The ego provides the lens through which we see all of life. If our lens is clean, we see clearly and can interact in a true way. To be arrogant or self-deprecating distorts our approach to life. Humility stands on a foundation of self-esteem, and is defined by how much space you occupy—being humble means occupying your rightful space, where "space" can be physical, verbal, emotional, financial, and so on."[155]

C. *Anavah*, approaching our lives with humility, means not taking up too much space, not trying to fool others with some disguise of our true selves; but to honestly offer our truest selves to the people and the work we encounter in our lives ... Cultivating *anavah* might support us in finding our soul's rightful place.[156]

D. A statement often attributed to C.S. Lewis puts it best: humility, it states, is not thinking less of yourself; it is thinking of yourself less ... Those who have humility are open to things greater than themselves while those who lack it are not ... those who lack it make you feel small, while those who have it make you feel enlarged.[157]

THINK ABOUT

I. Some rabbis interpret the word "*lecha*," "for yourself" in the verse, "You shall appoint magistrates and officials for yourself..." (16:18) as a call for each to judge her/himself, to judge our own actions. This notion

---

154 Rabbi Rami Shapiro, *The Sacred Art of Lovingkindness: Preparing to Practice*, Woodstock, VT: Skylight Paths Publishing, 2006, p. 136.

155 Alan Morinis, *Everyday Holiness: The Jewish Spiritual Path of Mussar*, Boston, MA: Trumpeter Books, 2007, p. 49.

156 Rabbi Michelle Pearlman and Rabbi Sharon Marx, *The Mussar Torah Commentary: A Spiritual Path to Living a Meaningful and Ethical Life*, Rabbi Barry H. Block, ed., New York, NY: CCAR Press, 2020, p. 6.

157 Rabbi Jonathan Sacks, *Essays on Ethics: A Weekly Reading of the Jewish Bible*, Jerusalem: Maggid Books, 2016, p. 230.

differs from that of appointing external judges to evaluate our behavior. There is value to both understandings.

Do you judge yourself or others more harshly?

2. 18:13 includes the instruction, "Be wholehearted with God." The Hebrew word for wholehearted, *tamim*, appears in the plural form. Are there many ways to be wholehearted?

3. One of the Four Children in the *Haggadah* is called *tam*, usually translated as "simple." During the Seder, the *Tam* Child asks: "What is this?" The "*tam*" child represents someone who easily trusts, and wants to learn.

4. In 20:8, commanding officers in wartime ask their troops, "Is there anyone afraid and disheartened? Let him go back to his home, lest the courage of his comrades flag like his." Is fear contagious? Courage doesn't mean being fearless but moving forward in spite of one's fear. Have there been times when you acted with courage—physical as well as emotional, moral, spiritual?

FOCUS PHRASE (21:9)

Tah'ah'seh ha'yashar—Do what is (up)right.

Ki Teitzei
(Deuteronomy 21:10–25:19)
"Compassion for Animals"

OVERVIEW

There are more laws and a wider range of laws in *Ki Teitzei* than in any *parsha*: laws prescribing humane treatment of animals, criminals, orphans, widows, strangers, slaves, and female captives. For example: You must pay out the wages due on the same day (24:15). You shall not plow with an ox and an ass together (animals of unequal strength) (22:10). You must have completely honest weights and completely honest measures (25:15). Other laws, which appear inhumane, reject cross-dressing (22:5) and sanction harsh punishment for what is viewed as disruptive behavior (21:18-21, 22:20-21, and 25:11-12).

In the Torah, there are thirty-six instances for which the death penalty is authorized. However, the Talmud asserts that the decision to execute requires a strict series of stipulations. Among other prerequisites, two eyewitnesses must have seen the crime committed, the perpetrators had to have been warned that the act was criminal and the punishment would be execution, and a panel of twenty-three judges had to hear the testimony with a majority of only one necessary to acquit.

In short, the rabbis' desire was to ensure the death penalty was virtually impossible to enact.

Most legislation in *Ki Teitzei* champions justice and compassion through honoring the sanctity of human and animal life. Prayers on *Yom Kippur*, the Day of Atonement reiterate these values, noting that God desires repentance, not punishment as atonement for transgressions.

STANDOUT VERSES

22:1-3 "If you see your fellow Israelite's ox or sheep gone astray, do not ignore it. You must take it back ... with their garment ... with anything that your fellow Israelite loses and you find: you must not remain indifferent." It is tempting to disregard or make light of someone else's problem. These verses mandate restoration regardless of inconvenience, expense, or the nature of one's relationship with the person who has lost something.

22:12 "You shall make tassels on the four corners of the garment with which you cover yourself." Numbers 15:37-41 designates tassels as reminders to uphold God's commandments. Over time, fulfillment of this commandment came through the creation of a rectangular cloth with tassels on its corners—a *tallit*. Some wear a *tallit katan*, a kind of undershirt with fringes hanging from the four corners, every day.

23:8 "You shall not abhor an Egyptian, for you were a stranger in that land." After being repeatedly reminded of how cruelly the Egyptians enslaved the Israelites, this verse comes as a surprise. How do you explain the prohibition against hating an Egyptian?

23:16-17 "You shall not turn over to the master a slave who seeks refuge with you ... you must not ill-treat them." It is uniformly accepted that this refers to slaves who fled to the land of Israel from foreign countries. This law refutes common practice in the ancient Near East, which forbade harboring runaway slaves.

TALK ABOUT

1. The portion opens with a discussion of Israelite practices when a warrior wishes to marry a female captive. The scenario is distressing, as are all realities of war. Here, the Torah mandates at least a modicum of compassion for the captured woman: She can regain some dignity through attention to her appearance. She has a few weeks' time to begin to adjust to her new surroundings while grieving her losses. If her would-be husband decides not to marry her, she may not be enslaved or sold for money.

The captive woman lives in her captor's home; thus, he presumably sees her anguish every day. Coming face to face with someone's suffering daily, do our hearts soften or harden? At what point do we start looking and start seeing; at what point do we stop looking and stop seeing?

2. 21:23 stipulates burying the corpse of an executed criminal. Eventually, this verse provided the basis for the Jewish practice of expedient ground burial for all human bodies. For generations, Jews shunned cremation. Now some Jewish communities find cremation acceptable. What is your view on this issue? What are the emotional advantages to a quick burial? Are there advantages to a delayed burial? What are reasons for

choosing ground burial instead of cremation, or cremation instead of ground burial?

3. *Ki Teitzei* mandates kindness to animals in 22:1, 22:4, 22:6-7, 22:10, and 25:4. Even though animals were sacrificed as a form of worship, the Torah repeatedly promotes compassion for animals. (e.g., Leviticus 22:28). What have domestic animals taught you about compassion, loyalty, and responsibility?

4. This portion also addresses false accusations and misused words. Our carelessness with words is a central concern during the High Holy Days. We take time to consider our indulgence of gossip, flattery, exaggeration, lying, and shaming. What is your relationship to words—to "rightful speech"?

5. A large section of this portion, 24:15-25:16, detail laws that protect vulnerable people, those who are economically disadvantaged and those who have no familial safety net. Consider these Torah laws in terms of current practices in our country (or more locally). What are basic, reasonable protections a humane society should guarantee? How do you compare the Torah laws that protect the vulnerable with the fate of the female prisoner of war whom we meet in 21:10-14?

THINK ABOUT

1. A commentary called *Zohar Chadash* considers that the opening words to this portion, "When you go out to do battle," refer to ongoing battles with the *yetzer hara* (often called the "evil inclination; I prefer the "destructive inclination"). What areas of your life never seem to get resolved? What situations repeat, year after year, and you can't seem to get a handle on them? For example, are friends always disappointing you? Do you continue to battle the same addiction? Do you start new projects before completing others?

2. Twice in chapter 22 we find variations on the word *"hit'a'lame"*: 22:1 *"v'hit'a'lam'ta"* and 22:3 *"l'hit'a'lame."* "Do not remain indifferent" provides a clear call for personal and social responsibility.

3. 21:20 describes a "glutton and a drunkard." In the High Holy Day *Al Chet* prayer, which enumerates ways we have missed the mark, we ask forgiveness for many offenses, including gluttony and alcohol abuse.

Are these behaviors problematic for you? What contributes to a healthy relationship to food and drink?

4. 22:13-29 lists laws regarding sexual misconduct. During the High Holy Days, we ask forgiveness for such behavior. If your behavior in the area of sexual matters warrants repair, how can you begin that process?

5. Chapter 24 begins with a discussion of divorce. The scenario is off-putting: "She fails to please him because he finds something obnoxious about her ..."

These verses invite us to reflect on our partnerships or marriages. Have these relationships been nurtured in the past year through shared activities, time away from stresses, and dedicated time to discuss areas of conflict? Have efforts been made to express love and concern? Do some relationship habits need to be critiqued or updated?

FOCUS PHRASE (22:3)

Lo tu'chal l'het'ah'leim—Do not remain indifferent.

Ki Tavo (Deuteronomy 26:1-29:8)
"Joy and Gratitude"

OVERVIEW

Ki Tavo, "When you enter ..." invites us to consider profound aspects of our lives. The portion begins with a ceremony of gratitude acknowledging the distance traveled to reach this moment, recognizing who and what has enabled success. After the ceremony, blessings and curses indicate the consequences of the people's behavior.

The detailed list of curses (Deut. 27:15-26 and 28:15-68) is difficult to hear. Can we reconcile harsh punishments with a loving God? For some, reconciliation is impossible. For others, relief comes by omitting the name of the person who chants this section during *Shabbat* services. The reader is called "one who wishes." They recite the curses in a low voice.

STANDOUT VERSES

26:5 "My father was a fugitive Aramean." The Torah consistently adjures the Israelites to remember their modest beginnings. "My father" could refer to Abraham, or Isaac, or Jacob (or all of them). These words form the opening text in the *Haggadah*.

26:11-12 "And you shall enjoy, together with the family of the Levite and the stranger in your midst, all the bounty ... Set aside in full the tenth part of your yield ... give it to the Levite, the stranger, the fatherless and the widow that they may eat their fill in your settlements." Celebrations are magnified when good fortune is shared with those who have less.

27:15 (and following) "*Amen.*" Derived from the Hebrew root meaning "firm," this word indicates agreement and endorsement. Muslims, Christians, and Jews use the word "*Amen*" at the end of prayers.

29:3 "Yet to this day YHVH has not given you a mind to understand or eyes to see or ears to hear." It is common not to fully understand the events in our lives until years later, with hindsight. Over time, we achieve some sense of comprehension and perspective. One response to this is: "If only I had known." Another response is: I couldn't have appreciated it then. A third response might be: Now that I understand, will anything change for me moving forward?

Talk About

1. 26:11 instructs, "... And you shall enjoy," employing the Hebrew word "v'sa'mach'ta." The word "simcha" describes a happy event built with intention and preparation. While simchas are always joyous occasions, they are different from occasions focused on fun. Simchas celebrate something accomplished; they celebrate a commitment. Does "celebration" fully describe a simcha?

2. 27:9 includes Moses telling the Israelites to "listen," "shema." Do you differentiate between hearing, listening, paying attention, and understanding? Which of these require the most acute focus? How do you feel when someone is truly listening to you? The blessing before sounding the Shofar commands us to "listen to its voice." Does your body, heart, mind, soul, or all respond to the Shofar? Is hearing the Shofar like anything else you have experienced?

3. 29:8 mandates, "Therefore observe faithfully all the terms of this covenant, that you may succeed in all that you undertake." What does it mean to succeed? Has your understanding of success changed over the years?

4. The list of curses in this portion is long. In some places, the curses are general: "Cursed shall you be in the city and cursed shall you be in the country" (28:16), and in some places, quite explicit: "YHVH will strike you with the Egyptian inflammation, with hemorrhoids, boil-scars, and itch, from which you shall never recover" (28:27).

It is difficult to select the most horrific scourges (possibly those dealing with one's children: 28:32 and 28:41), but I'd like to focus on those curses which consist of having one's efforts be frustrated: a house built but not inhabited, a vineyard planted but not harvested (28:30). These situations do not induce alarm; they induce despair: working hard and not reaping some reward; creating, but finding one's efforts thwarted. Many of us have experienced profound frustration in work, family life, or both. It takes courage and resilience to try again and remain optimistic when hope and trust are crushed.

THINK ABOUT

1. The first fruits and harvest mentioned in 26:1-2 refer to the agricultural staples of Israel: wheat, barley, grapes, figs, pomegranates, olives, and dates (mentioned in Deuteronomy 8:8). Enjoy these foods during the week they are mentioned in the Torah.

2. Read 26:1-11. It describes a ceremony of gratitude. What are you grateful for? How do you show gratitude publicly and privately?

3. In 26:5-9, the people are instructed to remember their history. Historical consciousness is a hallmark of the Jewish people. Recalling the past heightens self, communal, and national awareness, and pride. The Jewish people's birth is noted annually with a Passover Seder at which we read these verses.

Like the birth of a baby, the birth of a people includes moments of doubt and fear along with awe and wonder. Babies are born by coming through the birth canal. The Jewish people were "born" by proceeding through a passageway of dry land when (the story says), the seawaters were separated. The Israelites left "*Mitzrayim,*" a "narrow place," to achieve liberation. What are other hallmarks of new beginnings?

4. Consider 26:12-13. What types of *tzedakah* do you prioritize?

5. 26:16 ends with the phrase, "... with all your heart and soul." If we think of a person's heart as the location of love, what is located in the soul? When have you felt your soul touched? What fills it and what depletes it?

FOCUS PHRASE (29:8)

Tas'ki'lu et kol asher ta'a'soon—Succeed in all you undertake.

Nitzavim (Deuteronomy 29:9-30:20)
"Open Your Heart"

OVERVIEW

Nitzavim includes the covenant ceremony between God and the Israelites. Moses reminds them to be loyal to God; in return, God will grant prosperity. Moses exhorts, "Choose life by loving your God YHVH, heeding God's commands and holding fast to God."

Nitzavim and *Vayeilech* (the following portion) are usually read together.

Variations of the word *"t'shuvah"* occur eight times in ten verses of *Nitzavim* (30:1-10). *T'shuvah* is a central concern of the High Holy Day period. One way to describe *t'shuvah* is (re)appraisal resulting in transformation. As Moses nears the end of his life, he engages in (re)appraisal.

STANDOUT VERSES

29:13-14 "I make this covenant, with its sanctions, not with you alone, but with those who are standing with us this day before God YHVH and with those who are not with us here this day." How can a covenant be made with people who aren't present to agree to it? Jewish tradition understands this to mean that all future Jews will recognize the experience of a covenantal relationship with God *as if* they themselves made it. Other ancient Near Eastern treaties included the participants' descendants in binding treaties.

29:28 "Concealed acts concern our God YHVH but with overt acts, it is for us and our children ever to apply all the provisions of this Teaching." Most people want answers, and quick answers at that! Here the text is hinting: some things you may never understand. Judaism challenges us to use our intellects, to ponder, to search, and to question. But it holds out the possibility that some things are beyond our comprehension.

30:11-14 "Surely, this Instruction which I enjoin upon you this day is not too baffling for you, nor is it beyond reach. It is not in the heavens, that you should say, "Who among us can go up to the heavens and get it for us ... Neither is it beyond the sea ... No the thing is very close to you, in your mouth and in your heart, to observe it."

These beautiful verses indicate that the Torah is not for an elite intellectual class or for people who have attained lofty spiritual heights. It is a series of teachings for everyone, who can experience it through the lens of their own lived experience, in whatever ways they are able to best understand it.

30:19 "I have put before you life and death, blessing and curse. Choose life!" The Jewish celebratory toast, "*L'Chaim*," ("To Life") encapsulates our people's preoccupation with making the most of each precious day and year of life. Life is a gift to be cherished, and the longer one lives, the greater opportunity there is to create meaning and blessing.

TALK ABOUT

1. *Nitzavim* begins (Deuteronomy 29:9) by noting we stand before God. This awareness fades throughout much of the year, but during the High Holy Days, we find ourselves reawakened by this thought. Then we become freshly aware—we are accountable, our deeds and choices matter. What does it mean to "stand before God"?

2. 30:2 says "return to God," using the Hebrew word "*shav'ta*" which shares a root with "*t'shuvah*," "return." *T'shuvah* has been described in different ways, but it always includes an acknowledgement of wrongdoing, an effort to repair, and a commitment not to repeat the destructive act(s). Do you practice *t'shuvah* (reconciliation and realignment)? "*T'shuvah*-worthy" behaviors include lying, cheating, abusing power, withholding love.

3. God announces that the covenant with Israel is binding on those not yet born (29:14). It is understandable that some people balk at this: Why should people be expected to accept obligations they didn't choose? Some streams of Judaism encourage adherents to choose which aspects of Judaism they want to uphold.

What are the benefits and deficits to living in a Jewish community where people recognize similar obligations? What are the benefits and deficits of living in a Jewish community where people pick and choose traditions and norms to live by?

4. In 31:9-11, Moses writes down the Teaching, gives a copy to the priests and the elders, and instructs them to engage in a public reading every

seven years. Could he have done more to insure the Torah's centrality in Israelite life?

Today, some communities read from the Torah up to four times a week; others read a section once a week on Shabbat morning. What is enough, not enough, too much? How do you think communities should handle the less uplifting parts of the Torah—skip over them or shine a light on them?

5. The word "love" appears often in this *parsha*. Some people say that the Torah emphasizes justice but neglects love. In fact, the Torah regularly instructs us to love God, our neighbor, and the stranger. What do these types of love have in common? How do you define love?

THINK ABOUT

1. This portion is read on the Shabbat prior to *Rosh HaShanah*. What New Year themes do you find in *Nitzavim*? The root word of "*Nitzavim*," "standing," suggests "standing at attention," or "standing alertly." Does this describe your stance as the year begins? What are you ready to stand up for? About what are you standoffish? And how do you *understand* your identity as a parent, grandparent, child, sibling, friend, colleague, activist, caregiver, artist, etc.?

2. *T'shuvah* is not an event but a process: an awakening of mind or heart that something is off-center, toxic, or strangely exhausting. In whose presence do I pretend? Why do I make excuses about not showing up? About what issues have I become cynical? What painful truths about my life do I claim not to have time to explore? These are all questions for which *t'shuvah* may provide direction.

Awakening, naming, reflecting, evaluating, and imagining: these actions, not judging, criticizing, shaming, and blaming, are the keys to effective *t'shuvah*. Engaging in *t'shuvah* allows for the possibility of reconciliation, repair, and renewal.

3. Some people who choose Judaism as adults describe it as a homecoming. They say they "knew" something was missing in their lives, and discovering Judaism brought them a new sense of wholeness and being at home. They rejoice in their newfound extended family and become enthusiastic and dedicated participants in Jewish life. For others, becoming Jewish has been more treacherous in terms of navigating their childhood family or the family they are joining. What

has been the experience of your family members or friends who have chosen Judaism? In what ways is your community welcoming?

4. The words in 30:6 advise, "Open your heart." The Hebrew says, "Circumcise your heart." Circumcision cuts away an extra layer of flesh. It results in temporary bleeding (vulnerability) and greater sensitivity. What opens your heart and what closes it down?

5. The theme of 30:11-20 is choosing life and blessing. This section stresses that the choice is ours, not God's. God's teaching is not esoteric: "The thing is very close to you, in your mouth and in your heart." How have your commitments brought you life and blessing?

FOCUS PHRASE (30:6)

B'chol lva'vecha uv'chol nafshecha—With all your heart and soul.

Vayeilech
(Deuteronomy 31:1-30)
"Be Strong and Resolute"

OVERVIEW

At thirty verses, *Vayeilech* is the shortest Torah portion. Moses delivers an encouraging message to the Israelites, acknowledging he will be unable to join them in the Promised Land. Joshua becomes the primary leader. The opening tone, stabilizing and hopeful, darkens in the second part of the portion: God predicts the people will turn to other gods. Moses instructs people to gather every seven years to hear "every word of the Torah teaching."

STANDOUT VERSES

31:6 "Be strong and resolute, be not in fear or in dread ..." When recalling a time of apprehension, Moses spoke these very words to reassure the people of God's protection (Deuteronomy 1:21). This expression is characteristic of pronouncements made by deities in the ancient Near East, particularly in anticipation of war. It is a big ask to "fear not," but when it comes from a trusted loved one or worthy leader, the words "fear not" buttress confidence and commitment.

31:11 "... you shall read this Teaching aloud ..." For many people who attend services on *Shabbat* morning, the Torah reading (and its explication) is the most valued part of the worship experience. Even though people have a written text to view, there is something dramatic and memorable when the Torah scroll is taken from the ark and is chanted in Hebrew.

31:12 "Gather the people—men, women, children, and the strangers in your communities—that they may hear and so learn to revere your God YHVH ..." Here and in 29:9-10, Moses addresses a large collective.

TALK ABOUT

1. Moses says in 31:2, "I am now one hundred and twenty years old." This is the ideal life span noted in Genesis 6:3. Recently, more people

have become centenarians, and yet extreme old age still seems a marvel. Do you see old age as a blessing? What are the opportunities that are unavailable at younger ages? Can old age be uniquely productive? What do you wish your younger self had known?

2. The mantle of leadership passes from Moses to Joshua in 31:3. Although we sense that Moses doesn't want to die, he does not begrudge Joshua his new leadership role. It is challenging to walk away from a position of prominence or prestige. Even watching our children's primary allegiance move from us as their parents to their friends and partners can be difficult and feel threatening. Sometimes public figures set excellent examples by handling transitions with dignity. Sometimes it's embarrassing to see people unwilling to step aside when appropriate.

How have you handled public or private transitions? What creates a smooth transfer of responsibility?

3. In this portion, Moses learns again he will not reach the Promised Land, even though he devoted most of his life to this prospect. Moses represents the reality that we all die with at least some goals and wishes unfulfilled.

4. Moses instructs the people to gather every seven years to hear the Torah recited (31:10). Is hearing an address every seven years enough to sustain enthusiasm and belief? Some Jews only attend services during the High Holy Days and this sustains them. Is it enough for you? Other than services, what else satisfies your spiritual needs?

THINK ABOUT

1. Three times in *Vayeilech* we read, "Be strong and resolute" (31:6-7 and 31:23). These words build confidence. What do you tell yourself to build your confidence and how do you encourage others?

2. God says to Moses in 31:14, "The time is drawing near for you to die." When you have spoken to someone who has a terminal diagnosis, how have they managed it? What have you learned from observing or talking to someone who knows they will die shortly? If you can imagine being told you have six months to a year left to live, how would you approach this time? What do you think is a "good death"?

3. This *parsha* includes the phrase "Write for yourselves ..." the song of the Israelite people (referring to 32:1-52). Maimonides explains that

"Write for yourselves ..." means that each person should write a *Sefer Torah*.

But look at the verse, as directing each of us to write *our own* Torah scroll. This invites us to think of our lives as a collection of teachings—a kind of Torah. Carol Ochs wrote a book called, *Our Lives as Torah: Finding God in our Stories*, in which she documents the insight and healing that results when people view their lives as sacred text.[158]

4. This portion, usually combined with *Nitzavim*, is always read just before the High Holy Days begin. Do the High Holy Days usher in the Jewish New Year or your personal New Year?

FOCUS PHRASE (31:7)

Cha'zak ve'ah'mats—Be strong and secure.

---

158 San Francisco, CA: Josey-Bass, Inc., 2001.

Haazinu (Deuteronomy 32:1-52) "Active Listening"

OVERVIEW

Also called *Shirat Haazinu* ("the Song *Haazinu*"), this portion is a poem that begins by contrasting God and Israel. God is steadfast and Israel is fickle. God bestows blessings on the Israelites and they are disloyal. Moses' rebuke intensifies as he recognizes he will die soon. He describes God as lovingly devoted to the people. But God holds the people accountable for their lapses in allegiance.

STANDOUT VERSES

32:10 "God engirded them, watched over them; guarded them as the pupil of God's eye." In modern parlance, "the apple of their eye" refers to someone who is particularly cherished. The verse explains that God loves Israel with special devotion.

32:13 "Nursing them with honey from the crag ..." Specific female imagery for God is not common in the Torah, but here, we find a maternal metaphor to describe God's nourishing attention.

32:18 "... the God who labored to bring you forth." This is another example of God in the role of mother.

32:47 "For this is not a trifling thing for you: it is your very life." Torah teachings are not frivolous. They constitute the essence, the substance, and the core of a well-lived life.

TALK ABOUT

1. In 32:1 we read: "Give ear, O Heavens ..." These words, "I raise my hand to heaven ..." (32:40) are at the end of *Haazinu*. By invoking heaven twice, Moses tries to impress the Israelites with the covenant's eternal nature. What other words does Moses use to capture the people's attention?

2. Moses describes God as "perfect," "just," and "true," (32:4) and also as One who "wounds" and "punishes" (32:39 and 32:41). Is it possible to reconcile these polarized attributes of God? Some believe that God is just and merciful, but that God's justice and mercy will only be realized

in the *Olam haba*, the world to come. How do *you* address the reality of evil? How can a God of justice tolerate hunger, war, disease, or cruelty?

3. Why is there evil in the world? Nowhere does the Torah answer this question directly. Yet, Abraham and Moses, arguably the two most faithful followers of God, object to injustice. Abraham in Genesis 18:25, "Must not the Judge of all the earth do justly?" and Moses in Exodus 5:22, "Why did You bring harm upon this people?" Jeremiah, in the section of the Bible called "Prophets" challenges God even more directly, "Why are the wicked so prosperous? Why are evil people so happy?" Judaism welcomes questioning of God.

4. *Haazinu* is primarily a poem. Its dominant message is the singular relationship between God and the people of Israel. Is it a piece of love poetry? What does this portion have in common with love poetry?

5. In this portion, God is a warrior-king and also a nurturing parent. Is your understanding of God reflected in either of these metaphors?

6. Moses uses the word "see" in 32:39, and in 32:44 it says, "Moses came and recited all the words of this poem in the hearing of the people." An exact translation is "into the ears of the people." As Moses' final oration approaches, he calls on the Israelites to be extremely attentive to his words both through hearing and seeing. Do you sense Moses' urgency increasing elsewhere in this portion?

THINK ABOUT

1. Moses details the pivotal events in the Israelites' life, including the origins of God's relationship with Israel, their wanderings in the desert, and their acts of disloyalty. What are the pivotal events in your life? What were the early formative relationships inside and outside your family? Do any of these relationships affect your understanding of, or relationship with, God?

2. God is called "*Tsur*," "Rock," multiple times in this portion. What names of God resonate most with you? Here are some possibilities; feel free to add your own.

HaShem—The Name

HaMakom—The Place

HaShalom—The Peace

HaKodesh Baruch Hu—The Holy One, Blessed be the One

Ruach HaOlam—Spirit of the World

Boray HaOlam—Creator of the World

Shaddai—The Mountainous or Breasted One

YHWH—unpronounceable, but often read "Adonai." YHWH is based on the three tenses of the verb "to be": Was, Is, Will be.

Melech HaOlam—King/Sovereign of the World

Shechinah—In-Dwelling Presence

Ehyeh Asher Ehyeh—I will Be what I will Be

The liturgist Marcia Falk composed these fresh metaphors of God by drawing on a variety of biblical phrases:

Ein HaChayim—Well Spring or Source of Life

Nishmat Kol Chai—Breath of All Living Things

Nitzotzot HaNefesh—Sparks of the Inner, Unseen Self[59]

Do Falk's images speak to you?

3. In 32:15, Moses accuses the Israelites of becoming spoiled. They forget they owe their existence to God. In your experience, are successful people more or less likely to recall those who contributed to their accomplishments?

4. God tells Moses when and where he will die in 32:50, "You shall die on the mountain that you are about to ascend." Would you like to know when and where you will die? What would you do with that information?

5. In several places in the Torah, and in 32:50, being "gathered to your kin" is what transpires after death. Do you think you will be reunited with your family or loved ones after you die? Is this a comforting notion, or a disturbing thought?

---

159 "Toward a Feminist Jewish Reconstruction of Monotheism," in *Contemporary Jewish Theology: A Reader*, Elliott N. Dorff and Louis E. Newman, eds., New York, NY: Oxford University Press, 1999, p. 131.

6. *Parshat Haazinu* is read on *Shabbat Shuva*, the "Shabbat of Return" between *Rosh HaShanah* and *Yom Kippur*. There are several High Holy Day themes in this portion.

In the High Holy Day season, consider how you have grown and achieved your goals, and ways you have disappointed yourself or others. The High Holy Days provide a dedicated time to disclose heartfelt realizations to God or loved ones.

Focus Phrase (32:47)

Lo d'var reik hu, hu cha'yei'chem—For this is not a trifling thing for you; it is your very life.

V'zot Hab'rachah
(Deuteronomy 33:1–34:12)
"The Blessing of Endings"

OVERVIEW

This is the final portion in the Torah. It is read only on *Simchat Torah*, when the annual Torah reading cycle concludes and the new cycle, beginning with the first chapters of Genesis, commences. Moses delivers his final words, including a blessing for each tribe. The Torah ends not with fulfillment but with hope.

The blessing of the tribes serves as a reasonable conclusion to the Torah. It is reminiscent of Jacob blessing his sons at the end of Genesis (Genesis 49:1-28). In the closing verses of *V'zot Hab'rachah*, Moses dies. He has known God "face to face." God buries Moses, and a thirty-day period of mourning follows. Joshua's leadership begins.

STANDOUT VERSES

33:5 "... the tribes of Israel together." Throughout Jewish history there has been disunity and conflict among the "tribes" of the Jewish people: different sects, different leaders, different movements, different interpretations of sacred texts, different prayers, and different food customs. Yet many retain the aspiration that Jews find common ground and treat each other with respect. May this occur in our communities!

33:29 "O happy Israel!" What constitutes "happiness" in the Torah? See the preceding verse, 33:28: Israel dwelling in safety, in a land of grain and wine, under heavens dripping dew. It doesn't look like Eden, but the experience sounds paradise-like. Thus, the Torah begins with a picture-perfect home and concludes with the hope that such a home can be realized again.

34:7 "Moses was a hundred and twenty years when he died; his eyes were undimmed and his vigor unabated." This verse assures the reader that Moses was human: he was subject to death and he had a physical form.

34:10 "Never again did there arise in Israel a prophet like Moses—whom YHVH singled out, face to face." Although the prior verse asserts Moses' humanity, here the Torah insists on Moses' spiritual uniqueness.

TALK ABOUT

1. In 33:1, Moses is called "*ish haElohim*," "man of God." In 34:5, he is called "*eved YHVH*," "servant of God." In this portion, Moses rises above human status: God buries him (34:6) and he is described as the only prophet God singles out face to face (34:10 and Exodus 33:11). Yet, Moses' burial place is unknown. Why?

2. God is called "King" ("*melech*") in 33:5. Many are familiar with the "king" image from blessings, which begin, "*Baruch atah Adonai Eloheinu Melech haolam*." So it may be surprising to learn that God as King only appears three times in the Torah: in *V'Zot Hab'rachah*, in Exodus 15:18, and in Numbers 23:21. What is your reaction to God as "King"? God as "Queen"?

3. In 33:6-24, Moses blesses the tribes in somewhat similar fashion to how Jacob/Israel blesses his sons in Genesis 49:1-28. Moses' sons, Gershom and Eliezer, are not blessed. In fact, the Torah mentions them sparingly. Did the sons live in their powerful father's shadow? Was he an "absent father"?

    What are the challenges of having a well-known and widely admired parent, sibling, or spouse? Moses does not express regret about his sons' and wife's absence in his last days. Was Moses lonely or regretful? Commentators reflect on Moses' deep disappointment that he didn't enter Israel. I imagine he also felt remorse as a husband and father.

4. Compare the words used by Jacob in his sons' blessings (Genesis 49:1-28), and Moses' tribal blessing in Deuteronomy 33:6-24. What distinguishes the Genesis and Deuteronomy blessings from each other? I read the Genesis "blessings" as expressions of hope for the future and warnings of gloomy outcomes if the blessing-recipient does not refine his ways. The blessings in Deuteronomy are all laudatory and express confidence in the future.

5. In 34:5 it says that Moses died "at the command of YHVH." A closer translation of "*al pi YHVH*" is "by the mouth of YHVH." It is poignant that the final death noted in the Torah bears a resemblance to the first

"birth" described in the Torah: Adam, who was brought to life through an infusion of God's breath (Genesis 2:7).

THINK ABOUT

1. 34:7 functions as a kind of eulogy for Moses: "Moses was a hundred and twenty years old when he died; his eyes were undimmed and his vigor unabated." It is challenging to summarize a life in a brief eulogy. Can you recall words spoken at a funeral that succinctly described the person being remembered? Can you characterize yourself in a few sentences?

2. In 34:8 we are told that the Israelites mourned thirty days for Moses. In Numbers 20:29, thirty days is also allocated for mourning Aaron. It is Jewish practice to observe "sheloshim," thirty days of semi-mourning following the burial of a close family member. Most activities of daily life resume, but some people avoid parties, concerts, and entertainment. When you mourned, did your daily life change for the week of "shivah"? Is the anniversary ("yahrzeit") of a loved one's death a day you welcome (to remember them lovingly) or a day you dread (because it's hard to remember someone you loved a great deal, as well as someone about whom you are ambivalent)? What are ways you mark a loved one's yahrzeit?

3. Moses lived to 120. This number first appears in Genesis 6:3 where it says this is the limit of a human life. The birthday greeting "Ad meah v'esrim!" ("Until 120!") is derived from this verse. There are a few accounts of people living to 120, but it is still not an achievable age for most. We wish people "long life," without mentioning quality of life. It's likely that for most, some physical frailty and mental decline will accompany old age. What capacities of mind and body are most important to you?

4. Much of V'zot Hab'rachah consists of Moses blessing the tribes. How do you define "blessing"? In Hebrew, it is related to the word "knee," indicating a connection to humility (as in bending the knee). Is there a link between offering a blessing and being humble? (You may want to review descriptions of humility in the section on Shof'tim.)
    On Friday night, some bless their sons with the phrase, "May you be like Ephraim and Manasseh," and their daughters with "May you be like Sarah, Rebecca, Rachel, and Leah." Marcia Falk composed a blessing for both sons and daughters:

"Be who you are—
and may you be blessed
in all that you are.[160]

How does the traditional blessing and Falk's blessing differ?

5. When each book of the Torah is completed, people say, "*Chazak, Chazak V'Nitchazake*," which means, "Strength, strength, and let us strengthen each other." Having dedicated time to studying Torah, I hope you recognize it as a significant accomplishment. As you move forward, I wish you "*Chazak, Chazak!*" Thank you for being part of my Torah Study!

FOCUS PHRASE (34:9)

Mah'lei ruach choch'mah—The spirit of wisdom.

---

160 *The Book of Blessings: New Jewish Prayers for Daily Life, the Sabbath, and the New Moon Festival*, New York, NY: HarperCollins Publisher, Inc., 1996, p. 124.

Concluding Thoughts

Torah Tutor seeks to provide an accessible Torah Study resource for Jews, Christians, and the religiously unidentified. It is a guide to salient words, stories, and ideas in the first five books of the Hebrew Bible. I hope this book has enabled you to befriend the text and your learning companions. I hope this book has made you more comfortable with some of the Torah's esoteric language and bewildering practices.

I wrote this book not to answer questions, but to pose them. The purpose of this book is not to make you believe or change your beliefs, but to prompt your own reckoning with moral and spiritual issues. This book is not a manual but an *invitation* to risk exposure to an ancient text that has been a dominant cultural and religious force for over 2,000 years. Sadly, it is increasingly overlooked by non-fundamentalists today.

Along with my reflections, this book includes commentary from my favorite teachers, living and dead. I purposefully cited rabbis and scholars from various backgrounds and denominations. By presenting provocative insights from broadly-based sources, I have tried to show the wealth of Torah resources available, particularly from learned, text-passionate women.

I know many adults in multiple communities who showed up for Torah Study expecting to hear platitudes and admonitions. Instead, participants were challenged, stirred, and energized. They hadn't realized it was possible to read the biblical text with intellectual and moral honesty. They didn't expect the Torah to address issues that continue to confound us today. For some people, discussing biblical stories may have felt like a homecoming. For others, Torah Study felt unfamiliar but appealing.

For those inadequately served by their childhood Jewish education, it's not too late to expand your knowledge and fuel your curiosity. For those who are beginning their Jewish adventure as adults, welcome, and may you find many avenues for learning and spiritual growth.

What a relief in our scattered world to sit quietly and consider human existence, nature, social responsibility, and family dynamics. I hope *Torah Tutor* gave you time for internal and external conversations about important ideas. May your engagement with the Torah continue be open, exploratory, and even sacred. I hope that this book prompts learning about yourself and about the text, and that you will use what you learn to enrich your life in many dimensions.

Glossary

Akkadian — ancient Near Eastern language

Bar/Bat Mitzvah — son/daughter of the commandments, name of ceremony marking a boy or girl achieving the age of 13, and leading prayers in synagogue

B.C.E. — "before the Common/Christian Era," the accepted language in academic/scholarly discussion in place of B.C., which is a uniquely Christian way of identifying years

Bal Tashchit — "do not destroy," a Jewish law and ethical mandate based on Deuteronomy 20:19-20, also refers to not breaking vessels, tearing clothing, wasting food, and other unwarranted destruction of material things

B'rit — "covenant," also commonly used for "b'rit milah," full name of circumcision ritual

Cantorate — the profession of cantors who function as musically trained clergy in the synagogue

C.E. — "Common" or "Christian" Era, used by Jews and Muslims instead of A.D., which is an abbreviation for "Year of our Lord"

Chametz — leavened food not eaten during Passover, including wheat products such as bread, pastries, and cereals

Chavurah — from Hebrew word "friend," a group of friends who gather regularly for religious and/or social purposes

Chazak, chazak v'nitchazeik — "be strong, be strong, and strengthen one another," words spoken on completing each book of the Torah

Chesed — lovingkindness, selfless acts

Chevrah Kadishah — "holy society," voluntary communal group that prepares a body for burial according to Jewish law

Chumash — from Hebrew for "five," compilation of first five books of the Hebrew Bible with their corresponding readings from the Prophets, bound in a book, not a Torah scroll

Counting the Omer — blessing and "counting" each day of 49 days between Passover and Shavuot, considering it a journey from slavery to revelation, from a collection of refugees to a community with a sacred purpose

D'var Acher — "another thing," referring to a teaching related to main topic

D'var Torah (pl. divrei Torah) — "a word of Torah," referring to a brief talk based on weekly Torah portion

Eretz Yisrael — the Land of Israel

Get — Jewish divorce document

Haggadah (pl. Haggadot) — "Telling," book with stories and practices of Seder (Passover meal), used at family/communal gatherings

Hatikvah — "The Hope," Israeli national anthem

Havdalah Ceremony — "separation," or "division," brief ritual with wine, spices, and braided candle to mark end of Shabbat (Saturday sundown or later) or holiday

High Holy Days — 10-day period from Jewish New Year (Rosh haShanah) through Day of Atonement (Yom Kippur), devoted to personal and spiritual renewal, asking for forgiveness from others, doing good deeds and determining to live more reflectively and ethically in the year ahead

Ibn Ezra, Rabbi Abraham — important 12th century Spanish Torah commentator and philosopher

Kaddish — from word meaning "holy," a prayer, written mostly in Aramaic, associated with remembering departed loved ones, recited at conclusion of services, as well as frequently during first year of bereavement and on the anniversary ("yahrzeit") of loved one's death

Kohein/Kohanim — priests who were descendants of Aaron, some Jews today continue to be recognized as "koheins," which gives them dedicated honors during communal services

Kol Nidrei — "all vows," emotionally evocative prayer sung at beginning of Yom Kippur Eve (Erev Yom Kippur) services, sometimes used as name of Erev Yom Kippur service

Kosher, Kashrut — "proper," "fit," ritually correct Jewish dietary practices

Levite — descendent of the tribe of Levi, had specific duties in connection with the ancient Temples in Jerusalem

Maimonides, Rabbi Moses ben Maimon, also called "Rambam," — 1040-1105, greatest medieval Jewish scholar and philosopher, frequently cited and influential to this day

Matzah — unleavened flatbread associated with Passover and eaten at Seder and during Passover week

Menorah — seven-branched candelabrum used in the ancient Temple, a nine-branched candelabrum is used for Chanukah

Mensch — Yiddish for "person," but used specifically to describe a person of decency, modesty, and responsibility

Menschlichkeit — the qualities of being a mensch: honesty, kindness, and good conduct

Mezuzah — "doorpost," a small parchment scroll with selected Torah verses placed in a decorative container and affixed to doorpost outside a Jewish home, and sometimes on inside doorways as well

Middah (pl. middot) — virtue, attribute, characteristic

Midrash — from "to inquire," refers to classical and contemporary imaginative interpretation and exposition of Bible personalities and stories

Mikveh — a dedicated body of water descended into for the purpose of spiritual renewal, mostly associated with women who immerse following their monthly cycle

Mitzrayim — Hebrew for "Egypt"

Minyan — quorum of 10 Jews (for Orthodox Jews, 10 males) over the age of 13, required for certain prayers and rituals

Mishkan — the Tabernacle built by the Israelites to worship God while traveling in the wilderness

Mitzvah — "commandment," referring to God's specific commandments for the Jewish people, as well as a generic term for "good deeds"

Mussar — character development through spiritual practices based on 19th century Mussar Movement, intended to spur self-aware, ethical, modest living

Ner Tamid — "eternal flame," or "continual lamp," part of Tabernacle in wilderness, and part of every synagogue building today, usually in front of ark where Torah scrolls are kept

Parashah (pl. parashiyot) — Torah portion

Pirkei Avot — concise ethical teachings and maxims compiled during the Rabbinic period, c. 200 B.C.E.–c. 200 C.E.

Rabbinate — the profession of rabbis

Rashi — acronym for Rabbi Solomon ben Isaac, 1138–1204, greatest French medieval scholar, known for succinct and clear explanations of Torah text

Rosh Chodesh — "head of month," new moon celebrated as significant festival in ancient times, now mentioned in synagogue and noted on Jewish calendars, sometimes celebrated by women who gather for spiritual enrichment

Rosh HaShanah — the Jewish New Year, celebrated in September (occasionally in early October), a time of reflection and repentance

Seder — "order," referring to ritually orchestrated meal at the beginning of Passover (and sometimes repeated on second night or later in the week)

Sefer Torah — handwritten copy of first five books of the Hebrew Bible (the Pentateuch), written by trained scribe on special types of parchment with special ink in ornate script. The Sefer Torah is housed in an ark in a synagogue and. It is decorated and treated with great respect.

Shabbat (pl. Shabbatot) — "cease," or "rest," every seventh day dedicated to spiritual enrichment and distinguished from weekdays by special food, prayers, songs, and gatherings

Shabbat Shuvah — Sabbath of Return, the Shabbat that occurs between the holy days of Rosh HaShanah and Yom Kippur, a reflective time with special prayers focusing on repentance

Shechinah — "Dwelling," the feminine aspect of God

Sh'loshim — 30-day period of mourning following the burial of a close relative

Shofar — ancient musical horn (made from horn of a ram or related animal) used by Israelites in the Hebrew Bible for important announcements. Today, it is sounded in preparation during the month leading up to High Holy Days and during Rosh haShanah and Yom Kippur services. The shofar has a uniquely penetrating sound.

Sidrah (pl. sidrot) — from Aramaic, "Torah portion"

Simchah — a happy occasion shared with others, a time of rejoicing for something accomplished

Simchat Torah — "rejoicing in the Torah," the name of the holiday at the end of Sukkot harvest festival, the last section of Deuteronomy and the first section of Genesis are read to indicate continual cycle of Torah reading. People literally dance with the Torah Scrolls (sifrei Torah) and it is a lively celebration.

Spinoza, Baruch — (1632–1677), prominent Dutch Jewish philosopher, an early proponent of biblical criticism

Tabernacle — the portable sanctuary built by the Israelites for worship and convocation during the period of wilderness wandering before entry to the Promised Land

Tallit — prayer shawl worn during morning prayers at home or synagogue

Tanakh — acronym for the Hebrew Bible, formed by using first letters of three sections of the Hebrew Bible: "T" for Torah, "N" for Nevi'im (the Prophetic books) and "K" for Ketuvim (Writings)

T'fillin — small leather boxes with printed Torah verses in them, placed on the forehead and arm during morning prayers, as a reminder to follow commandments

The Rabbis — with some variations, generally refers to the sages of Talmudic times, c. 70–500 C.E.

The Talmud — the most significant collection of Jewish oral teachings and traditions of Torah interpretation, compiled over hundreds of years, finished in 6th century C.E.

The Temple — site of ancient Israelite and later Jewish worship and national identity, destroyed twice and rebuilt in same location, the Western Wall in Israel today (also called "The Kotel") is the only remaining part of any structure connected to The Temple

Torah — in the narrow sense, the first five books of the Hebrew Bible, in a more expansive sense, all teachings related to Jewish life

T'shuvah — repentance and repair through acts of spiritual, emotional repair and material reparation

Tzedakah — from the word for "justice," providing for those in need

Tzitzit — specially knotted ritual fringes or tassels worn in antiquity by Israelites and today by observant Jews. Wearing tzitzit serves as a reminder of all the commandments.

Yetzer hara — the human inclination to negativity, destruction, desecrating pursuits

Yetzer hatov — the human inclination to goodness, creativity, noble pursuits

YHVH — primary name for God in the Hebrew Bible, based on four consonants (therefore, also called "The Tetragrammaton"), not pronounced as is, but substitute names are used such as "Adonai," or "HaShem"

Yom Kippur — "Day of Atonement," the holiest day of the Jewish year; many Jews fast, pray, and review their actions over the past year

Bibliography

Abrams, Judith Z. *Torah and Company*. Teaneck, NJ: Ben Yehuda Press, 2006.

Adelman, Penina V. *Miriam's Well: Rituals for Jewish Women Around the Year*. New York, NY: Biblio Press, 1990.

Adler, Rachel. *Engendering Judaism: An Inclusive Theology and Ethics*. Philadelphia: Jewish Publication Society, 1998.

Antonelli, Judith S. *In the Image of God: A Feminist Commentary on the Torah*. Northvale, N.J.: Jason Aronson, 1997.

Alter, Robert. *The Art of Biblical Narrative (revised)*. New York, NY: Basic Books, 2011.

_____ *The Hebrew Bible, Volume 1: The Five Books of Moses*. New York: W.W. Norton & Company, 2019.

Bal, Mieke. *Lethal Love: Feminist Literary Readings of Biblical Love Stories*. Bloomington and Indianapolis: Indiana University Press, 1987.

Barenblat, Rachel. *Toward Sinai: Omer Poems*. Lanesboro, MA: Velveteen Rabbi Press, 2021.

Berlin, Adele. *Poetics and Interpretation of Biblical Narrative*. Winona Lake, IN: The Almond Press, 1983.

Block, Barry H. Ed., *The Mussar Torah Commentary: A Spiritual Path to Living a Meaningful and Ethical Life*. New York: Central Conference of American Rabbis, 2020.

Berrin, Susan, Ed., *Celebrating the New Moon*, Lanham, MD: Rowman & Littlefield Publishers, Inc., 1996.

Brown, Erica. *Leadership in the Wilderness: Authority and Anarchy in the Book of Numbers*. Jerusalem: Maggid Books, 2013.

Buchmann, Christina and Celina Spiegel, Ed., *Out of the Garden: Women Writers on the Bible*. New York: Ballantine Books, 1994.

Cahill, Thomas. *The Gifts of the Jews: How a Tribe of Desert Nomads Changed the Way Everyone Think and Feels*. New York, NY: Anchor Books, 1998.

Comins, Rabbi Mike. *A Wild Faith: Jewish Ways into the Wilderness, Wilderness Ways into Judaism*. Woodstock, VT: Jewish Lights Publishing, 2007.

Cox, Harvey. *Common Prayers: Faith, Family, and a Christian's Journey Through the Jewish Year*. New York: Houghton Mifflin Company, 2001.

Daly, Mary. *Beyond God the Father: Toward a Philosophy of Women's Liberation*. Boston: Beacon Press, 1973.

Diamant, Anita. *The Red Tent*. New York, NY: Picador, 1997.

Dorff, Elliott N. and Louis E. Newman, Eds., *Contemporary Jewish Theology: A Reader*. New York, NY: Oxford University Press, 1999.

Douglas, Mary. *Purity and Danger: An Analysis of Concept of Pollution and Taboo*. New York, NY: Routledge Classics, 1966.

Drinkwater, Gregg, Joshua Lesser and David Shneer, Ed. *Torah Queeries: Weekly Commentaries on the Hebrew Bible*. New York, NY: New York University Press, 2009.

Engelmayer, Shammai, Ozarowski, Joseph S. and Sofian, David M. *Common Ground: The Weekly Torah Portion Through the Eyes of a Conservative, Orthodox and Reform Rabbi*. Northvale, NJ: Jason Aronson Inc., 1997.

Falk, Marcia. *The Book of Blessings: New Jewish Prayers for Daily Life, The Sabbath, and the New Moon Festival*. New York, NY: HarperCollins Publishers, Inc., 1996.

Feld, Merle. *A Spiritual Life: A Jewish Feminist Journey*. New York, NY: SUNY Press, 1999.

Foer, Jonathan Safran and Nathan Englander, ed. *New American Haggadah*. New York: NY: Little, Brown and Company, 2012.

Fox, Everett. *The Five Books of Moses*. New York, NY: Schocken Books, Inc. 1995.

Frankel, Ellen. *The Five Books of Miriam: A Woman's Commentary on the Torah*. New York, NY: Putnam Books, 1996.

Friedman, Richard Elliott. *Commentary on the Torah*. New York, NY: HarperCollins, 2001.

Frymer-Kensky, Tikva. *Reading the Women of the Bible: A New Interpretation of Their Stories*. New York, NY: Schocken Books, 2002.

Gelernter, David. *Judaism: A Way of Being*. New Haven and London: Yale University Press, 2009.

Gold, Rabbi Shefa. *Torah Journeys: The Inner Path to the Promised Land*. Teaneck, NJ: Ben Yehuda Press, 2006.

Goldstein, Elyse. *ReVisions: Seeing Torah Through a Feminist Lens*. Woodstock, VT: Jewish Lights Publishing, 1998.

_____. *The Women's Torah Commentary: New Insights from Women Rabbis on the 54 Weekly Torah Portions*. Woodstock, VT: Jewish Lights Publishing, 2000.

Gottlieb, Roger S., Ed. *This Sacred Earth: Religion, Nature, Environment*. New York, NY: Routledge, 1996.

Greenberg, Irving. *The Jewish Way: Living the Holidays*. New York: Summit Books, 1988.

Haberman, Bonna Devora. "Difficult Texts." *Sh'ma: An On-Line Journal of Jewish Responsibility* (April 2001). http://www.shma.com/apr01/index. htm.

Haberman, Joshua O., Ed., *The God I Believe In: Conversations About Judaism*. New York, NY: The Free Press, 1994.

Hartman, David. *A Living Covenant: The Innovative Spirit in Traditional Judaism*. Woodstock, VT: Jewish Lights Publishing, 1997.

Hattin, Michael. *Passages: Text and Transformation in the Parsha*. Jerusalem: Urim Publishers, 2012.

Hazony, David. *The Ten Commandments: How Our Most Ancient Moral Text Can Renew Modern Life*. New York, NY: Scribner, 2010.

Hazony, Yoram. *The Philosophy of Hebrew Scripture*. New York, NY: Cambridge University Press, 2012.

Held, Rabbi Shai. *The Heart of Torah: Volume 1, Essays on the Weekly Torah Portion: Genesis and Exodus*. Philadelphia: The Jewish Publication Society, 2017

_____ *The Heart of Torah: Volume 2, Essays on the Weekly Torah Portion: Levitius, Numbers and Deuteronomy*. Philadelphia: The Jewish Publication Society, 2017.

Kamlonkowski, Tamar S. *Leviticus (Volume 3 Wisdom Commentary Series)*, Collegeville, MN: Liturgical Press, 2018.

Kedar, Rabbi Karyn D. *Omer: A Counting*. New York, NY: CCAR Press, 2014.

Kissileff, Beth, Ed., *Reading Genesis: Beginnings*. New York, NY: Bloomsbury Publishing, 2016.

Kligler, Jonathan. *Turn It and Turn It For Everything Is In It: Essays on the Weekly Torah Portion*. Eugene, OR: Reconstructionist Press, 2019.

Klitsner, Judy. *Subversive Sequels in the Bible: How Biblical Stories Mine and Undermine Each Other*. Jerusalem: Maggid Books, 2019.

Korngold, Jamie S. *God in the Wilderness: Rediscovering the Spirituality of the Great Outdoors with the Adventure Rabbi*. New York: Doubleday, 2007.

Kugel, James L. *How to Read the Bible: A Guide to Scripture, Then and Now*. New York: Free Press, 2007.

_____. *On Being a Jew: What does it Mean to be a Jew? A Conversation about Judaism and its Practice in Today's World*. New York, NY: HarperCollins Publishers, 1990.

Kula, Irwin. *Yearnings: Embracing the Sacred Messiness of Life*. New York, NY: Hachette Books, 2006.

Kushner, Lawrence. *God was in this Place & I, I did not know: Finding Self, Spirituality and Ultimate Meaning*. 25th Anniversary Edition. Woodstock, VT: Jewish Lights Publishing, 2016.

Leibowitz, Nehama. *Studies in Bemidbar*. Jerusalem: World Zionist Organization, 1980.

_____. *Studies in Genesis*. Jerusalem: World Zionist Organization, 1972.

_____ . *Studies in Shemot (Exodus)*. Jerusalem: The World Zionist Organization, 1981.

Levine, Baruch. *The JPS Torah Commentary: Leviticus*. Philadelphia: The Jewish Publication Society,

Lew, Alan. *Be Still and Get Going: A Jewish Meditation Practice for Real Life*. New York, NY: Little, Brown and Company, 2005.

_____ *This is Real and You Are Completely Unprepared: The Days of Awe as a Journey of Transformation*. New York: Back Bay Books, 2003.

Milgrom, Jacob. *The JPS Torah Commentary: Numbers*. Philadelphia: The Jewish Publication Society, 2003.

Mitchell, Stephen. *Genesis: A New Translation of the Classic Biblical Stories*. New York, NY: HarperCollins Publishers, 1996.

_____. *Joseph and the Way of Forgiveness*. New York, NY: St. Martin's Publishing Group, 2019.

Mogel, Wendy. *The Blessing of a Skinned Knee: Using Jewish Teachings to Raise Self-Reliant Children*. New York, NY: Compass, 2001.

Morinis, Alan. *Everyday Holiness: The Jewish Spiritual Path of Mussar*. Boston, MA Trumpeter Books, 2007.

Ner-David, Haviva. *Life on the Fringes: A Feminist Journey Toward Traditional Rabbinic Ordination*. Teaneck, NJ: Ben Yehuda Press, 2014.

Newman, Louis E. *Repentance: The Meaning and Practice of Teshuvah*. Woodstock, VT: Jewish Lights Publishing, 2010.

Nouwen, Henri J.M. *Solitude: Three Meditations on the Christian Life*. Notre Dame, IN: Ave Maria Press, 1974.

Ochs, Carol and Kerry M. Olitzky. *Jewish Spiritual Guidance: Finding Our Way to God*. San Francisco, CA: Jossey-Bass Inc., Publishers, 1997.

Perlberger, Hanna. *A Year of Sacred Moments: The Soul Seeker's Guide to Inspired Living*. Bloomington, IN: Balboa Press, 2017.

Perlman, Debbie. *Flames to Heaven: New Psalms for Healing & Praise*. Wilmette, IL: RadPublishers, 1998.

Person, Hara E., Ed., *Voices of Torah: A Treasury of Rabbinic Gleanings on the Weekly Portions, Holidays and Special Shabbatot.* NY: CCAR Press, 2011.

Pinchas, Peli. *Torah Today: A Renewed Encounter with Scripture.* Washington, D.C.: B'nai B'rith Books, 1987.

Plaskow, Judith. *Standing Again at Sinai: Judaism from a Feminist Perspective.* San Francisco: Harper and Row, 1990.

Prager, Rabbi Marcia. *The Path of Blessing: Experiencing the Energy and Abundance of the Divine.* Woodstock, VT: Jewish Lights Publishing. 1983.

Robinson, George. *Essential Torah: A Complete Guide to the Five Books of Moses.* New York: Schocken Books, 2006.

Rosenblatt, Naomi H. *Wrestling with Angels: What Genesis Teaches Us About Our Spiritual Identity, Sexuality, and Personal Relationships.* New York, NY: Dell Publishing, 1995.

Reuben, Rabbi Steven Carr. *A Year with Mordecai Kaplan: Wisdom on the Weekly Torah Portion.* Philadelphia: The Jewish Publication Society, 2019.

Sacks, Rabbi Jonathan. *Covenant and Conversation: A Weekly Reading of the Jewish Bible.* Jerusalem: KorenBooks, 2010.

_____. *Essays on Ethics: A Weekly Reading of the Jewish Bible.* Jerusalem: Maggid Books, 2016.

Sarna, Nahum M. *JPS Commentary: Genesis.* Philadelphia: Jewish Publication Society, 1989.

Scherman, Rabbi Nosson. *The Chumash, Stone Edition.* Brooklyn, NY: Mesorah Publications, Ltd., 1993.

Schorr, Rabbi Rebecca Einstein and Rabbi Alysa Mendelson Graf, eds. *The Sacred Calling: Four Decades of Women in the Rabbinate.* New York, NY: CCAR Press, 2016.

Seeskin, Kenneth. *No Other Gods: The Modern Struggle Against Idolatry.* West Orange, New Jersey: Behrman House, 1995.

Shalev, Meir. *Beginnings: The First Love, the First Hate, the First Dream ... Reflections on the Bible's Intriguing Firsts.* NY: Random House, 2011.

Shapiro, Rami. *The Sacred Art of Lovingkindness: Preparing to Practice.* Woodstock, VT: SkyLight Paths Publishing, 2006.

Sherwin, Byron L. and Seymour J. Cohen. *Creating an Ethical Jewish Life: A Practical Introduction to Classic Teachings on How to Be a Jew*. Woodstock, VT: Jewish Lights Publishing, 2001.

Soelle, Dorothee with Shirley A. Cloyes. *To Work and To Love: A Theology of Creation*. Philadelphia, PA: Fortress Press, 1984.

Soloveitchik, Rabbi Joseph B. *The Emergence of Ethical Man*. New York, NY: Toras HoRav Foundation, 2005.

Solomon, Judith Y. *The Rosh Hodesh Table: Foods at the New Moon*. New York, NY: Biblio Press, 1995.

Telushkin, Rabbi Joseph. *A Code of Jewish Ethics: You Shall Be Holy*, Vol. 1. New York: Bell Tower, 2006.

_____. *Words that Hurt, Words that Heal: How the Words You Choose Shape Your Destiny*. New York, NY: HarperCollins Publishers, 1996.

Teubal, Savina. *Hagar the Egyptian: The Lost Tradition of the Matriarchs*. New York: Harper and Row, 1990.

Teutsch, David A. *Ethics of Speech*. Wyncote, PA: Reconstructionist Rabbinical College Press, 2006.

_____, Ed., *Kol Haneshama: Shabbat Vehagim*. Elkins Park, PA: The Reconstructionist Press, 2004.

Tigay, Jeffrey H. *The JPS Torah Commentary: Deuteronomy*. Philadelphia: The Jewish Publication Society, 1996.

Trible, Phyllis. *God and the Rhetoric of Sexuality*. Philadelphia: Fortress Press, 1978.

_____. *Texts of Terror: Literary-Feminist Readings of Biblical Narratives*. Philadelphia: Fortress Press, 1984.

Tucker, Gordon. *Torah for its Intended Purpose: Selected Writings (1998–2013)*. New York: Ktav Publishing House, 2014.

Woflson, Ron. *The Seven Questions You're Asked in Heaven: Reviewing and Renewing Your Life on Earth*. Woodstock, VT: Jewish Lights Publishing, 2009.

Yehoshua, A.B. Translated by Stuart Schoffman. *Friendly Fire*. New York, NY: Houghton Mifflin Harcourt Publishing Company, 2007.

Zion, Noam and David Dishon. *A Different Night: The Family Participation Haggadah*. Jerusalem, Israel: Shalom Hartman Institute, 1997.

Zornberg, Avivah Gottlieb. *Bewilderments: Reflections on the Book of Numbers*. New York, NY: Schocken Books, 2015.

_____. *Genesis: The Beginning of Desire*. Philadelphia: Jewish Publication Society, 1995.

_____. *The Particulars of Rapture: Reflections on Exodus*. New York: Doubleday, 2001.

Acknowledgements

My Dad, Fred Bohm, was a profoundly compassionate person, shaped by his childhood and youth in Vienna and his fraught immigration to this country to escape the Nazi scourge. He was light-hearted, optimistic, and idealistic. He was a political and visual artist, drawn to beauty in form and purpose in function.

My Mom, Trudie Tauscher Bohm, died while this book was in production. I am so grateful she read parts of it and expressed appreciation for it. Her strong character and elevated sense of personal and social responsibility resonates throughout our family. She was a dedicated teacher and cherished Oma.

My beloved Aunt Alice (Morawetz), at 93, retains a wise, kind, and grateful spirit. Your encouragement throughout my life has made all the difference.

My sister, Erica, is a person of unusual modesty and emotional generosity. You held my hand as a child, and you stand by my side as an adult. It has been a wonderful gift to grow closer through the years.

My children and their spouses/partners remind me what is most valuable in life. You challenge me and help me grow. I pray that your lives remain filled with love and meaning. May the future hold unexpected and beckoning opportunities!

My grandchildren—open-hearted Netalli, exuberant Ellie, gentle Rory, discerning Harlan, expressive Julie (my Omer Buddy), loves-to-learn Julianna, and overflowing Will: you each bring me light and delight. What a privilege it is to watch you unfold into your lives!

Since 1970, Jill Hanken has been a touchstone for every aspect of my life. Thank you for your loyal, honest, and tender friendship.

My friends Ellen and Steve Fox are models of *chesed* and *menschlichkeit*. How you live inspires me. I am so grateful for your friendship for over 30 years.

My first job as an ordained rabbi was at Congregation Beth Israel in San Diego, in 1982. I have been fortunate to retain rabbinic and friendship connections with CBI. In 2011, I began teaching Torah Study at CBI. This book is a direct outgrowth of my preparation for those sessions. Thank you to the dedicated Torah Study participants whose wonderful comments and questions push me to dig deeper and wider.

I am grateful to Temple Solel in North County. I loved being your rabbi, and I cherish many friendships developed over the years. I am grateful to Rabbi Alexis Berk and Cantor Billy Tiep for inviting me to teach and participate in meaningful ways. Thank you to Solel's Torah Study group, which has also contributed to this book through its weekly engagement with the text.

Thank you to Diana Lerner and the hundreds of participants in Camp Mountain Chai's Women's Weekends for cheering my creative interactions with the Torah.

Rabbi Eugene Lipman was the first person I knew who lived a serious, passionate Jewish life. He was a wonderful role model.

Rabbi Simcha Weiser, Headmaster at Soille Hebrew Day School, demonstrates the exquisite reach of Torah through his dedication to students and lifelong Jewish learning.

I am grateful to Rabbi Jack Riemer, Rabbi Debbie Prinz, Rabbi Susan Freeman, Rabbi Rami Shapiro, Rabbi Gila Ruskin, and Rabbi Karyn Kedar who encouraged me to write this book. Liz Levine brought needed support along the way.

Thank you, Rabbi Beth Lieberman, for your early guidance.

Thank you, Martin and Andrew Davis, for your work in securing permissions.

Thank you to many colleagues and teachers for allowing me to include your thoughtful reflections on the portions.

Thank you David Crumm and Front Edge Publishing for your encouragement and professionalism, and for the beautiful vision which guides your enterprise.

I am grateful to teachers from Hebrew Union College, CCAR colleagues, WRN, the Shalem Institute, the Institute for Jewish Spirituality, Pardes, and the Women's and Gender Studies in Religion program at Claremont Graduate University.

Additional people—too many to mention here—have taught and nurtured me Jewishly and otherwise. I am grateful that our life paths crossed, and that you shared your time, knowledge, and experience with me.

I have attended hundreds of classes, lectures, and seminars over the years, and have read commentaries and *Divrei Torah* from many sources. If I have not appropriately acknowledged an idea, it is an oversight for which I am both responsible and regretful.

Finally, I am grateful to my husband, David. Your loving, artful, careful eye perused this manuscript multiple times, and your editorial suggestions strengthened it immeasurably. In generous and selfless fashion, you support my thinking and writing. Thank you for providing an ideal environment for me to look inside the text and myself. Thank you for widening my horizons in multiple areas, for laughing with me, and for being my home and haven.

About the Author

Rabbi Lenore Bohm was born in New York to Viennese refugees. She was ordained from Hebrew Union College-Jewish Institute of Religion (HUC-JIR) in 1982, among the first 50 women to become rabbis.

Most of Lenore's career has been spent in San Diego, California, as a pulpit rabbi and as a Jewish Educator for a variety of non-profit organizations, including Jewish Family Service, the Jewish Community Center and the Leichtag Foundation. For two years, Lenore served Congregation Beit Shalom in Adelaide, Australia. Lenore was part of the first rabbinic cohort of the Institute for Jewish Spirituality. Lenore studied Contemplative Spiritual Leadership at The Shalem Institute for Spiritual Formation in Washington, DC, and Spiritual Direction at the University of San Diego. She studied Christian Feminist Theology at Claremont Graduate University.

Lenore earned her BA in English from Carnegie Mellon University. For two years, she attended an innovative interfaith seminary in Washington, D.C., called INTERMET in which aspiring rabbis, ministers and priests studied the Bible, pastoral care and social justice issues together, while each interned at a congregation of their own denomination. She received her MA in Hebrew Letters from HUC. Lenore received her Doctor of Divinity from HUC-JIR in 2007.

Currently, she serves as Rabbi-in-Residence at Temple Solel in Cardiff-by-the-Sea. She also leads Torah Study at Congregation Beth Israel in San Diego.

Lenore has four adult children and seven grandchildren.

About the Cover

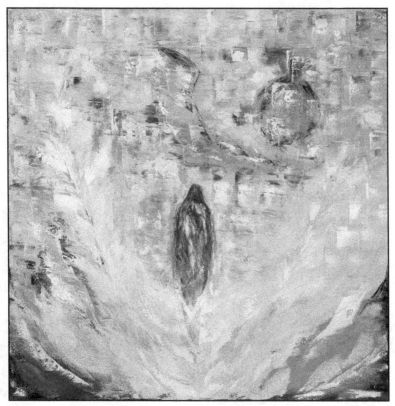

The cover art is a detail from "Fire of Torah" by Kreina Haviv.

Kreina Haviv is an artist who grew up in France and now lives in Israel. Kreina's message is both ancient and as new as what is happening today. She addresses the nobility of our inner soul. Kreina's elegant gestures bring a fresh dimension to Jewish art. Her works appear in private collections in Israel, Europe and North America.

Thank you!

Thank you for exploring Torah with me. I hope *Torah Tutor* was a valuable companion on your journey. If you enjoyed your experience, I encourage you to tell friends in your community. Book reviews are also a great way to let others know about this resource. Please consider writing a book review on the retail platform of your choice, or Goodreads.com.

For information about book signings or study sessions, you can reach me at RabbiLenore@TorahTutorBook.com. You will find more resources on the book's website, TorahTutorBook.com.

Contact info@frontedgepublishing.com to place bulk orders for *Torah Tutor* or to learn how to order specially modified editions that can include your organization's logo on the cover and/or additional information inside the book.

Recommended Reading

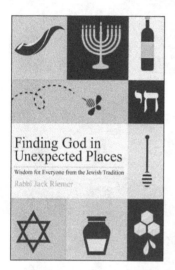

Finding God in Unexpected Places

by Rabbi Jack Riemer

"Rabbi Riemer offers us the kind of wisdom that we need in order to survive and thrive," writes Dr. Bernie Siegel, best-selling author of a dozen books about spirituality and healing. The late Nobel laureate Elie Wiesel adds, "Jack Riemer's words are songs of hope and faith. Listen to them as I do."

Word of warning: The stories in this book may surprise you and perhaps make you chuckle, but they could change your life, as well.

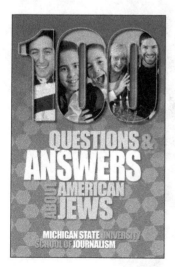

100 Questions and Answers about American Jews

by the Michigan State University School of Journalism

This simple, introductory guide answers 100 of the basic questions non-Jews ask in everyday conversation. It has answers about Judaism and Jewish culture, customs, identity, language, stereotypes, politics, education, work, families and food. This guide is meant as a quick introduction for non-Jews who need a starting point in learning about their Jewish neighbors and co-workers.

Front Edge Publishing books and ebooks are available on retail platforms worldwide, including Amazon.com and BarnesandNoble.com. Contact info@FrontEdgePublishing.com to inquire about bulk order rates.

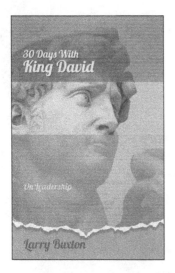

Thirty Days with King David

by Larry Buxton

In turbulent times, King David united a nation—and his hard-earned wisdom can bring us together today. David ranks among the world's greatest heroes for defeating Goliath and best-selling authors for writing Psalms. He is honored by Jews, Christians and Muslims. In this book, pastor, educator and leadership coach Larry Buxton shows us how David embodies 14 crucial values shared by effective leaders to this day.

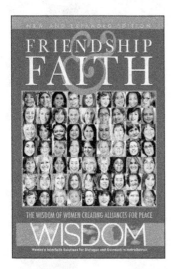

Friendship & Faith, 2nd Edition

by the Women of WISDOM

This is a book about making friends, which may be the most important thing you can do to make the world a better place—and transform your own life in the process. Making a new friend often is tricky, as you'll discover in these dozens of real-life stories by women from a wide variety of religious and ethnic backgrounds. But, crossing lines of religion, race and culture is worth the effort, often forming some of life's deepest friendships, these women have found.

CPSIA information can be obtained
at www.ICGtesting.com
Printed in the USA
JSHW040210020722
27595JS00002B/162